Behaviorism

and Phenomenology

CONTRIBUTORS

SIGMUND KOCH

R. B. MAC LEOD

NORMAN MALCOLM

CARL R. ROGERS

MICHAEL SCRIVEN

B. F. SKINNER

Behaviorism
and Phenomenology

CONTRASTING BASES
FOR MODERN PSYCHOLOGY

Edited by
T. W. WANN

THE UNIVERSITY OF CHICAGO PRESS

CHICAGO & LONDON

ISBN: 0–226–87282–3 (clothbound); 0–226–87283–1 (paperbound)
THE UNIVERSITY OF CHICAGO PRESS, CHICAGO 60637
The University of Chicago Press, Ltd., London

W HEN ENGAGING in any endeavor, no matter how simple, with active, creative men, one should not be too surprised to find that things do not work out exactly as planned. Whatever else is contained in the meaning of "creative," change is one of the major results of creative efforts. The blunting rather than sharpening of the contrasts between behaviorism and phenomenology that took place in this symposium seems such a change.

To say that things did not work out exactly as planned is not to say they did not work out. In fact, by the simple but admittedly devious stratagem of changing the title of the symposium to "Behaviorism and Phenomenology: Complementary Bases for Modern Psychology, with One or Two Dissents," one could bring all into order.

Professors MacLeod, Malcolm, Rogers, and Scriven, in one way or another, suggest the possibility of coexistence. MacLeod says, "The topic . . . of the symposium . . . was the contrasts, or the alternatives if you like, between behaviorism and phenomenology. . . . I would certainly suggest that these are not really two alternatives at all. They are two interesting approaches" (p. 184). Malcolm feels that there is a "hard core of logical truth contained in behaviorism," but that "The Achilles' heel of this doctrine lies in its treatment of psychological sentences in the first-person present tense" (p. 149). Rogers says, "There is a lot about behaviorism that I accept. I was simply trying to go beyond it" (p. 157). Scriven hopes to get across "some feeling for the ways in which I think that one can carry through the program of reconciliation of the *defensible* forms of phenomenology and behaviorism" (p. 180).

One of the dissents is equally clear. Professor Koch remained, to the end, delightfully intransigent. Illustrative of this dissent is the comment, "I would be happy to say what we have been hearing could be characterized as the death rattle of behaviorism, but this would be a rather more dignified statement than I should like to sponsor, because death is, at least, a dignified process" (p. 162).

Whether Professor Skinner is in dissent is not as clear. He does say, ". . . I am *not* convinced that the things that Dr. Rogers sees and infers are the primary moving forces. They seem to me to be epiphenomenal in a philosophical sense or at least something which occurs after the important fact" (p. 135). However, he also says, "They [internal states] exist—we can create a vocabulary for talking about them and part of human progress has been the improvement of our description of these things" (p. 106), and, "No entity or process which has any useful explanatory force is to be rejected on the ground that it is subjective or mental. The data which have made it important must, however, be studied and formulated in effective ways" (p. 96). The reader must decide.

Included in the letters of invitation sent to the participants is the sentence: "We chose this format not so much to encourage controversy (we will do nothing to avoid it) as to examine some basic problems in psychology in a context of questioning." The delivered papers supply the examination of some basic problems in a context of questioning. The discussions supply the controversy (apparently, at the base, about the nature of knowledge—which should come as no surprise). They are here published in a paraphrased total.[1] I have tried to rob them of the vagaries of the extemporaneous, while maintaining both the intent and the personal style of the speaker. The possibility that I have succeeded in achieving the reverse of what was desired is always with us, in which case the speakers are not culpable. Again, the reader must decide.

The program for the symposium contained the statement: "Rice University is pleased that this symposium, which forms a part of its own semicentennial celebration, has been chosen by the Division on Philosophical Psychology to mark its inception as a new division of the American Psychological Association. In recognition of this event, the officials of the new Division are chairmen of the several sessions." These officials, members of the Steering Committee for the new division, in order of their appearance on the podium, were: Dr. Joseph R. Royce, Chairman, Department of Psychology, University of Alberta; Dr. Edward M. Scott, Clinical Psychologist, Mental Health Division, Oregon State Board of Control; and Dr. James Royce, Chairman, Department of Psychology, Seattle University. We thank

---

[1] The papers of Professor Koch and Professor MacLeod were delivered on the opening day of the symposium. The time available for discussion of their papers was unavoidably, and unfortunately, shortened by the intrusion of other scheduled activities.

them for their care and kindness, as we thank the Rice University Semicentennial Committee for its generosity.

Speaking of thanks, I am thankful these lines are finally being written, thankful to Dr. James Street Fulton, Chairman, Department of Philosophy, Psychology, and Education, Rice University, for his calming support; to Miss Gail Hoechstetter, departmental secretary, for her incredible efficiency; and to my wife for her absolutely necessary, puzzled patience.

To the participants—our respectful gratitude.

T. W. WANN

Contents

SIGMUND KOCH

Psychology and Emerging Conceptions of Knowledge as Unitary[1]

I. INTRODUCTION

I CAN ONLY BELIEVE that my title, submitted some months ago, was the product of a burst of sabbatical-induced euphoria. It would perhaps be well to neglect entirely what I had in mind by using this title, but that degree of sobriety I cannot achieve. Behaviorism is a position whose implications transcend psychology. It is also one which has leaned heavily on extra-psychological sources of support and, indeed, owes its origin in large part to trends in the history of ideas that have formed modern man's general conception of the nature of knowledge. The career of behaviorism having thus been bound up with that of a widely deployed movement in recent culture, it is hardly likely that its fate will not be similarly bound. I propose, then, to honor the present title, if only to the extent of a few paragraphs which attempt to record what in some contexts is known to all of you but is not always sufficiently stressed in considerations of behaviorism: that there is currently taking place a sweeping redefinition by man of the nature of his own knowledge. An era in thought-about-thought is breaking up. A new one, with implications that justify the often abused adjective "revolutionary," is under way.

For more than a decade, processes of reappraisal have been going

SIGMUND KOCH, Professor, Department of Psychology, Duke University.

[1] The description, in the early paragraphs of this paper, of the ongoing revolution in conceptions of inquiry and knowledge is based on my draft-in-progress of *Psychology and the Human Agent* (the "postscript" volume to *Psychology: A Study of a Science*). More detailed analyses of the history of behaviorism reflecting a point of view similar to the one taken in this paper may be found in the following sources: *Encyclopaedia Britannica* article on "Behaviorism"; "Epilogue" to Study I of *Psychology: A Study of a Science* (especially pp. 733–49 and 752–69); and "Clark L. Hull" (Koch, 1961, 1959, 1954, respectively).

forward in almost every branch of intellectual activity, which, taken together, lend more than modest credence to the diagnosis just made. In science—despite a rate of technological and even fundamental advance almost incredible relative to past history—a new humility has become evident. In both the natural and biological sciences there are conspicuous tendencies to perceive and point up limits; to acknowledge, in the very conception of inquiry, the importance of the uncodifiable; to view with respect other domains of cognitive activity, and to search for and recognize continuities with such domains. In literature, the congealed standards of the first half of the century are under scrutiny: some voices no longer fear to question the sententious judgmentalism of those who have defined "the modern tradition"; there is restiveness over certain consequences, if not always claims, of formalism and experimentalism; there is a disposition to surrender some of the hypothetical riches of "ambiguity" for the austerities of meaning and to exchange the insularities of aesthetic cliquism for committedness to life and its predicaments. One discerns similar evidences in the visual arts—even if more submerged by certain last-ditch assertions of the earlier twentieth-century values than in the case of literature. In reaction to the glut of "anti-art" produced by such noisy movements as abstract expressionism and action painting, voices here and there are beginning to decry the hegemony of "movements," and the restrictive aesthetic mystiques that have at once instigated and fed on them.

In the scholarly humanities, there is a new and constructive intransigence: a determination no longer to accept the indifference of a society whose values derive from idolatry of science; at the same time, a resolve not to find consolation in a philosophy of contempt for the uninitiate, but to re-examine rationales in such a way as to promote the spread of the humanist perspective in a world which much needs it and to discover the location and involvements of the humanities in the organism of knowledge. In education, there is much casting about—but in no direction so much as in that which seeks to embed particular knowledge in generality of purview, and to salvage that classical conception which sees knowledge not merely as instrumental or decorative, but as a terminal good.

In philosophy, the indications are perhaps most compelling of all. An era during which philosophy almost voted itself out of existence in its fervor for security is almost ended. Its surrender of its history, its shedding of metaphysics and axiology, its flight from substantive problems to those of method, its reduction of those of method to those of language—all these have come increasingly under question. Logical positivism is no longer with us. Analytic philosophy, which, on the surface, seemed to broaden the purview of positivism by extending analysis from scientific to natural languages but which at times achieved an even greater constriction by conceiving natural language as that of "common sense" per se, is in process of inviting back many of the recently proscribed fields and problems of philosophy. Ethics and value studies in general are back. Contraries of virtually every canonical resolution of specific epistemological problems, of the sort that held sway for thirty or forty years, are back. And they have been brought back in the hands of former logical positivists and current analytic philosophers—as well as by others.

Along with these local but cognate processes of reappraisal, interests in the total articulation of knowledge have been conspicuous for the past decade or so. Those asserting such interests have originated in each of the fields mentioned and in some few not noted. The area of concern is often couched in such terms as "the relations of the sciences and the humanities." It is widely supposed that *Year 1* of this concern commenced with C. P. Snow's Rede Lecture (60), which gave currency to the phrase "the two cultures." One intends nothing invidious in noting that an explicit interest in similar problems has never been wholly absent since that point in history at which it became possible to discriminate "the sciences" from "the humanities," and further, that though such interests have been submerged during much of the present century, they were pursued with some ardor by the beginning of the fifties, if not before. In any event, there is by now more than a small literature (and in my opinion, a portentous one) the tendency of which is to seek reassessment of recently reigning conceptions of human knowledge in a way sensitized to the continuities within the processes that mediate inquiry in *all* fields and to the possible arbitrariness of such boundaries as those currently drawn to separate the major divisions of knowledge.

To this reinspection of the texture of knowledge, the major contributions have come, significantly enough, from physical scientists: outstandingly, Michael Polanyi (54, 55, 56), but also men like Sir George Thompson (62), J. Robert Oppenheimer (52, 53), J. B. Conant (15, 16), Gerald Holton (28, 29), Harold Gomes Cassidy (12), and the Bridgman who wrote *The Way Things Are* (5). The same context of thinking has been joined by scientists from other fields: e.g., the microbiologist René Dubos (17), the paleontologist Loren Eiseley (19, 20, 21), the mathematician (also literary critic and historian of ideas) J. Bronowski (6, 7, 8). Again, this same context of thinking has been fed, perhaps less directly but with comparable significance, by those among the historians of science whose tendency—either explicit or implicit—has been to test reigning conceptions of the nature of science against the *facts* of inquiry [e.g., Alexandre Koyré (40, 41), I. B. Cohen (13), Herbert Butterfield (9), Charles Coulston Gillispie (23), Thomas S. Kuhn (42)], and those among the philosophers of science who seem most eager to adjust their view of science to the particularities of history, e.g., Stephen Toulmin (70, 71, 72) and N. R. Hanson (25). This line of questioning has also received profit from the works of men who have sharply called recent philosophical orthodoxies into question, e.g., Brand Blanshard (3) and Ernest Gellner (22).

To such contributions there may of course be added those of the many individuals who have been drawn to a concern with "science-humanities relations" by Snow's controversial lecture (60). The issue, as posed by Snow, has certainly become a *cause célèbre*. It has been the object of widespread comment in the popular and intellectual press and has set the topic for countless university symposia and pronouncements by educators. It has led to reassessments of the objectives of education by special study commissions [e.g., Leverhulme Study Group (45)], and inspired revisions—at the level of planning and sometimes of practice—of university curricula. It has even spawned several anthologies which seek to demonstrate the unity of knowledge by the culling of poems about science [e.g., Eastwood (18)], and at least one book which analyzes the artistic propensities of scientists as revealed in their technical drawings [Lapage (43)]. One rather expects that the number of art exhibits sponsored by medical and dental associations is due for a sharp increase and that some enterprising theoretical physicists will soon be addressing the nature of things in the mode of Lucretius. Whatever the final value of this Snow-flurry, it is entirely evident that Snow had, in his phrase, "touched a nerve," indeed a massive and international one. And it would be unfair to leave any impression that the resulting discussion has been altogether fallow; not a few of the ideas have been constructive or clarifying.

While this wave of interest has gathered, psychology and the social sciences have stood on shore, almost untouched by the spray. Those who know the history of modern psychology (I will not speak for the social sciences, though I suspect that much of what I have to say is relevant) will find little cause for surprise in this. We are not known for our readiness to be in the wavefront of history. It could almost be maintained that modern psychology ran out of its independence at the moment of declaring it. In every period of our history, we have looked to external sources in the scholarly culture—especially natural science and the philosophy of science—for our sense of direction. And typically we have embraced policies long out of date in those very sources. What is unique about our present lag relative to the rest of scholarly culture is that each branch of the latter seems to be either working toward, or inviting into existence, a redefinition of knowledge based on an *empirical* analysis of inquiry of a sort which must largely depend on *psychological* modes of analysis. Indeed, extant efforts in this direction everywhere involve psychological commitments, often of a rough and ready sort. Yet psychology seems hardly cognizant of the challenge implicit in these circumstances. Or of the circumstances.

More curiously still, the emerging redefinition of knowledge is already at a phase, in its understanding of the particularities of inquiry, which renders markedly obsolete that view of science still regulative of inquiring practice in psychology. This can be said in utter literalness, for the view in question was imported, with undisguised gratitude, from the philosophy of science and related sources some three decades ago but, while remaining more or less congealed in psychology, was subjected to such attrition in the areas of its origin that in those areas it can no longer properly be said to exist. Psychology is thus in the unenviable position of standing on philosophical foundations which began to be vacated by philosophy almost as soon as the former had borrowed them. The paradox is now compounded: philosophy and, more generally, the methodology of science are beginning to stand on foundations that only psychology could render secure.

Strongest of all, the new interests in the particularities of inquiry and the interrelations of the resulting knowledge invite into existence precisely those curiosities, neglect of which has most thwarted the historically constituted aims of psychology. Whether these aims be stated in terms of the total functioning of the organism or in any others given by history, it is clear that problem selection has tended to be guided by simplistic presuppositions and that we have addressed only glancingly, if at all, those contexts of human function which are most valued by the judgment of civilization. It is precisely such knowledge which is now most wanted by the culture at large. But it is precisely such knowledge that is most wanting in psychology.

There is a strange circularity, then, in the predicament of psychology. Psychology has long been hamstrung by an inadequate conception of the nature of knowledge, one not of its own making. A world now in motion toward a more adequate conception begins to perceive that only psychology can implement it. Yet psychology is prevented from doing so because, almost alone in the scholarly community, it remains in the grip of the old conception. But this state of affairs could lead to a happy consequence: should psychology break out of the circle just described, it could at one and the same time assume leadership in pressing toward resolution of the central intellectual problem of our time *and* liberate itself for the engagement of bypassed, but important and intensely interesting, ranges of its own subject matter. Moreover, it can find courage to do these things in the circumstance that the very sources upon which it has most leaned for authority—physics and the philosophy of science—are, together with the rest of the scholarly community, urgently inviting them to be done.

Perhaps the most important *immediate* thing that could be done toward breaking out of this circle would be to lay, once and for all, the incubus of behaviorism. In recent years, behaviorism has—reflexively as it were—almost accomplished such a maneuver on its own. But it has not gone at the matter with true *élan*. It needs help.

Behaviorism has been given a hearing for fifty years. I think this generous. I shall urge that it is essentially a role-playing position which has outlived whatever usefulness its role might once have had. If you expect me to support this statement via a final and crushing refutation of behaviorist epistemology, you will be disappointed. I suspect that there is a class of positions that are wrong but not refutable and that behaviorism may be in such a class. For many methodological proposals and for certain positions of metaphysical or even empirical import, I am not even sure what a "refutation" would mean. If behaviorism is advanced as a *metaphysical* thesis, I do not see what, in final analysis, can be done for a truly obstinate disbeliever in mind or experience, even by way of therapy. If it is advanced as a *methodological* thesis, I think it can be shown that (*a*) the conception of science which it presupposes (especially of concept definition and application and of verification) does not accord with practice even in those sciences which the position most wishes to emulate, and (*b*) that its methodic proposals have had extremely restrictive consequences for empirical problem selection and a trivializing effect upon the character of what are accepted as "solutions" by a large segment of the psychological community. More than this, I think that for both metaphysical and methodological variants of behaviorism (and I am not convinced that the methodological variety is quite so "uncontaminated" with metaphysics as stereotype would have it), the following can be said: These are essentially irrational positions (like, e.g., solipsism) which start with a denial of something much like a foundation-tenet of common sense, which *can*, in the abstract, be "rationally" defended for however long one wishes to persist in one's superordinate irrationality, but which cannot be *implemented* without brooking self-contradiction. The exhibition of such self-contradictions is, I think, as close to a "refutation" of behaviorism as one can reasonably get. But the task is made cumbrous, of course, by the behaviorist's tendency to cover up such discrepancies between precept and practice by artfully concealing both his analytic elisions and extra-systemic importations of experiential meanings (often effecting their invisibility even to himself). The usual device is a shifting use of an extraordinarily non-particulate and crassly defined technical vocabulary.

I cannot, in the present paper, develop all of the preceding lines of consideration or, indeed, any of them in the detail that would be desirable. I shall concentrate primarily on exhibiting the outmoded and inadequate character of the view of science to which most behaviorists still appeal in support of their epistemology and on certain of the pragmatic effects of that epistemology on problem selection and treatment. Since I have been asked to give my presentation a historical cast, I shall begin with a shamelessly abstract historical rundown of the chief phases of behaviorism in American psychology, and shall consider further topics via a medley of briefly considered illustrations, so that a broad historical picture may be suggested, if only dimly. If time remains, I should like to close with a few comments concerning phenomenological alternatives to behaviorism as they are currently shaping up.

II. BEHAVIORISM

1. Historical

The story of the rise of behaviorism and of the neobehaviorist succession is familiar. But certain strands of it, especially if brought into relation with developments since about 1950, can yet be instructive. And the tendency of this latter interval—which can be called the period of neo-neobehaviorism—is perhaps not familiar, especially to the philosophers in the audience.

Classical Behaviorism

Classical behaviorism (1912–30) is best understood as a set of widely shared, if variably interpreted, orienting attitudes toward the business of psychology. As is well known, these included:

a) Objectivism: The insistence on objective techniques for securing data and the corollary disposition to (in Watson's phrase) "bury subjective subject matter." Again in the aseptic language of Watson, behaviorism "attempted to make a fresh, clean start in psychology, breaking both with current theories and with traditional concepts and terminology" (79, p. 4). Only such observations were to be considered admissible as can be made by independent observers upon the same object or event—exactly as in physics or chemistry. Most of the time, Watson defended his central thesis on methodological grounds, but sometimes a metaphysical judgment to the effect that "mind" or "consciousness" does not exist is suggested. And there were other behaviorists in the classical interval, for example, A. P. Weiss, who were consistently and uncompromisingly metaphysical materialists.

b) S-R orientation: All lawful psychological statements are to be expressed in terms of stimulus and response. Watson's ambiguities in respect to the definition of these terms—his vagrant fluctuation between physical and molar-situational criteria of S and physiological versus molar-behavioral criteria of R—are notorious. The problems thereby raised plagued subsequent behaviorist writers, "classical" and "neo." As early as 1922, Tolman was exercised by such ambiguities and asserted his advocacy of a consistently "non-physiological behaviorism" (63). Yet the issue received nothing resembling a consensus until the nineteen-fifties, and "resembling" is used advisedly.

c) Peripheralism: Watson's program necessitated that he consider how phenomena traditionally classed as "mental" might be treated in objective *S-R* terms. Most of his positive systematic ideas are thus attempts to show that processes formerly conceived as determined primarily by the brain could be better understood if allocated mainly to receptors, effectors, and their most direct nerve connections. Best known in this connection are Watson's motor theories of imagery and thinking, of feeling and of emotion. Somewhat more elaborated peripheralistic hypotheses were put forward during the classical interval by such writers as Smith and Guthrie [who, already in 1921, presaged, in such notions as the "maintaining stimulus," "pre-current response," and "readiness," peripheral mechanisms very much like Hull's S_D and r_G; cf. Smith and Guthrie (59)].

d) Emphasis on learning and on some form of S-R associationism as the basic laws of learning: Traditional psychology approached learning as subsidiary to sensory and perceptual problems. But an *S-R* psychology, by side-stepping perception, is prone to place central emphasis on learning. Moreover, by 1913 (the year that marks the formal advent of behaviorism), learning had proven a field eminently open to objective study. The story of how Watson came to fix on *conditioned reflex* principles as the basic laws of learning is of interest, from a "sociology of science" point of view. Some years ago, Lashley told it to Karl Zener and me on one of his visits to Duke. Watson spent much of the summer of 1916 in a frantic effort to obtain photographic records of implicit speech movements. The hope was to present such pictures of the physical basis of thinking in his presidential address to the American Psychological Association which he was to give that fall. But about two weeks before the scheduled time for the address, it became apparent that success was not likely to be forthcoming. Watson rapidly shifted tack. Lashley, then a student in his laboratory, had been doing work on human salivary and motor conditioning. For his address, Watson (77) hurriedly wrote up this research, along with a vigorous recommendation of the use of conditioning methods (then but slightly known outside of Russia). Thereafter, he assigned progressively greater importance, not only to the utility of the *methods* (e.g., for the study of animal sensory acuity), but to the value of conditioning *principles* for the explanation of behavior. By 1924, he was prepared to phrase *all* problems of learning in terms of "conditioning."

e) Environmentalism: This hardly requires development. Watson's extreme position is well known. What is not comparably well known is that his unbridled assessment of the extent to which environmental "shaping" is possible did not become explicit in his writing until close to the end of his career as psychologist.

Neobehaviorism

Classical behaviorism had been an attempt to escape the stagnation of the subjectivist psychologies then prevailing by providing psychology with a *decision procedure*, which, it was hoped, would make forward movement inevitable. But though the position soon attained hegemony—Watson was correctly reporting the trend when, in 1924, he said, "Most of the younger psychologists realize that some such formulation as behaviorism is the only road leading to science" (78, p. vii)—it degenerated with comparable celerity into polemicism and inflated program-making. Neobehaviorism may be seen as a second attempt to provide psychology with a decision procedure—this time an effective one that would conserve the orienting attitudes of behaviorism but recast them in such a way as to give them teeth.

By the late twenties, there was much "objective" experimentation but few bodies of clearly stated predictive principles comparable to the crowning achievement of physics: its theories. Instead, experimentation seemed aimless, "theoretical" hypotheses but loosely related to data, and debate idle. The search for a "decision procedure" thus became a search for a formulary of the techniques for "constructing" *rigorous theory*. The incidence of the search for *objectivity* now shifts. Early behaviorism had primarily involved attempts to guarantee the objectivity of the descriptive (first-order) concepts used for empirical data. While not giving up this objective (and indeed trying to place its pursuit on a more secure footing), neobehaviorism sought to realize and implement objectivism at the level of theory. The idea was to insure that all elements of a system language be "securely anchored" by explicit linkages to antecedent independent and consequent dependent variables and, in general, to effect a point-for-point correspondence of the logical properties of systematic formulations of psychology with those of psychology's traditional emulation-model, physics. In pursuit of these ends, psychology did not go directly to physics but turned instead for its directives to middlemen. These were, for the most part, philosophers of science (especially logical positivists) and a number of physical science methodologists who had been codifying a synoptic view of the nature of science and who, by the early thirties, were actively exporting that view from their specialties to the scholarly community at large. The view was based on a "rational reconstruction" of a few selected formulations in theoretical physics and put forward a detailed model of the scientific enterprise which came to be known as the "hypothetico-deductive method."

It would be revealing to reconstruct a little of the early history of this interaction between psychology and the "science of science." But I must hold myself to a few points:

The sources to which psychology turned in the early thirties for its model of science were primarily logical positivism, neopragmatism, and operationism. Because of objective consonances among these positions and certain sympathetic interactions among their holders, a complex and uneven fusion (to which the dominant contours were given by logical positivism) began to take place from the late twenties onward. It should be observed that psychology's selections from this cluster of formulations were spotty, adventitiously determined, and not supported by especially expert scholarship in the relevant sources.

The neobehaviorist period was ushered in by Hull's advocacy of hypothetico-deductive method. His advocacy, though fervent, was not sounded in the *technical* terms of the concurrent philosophical developments. Also, Hull's frequent recommendations and illustrations of axiomatic method during the early thirties tended not to include sustained consideration of problems of empirical definition. Though Bridgman's work (4) had been cited by H. M. Johnson as early as 1930 (33), it was not until the mid-thirties that a spate of articles on "operational definition" directed the attention of psychologists to empirical definition and produced the widespread impression that objectivism could be finally implemented only by careful "operational" practice. It was not until the late thirties that the preceding contexts of discussion were supplemented by analyses which explicitly took the logical-positivist model of science as regulative. Though initially recommendations of axiomatic method and discussions about operational strategy had tended to occur in somewhat separated contexts, both of these topics found an integrative framework in the formulations of logical positivism. Discussions and applications of positivistic meaning criteria soon began to appear in the literature side by side with operationist analyses. Throughout this entire sequence and down to this very day, no great clarity was achieved about these imported ideas: witness the tendency still prevailing on the part of many to use "logical positivism" and "operationism" interchangeably.

What in fact seems to have been the case is that psychology was enthralled by the apparent authority of these ideas, not their content. The large methodological literature by which they were conveyed from the glittering areas of their origin to psychology was prescriptive and zealous but, when written by psychologists, marked by modest orders of philosophical sophistication and, when written for psychologists by philosophers, vitiated by limited familiarity with the research problems of our science. What seems to have been imparted to the typical psychologist might be characterized as an ocean of awe surrounding a few islands of sloganized information, as for instance, that a theory is an "interpreted formal system," that such systems are constituted by such and such "elements," that a theory makes contact with "observable states of affairs" via a specification of experimental "operations" or by means of a cryptic device known as the "reduction sentence."

Be all this as it may, psychology, in America at least, soon stabilized itself within the ambiance of the positivist-neopragmatist-operationist view of science (let us call it the "new view"). The hypothetico-deductive reconstruction of science that it put forward was open to the interpretation that properly rule-regulated scientific work was *self-corrective*, and thus it seemed to offer a more or less sure-fire instrumentality for scientific advance. Though neobehaviorists took the initiative in wiring the elements of this model into their scientific sensibilities, psychologists of other conceptual tendency followed suit in accepting the hypothetico-deductive model and other aspects of the "new view" in one or another degree.

A period of comparative optimism, which I have called in another connection the "Age of Theory," soon supervened: it was marked by a general feeling that psychology had finally arrived at the phase of progressive science. "Theory" tended to be conceived of as a *commodity*, the production of which could be scheduled by educating the work-force into the presumptive dictates of the "new view" of science. Theoretical publications in psychology tended increasingly to divide concern between translating the new view into stipulations of the objectives of "sound theory" for psychology and presentation of formulations intended to approximate such objectives.

It is hardly necessary to reconstruct the atmosphere of the Age of Theory, particularly that of its classical interval, say, from the mid-thirties to the mid-forties. The regulation of systematic work by the directives and imagery of hypothetico-deduction, the sub-culture surrounding operational definition, the lore concerning the intervening variable, the belief in the imminence (if not achievement) of precisely quantitative behavioral theory of comprehensive scope, the broadly shared judgments with respect to strategic foundation data, the belief in automatic refinement and convergence of theories by the device of "differential test," the fixed vocabulary for the comparative dissection and analysis of theory—all of these are easily recalled, if indeed recall is necessary. The rather stable geography of dominating theoretical positions and the standard contexts of apposition and opposition will also come easily to mind. These scattered fragments define an ideology not wholly discontinuous with that of the present.

In broad aspect, neobehaviorism may be seen as a marriage between the orienting attitudes of classical behaviorism and one or another interpretation of the "new" model of science. The general orienting attitudes are to be implemented by translation into theory, or theory-like formulations, in accord with the requirements of the model. As a result, the earlier attitudes are reasserted but in altered form. Thus, for instance, re *objectivism*, the metaphysical overtones of classical behaviorism are, at least by frequent asseveration, sloughed off and attempts are made in a variety of directions to find rationales for a consistently *methodological* objectivism. With respect to the earlier homogeneously *S and R framework*, it can be said that though S and R are retained as the end-terms of psychological analysis, most neo-behaviorists sub-specify this framework at least to the extent of introducing into the causal equation for behavior certain concepts ("intervening variables") meant to represent "internal" behavior determinants. It is worth noting that in some neobehavioristic formulations there may be discerned a number of intervening variables (e.g., aspects of Hull's D, also I_R and $_sO_R$) which are not uniquely determined by (or inferable from) antecedent "stimulus" variables. In respect to the classical emphasis on *learning*, it is of course no secret that neo-behaviorism preserved and perhaps heightened this emphasis, most neobehaviorist formulations being essentially "theories" of learning. At the same time, Watson's emphasis on Pavlovian *conditioning* principles gives way to a variety of emphases in which classical condition-ing is subsumed under more general principles, supplemented, or re-interpreted. Most such emphases are further characterized by the attempt to achieve finer, more rigorous, and, hopefully, quantitative specification of the conditions of learning. The *peripheralism* of clas-sical behaviorism is, of course, also retained, but with the difference that attempts toward more particulate analyses of the consequences for behavior dynamics of certain peripheral "mechanisms" are made by some neobehaviorists, while the peripheralism of others of some-what stronger "empty organism" predilection assumes the more pure-ly methodological guise of restricting causal statements entirely to "observable events" at the periphery of the organism.

Adequate portrayal of neobehaviorism would, of course, demand lengthy development, not only of the preceding generalizations, but of others which would be needed to describe comparably definitive features. Here, however, I should like to expand very briefly upon a few characteristic aspects of neobehaviorism's defense of its *objec-tivist* epistemology, which topic is, after all, fundamental to assess-ment of the position.

Two of the outstanding contexts in which neobehaviorism has over the years tried to define and defend its *methodological objectivism* have been (*a*) a set of loose agreements concerning the legitimate *observation base* of psychology, and (*b*) the lore surrounding the *intervening variable paradigm* of theory construction.

a) *Observation base:* As already implied, the interval leading into the Age of Theory was marked by uneasiness over the mixed meta-physical-methodological grounds and the inconstant criteria devel-oped by classical behaviorism in defense of its epistemology. Psychol-ogy needed a clear and, so to say, "connotationally uncontaminated" rationale for objectivism, a *consistently* methodological one. The "operational" criterion seemed to provide this, as did later certain other formulations of the empirical criterion of meaningfulness of the sort developed by logical positivism.

Though interpretations of technical meaning criteria imported from the philosophy of science were free and various, certain core beliefs concerning the legitimate observation base for psychological state-ments were common to all of them. It is significant that these commit-ments were historically prior to the importation of such criteria, and, after importation, they remained untouched by the frequent and radical changes in meaning theory which continued in normal course of professional epistemological scholarship.

Such rock-bottom commitments concerning the observation base may be suggested via the following reconstructions:

1. All lawlike statements of psychology containing *dependent variables* not expressible in, or reducible to, publicly verifiable and thus "objectively" observable *behavior* indexes are to be excluded as illegitimate. Such dependent variable terms are to be defined in the same observation terms as are at the basis of physical science (weak form) and, perhaps, are even translatable into, or reducible to, actual descriptive and explanatory concepts of physics (strong form). The prototypical case of an admissible dependent variable is, of course, the notion of *response* or, more specifically, a "measurable" index of response, in some one of the varied, if often unspecified, meanings of "response."

2. Similarly, it is demanded that legitimate *independent variables* of psychology designate referents which can pass the test of independent, simultaneous observability *and* are definable in either the observation language of physical science or the concepts of physics. The prototypical case of an admissible independent variable is, of course, the notion of the *stimulus,* again in some one of many rather unseparated meanings. It should be noted that, in the case of the independent variable, the strong-form requirement of translatability into (or "connectability," in some strong sense, to) the concepts of physics has retained more general currency (as, e.g., in the "physical energy" criterion for the definition of the stimulus) than the analogous requirement for the dependent variable.

During the Age of Theory, these assumptions were embedded in, or rendered into the language of, the various "operational" or empirical meaning criteria imported from the methodology of science. The rather casual character of the relation between such technical criteria and these commitments concerning the observation base is indicated by the widespread presumption that the mere use of a language of stimulation and behavior, S and R, entails a built-in guarantee of semantic significance. Yet it must be noted that during most of the Age of Theory no great progress was made toward resolving the ambiguities in the definitions of S and R bequeathed by classical behaviorism. Hull, for instance, fluctuated between physicalistic and molar-behavioral (and in practice, experimenter-perceived) criteria of S and R as vagrantly as did Watson. Such tendencies are strikingly epitomized in Hull's theory by the fact that, though he carefully specified four response *measures* of the major dependent variables of his system (32; cf. p. 383), there is virtually no consideration of the R-term which the "measures" measure, nor is much concern given to estimating the empirical plausibility that the measures will co-vary. Guthrie was disposed to hold consistently to a physicalistic usage of S and R, but, as we shall see later, he himself makes clear in his last published article that his practice could not conceivably have been consistent with such usage. I am constantly told that Skinner has all along merited a clean bill of health in his "generic" concept of reflex and his analyses of the character of operant behavior. Perhaps this is so, but I must frankly confess that I have never been able to read his statements about his own scientific behavior in a univocal way and, further, that I suspect that though a definition of an *R*-class in terms of a physically specifiable "property upon which reinforcement is contingent" (58, p. 66) may not create especial trouble when that class is apparatus-determined (as in the Skinner box), it can run into trouble in the context of such remote extrapolations of his principles as are involved in the analysis of "verbal behavior" and other citizenly pursuits.

b) The intervening variable paradigm: Nowhere is the intersection between the autisms of the Age of Theory and the "new view" of science better symbolized than in the *intervening variable paradigm.* Its appeal to Age of Theory systematists was twofold. First, it seemed to offer a guarantee of objectivism *at the level of theory.* The criterion of "firm anchorage" of theoretical concepts via explicit functional relations to antecedent and consequent "observables," beautifully fulfilled the yearning of the Age for a theoretical *decision procedure.* If inferred explanatory concepts were to be unequivocally linked to observables, no longer need there be fear of irresponsible constructions whose role within the theory is instant to the whim of the theorist (what Hull called "anthropomorphism . . . in behavior theory"). At the same time, the paradigm seemed to render into orderly and intelligible terms the problems confronting the psychological theorist: he needed three classes of variables; he needed the interconnecting "functions"; he needed a mode of inferring or constructing those functions, etc. Moreover, the schema was readily reconcilable with various elements of the "new view." The statements interlinking the three classes of variables could, if one so desired, be asserted as *postulates*, thereby making place for the paraphernalia and imagery of hypothetico-deductive method. The fervent drive toward *quantification* of systematic relationships could become the quest for quantitatively specified intervening variable functions. Of especial significance to our present concern, the demand for explicit linkages with observables could be equated with the demand for *operational* (or "satisfactory" empirical) *definition.* And, relative to all these happy desiderata, the schema included a built-in guarantor of success: a standard method—the "defining experiment"—for inferring postulates from experimental evidence. In briefest terms, the method was to select or design a series of experiments, the empirical variables of which would be placed in correspondence with (that is, "represent" or "realize") the *theoretical* variables whose relations were in question. Standard curve-fitting techniques were to be applied to the experimental data. The resulting equations or "curves" were then presumably to hold for the theoretical variables whose relations were at issue. Though such a strategy can be (and has been) elaborated in differing ways, its rationale has rarely been questioned.

Here we note only that the vocabulary and directives of intervening variable strategy were legislative for many during much of the Age of Theory. Originally proposed by Tolman (64, 65, 66, 67, 68), it was taken over in modified form by Hull (32) and the many under his influence [e.g., Spence (61) and Miller (50)]. They (and others even outside the behaviorist tradition) attempted to conform to the paradigm in the arrangement of variables in their theories and in the specification of intervening variable functions. These latter were often of unrestricted generality and sometimes were put forward in mathematical, or apparently mathematical, form.

We will chronicle certain of the more recent vicissitudes of the ideology concerning the *observation base* and the *intervening variable paradigm* in the discussion of neo-neobehaviorism that follows.

Neo-neobehaviorism

Such general emphases of neobehaviorism as have been mentioned remained relatively stable until the mid-forties. But they came increasingly under question during the late forties and fifties. This resulted partly from the failure of neobehaviorist systems to realize the theoretical and practical objectives announced in the thirties. But more generally, this interval saw profound changes in psychology, in the course of which neobehaviorist positions were modified and liberalized. The pressures toward "liberalization" were partly internal to behaviorism, arising from the interaction between theory and research (especially where theoretical ideas were extended to man-pertinent problems). But many extrinsic developments invited or enforced modifications of neobehaviorism. These I can illustrate only in passing: e.g., a resurgence of interest in such bypassed areas as instinctive behavior, perception, complex motivational processes, and thinking; a revivified concern with the physiological basis of behavior, which both reflected and augmented significant new knowledge about the nervous system; a wider excursion of theoretical ideas than in previous decades (e.g., Hebb, Gibson); growth in influence of established non-behaviorist formulations (e.g., Gestalt viewpoints, psychoanalytic and other personality theories stressing experiential analysis, for instance, Murray's and Rogers'); development of new approaches to behavioral analysis (e.g., sensory processes, communication, simple learning) via a wide range of formal and mathematical models drawing on systems-engineering and probability mathematics.

In responding to such trends, "liberalized" neobehaviorism all but lost its identifying characteristics. Certainly the position has so changed as to merit the addition of a new "neo" to its title. The changes are especially evident in the volumes of *Psychology: A Study of a Science* [especially Study I (37)], in which many influential theorists, including neobehaviorists, present detailed retrospective analyses of their positions. Major orienting attitudes of classical behaviorism and neobehaviorist modifications thereof can be seen to be watered down to a point such that distinctiveness is threatened. I confine myself to a cursory sampling of evidences of the attenuation of attitudes which seek to enforce *objectivism*, in the two contexts that were broached a few paragraphs back: commitments concerning the *observation base* and the *intervening variable paradigm*.

a) Changing trends re objectivism: With respect to the *observation base*, among the more dramatic of these evidences is the radical re-analysis of S and R evident in many of the essays. Though S and R have in some sense always been under re-analysis, it is rare that the enterprise has proceeded with the present abandon. For instance, Guthrie, whose career overlaps classical and neobehaviorism, once and for all abandons the persistent behaviorist hope that stimuli may be uniformly reducible to *physical* description, and response, to "movement in space." Rather, "we find ourselves inevitably describing [stimuli] in perceptual terms"; moreover, "it is . . . necessary that they have *meaning* for the responding organism" (24, p. 165; italics mine). With regard to response, "we cannot reduce the classes of psychological facts which . . . we must deal with to component movements in space" (24, p. 165). In the same volume, Neal Miller points out, in a sweeping assessment of past practice, that "stimulus-response psychologists may be said to know and care relatively little about either stimuli or responses; they are specialists on the hyphen between the S and R and could more aptly be called 'hyphen psychologists,' or to use Thorndike's term, 'connectionists'" (51, p. 242). By way of reconstruction, Miller presents, perhaps more sharply than in previous writings, his method of "functional behavioral definition," which holds that "a response is any activity by or within the individual which can become functionally connected with an antecedent event through learning; a stimulus is any event to which a response can be so connected" (51, p. 239). In the same paper, Miller gives painstaking attention to *central processes*, and remains a peripheralist only to the extent of phrasing them in terms of the "central response," a type of "response" certainly not, either in fact or by Miller's intention, identifiable with muscle contraction or gland secretion. Indeed, he points out that this concept allows "the theory to exploit images, . . . perceptual responses, . . . and the possibility that central responses can contribute to the focusing of attention" (51, p. 242). Tolman, in his contribution to Study I (69), re-evaluates his objectivistic theory of purposive behavior, indicating repeatedly that his major theoretical concepts (intervening variables) come from his "own phenomenology," and expressing serious doubt as to whether such concepts can even be *applied* objectively (i.e., according to fixed rules which link them to behavioral "pointer readings"). This last illustration takes us by a natural transition to the topic of the *intervening variable paradigm*.

With respect to the *intervening variable paradigm*, it may be said that the trend of *Psychology: A Study of a Science* is to call it and much of the associated doctrine sharply into question; to do this in almost every sense in which questioning is possible. Thus, for instance, the originator of the doctrine, Tolman, has now come full circle relative to the feasibility of "standard" *defining experiments*. He now adduces strong grounds for doubting the trans-situational generality of any theoretical function based on the particularities (i.e., the obtained co-variations of empirical variables) of "standard" defining experiments. Moreover, Tolman's general conception of the significance of intervening variables in his theory has dramatically changed: no longer are they determinately linked to "the empirically stipulated independent and dependent variables" (i.e., observables, operational or reductive symptoms); rather, "they are merely an aid to thinking ('my thinking,' if you will)"—"a tentative logic (or psychologic) of my own" (69, p. 148). Interestingly, Lazarsfeld (44), in discussing the need for progress in the methodology of social science index formation, makes precisely the same evaluation of the defining experiment. Again, Neal Miller calls sharply into question the empirically warranted *generality* of all intervening variable functions thus far put forward by *any* theorist by making an acute analysis of "the experimental design required but seldom used to justify intervening variables" (51, pp. 276–80). The design stipulated by Miller (essentially use of two or more independent experimental "operations" and "measures," respectively) can be seen to require an exceedingly weak warrant of generality; yet it is only Miller himself who has applied this design, and this only at *qualitative* levels in a few simple situations where the "intervening variable" was a single primary drive like hunger or thirst. Moreover, even in such instances, Miller by no means always finds the necessary co-variation. All is not calm, even in the presumably unruffled area of sensory psychology. Thus Licklider (46), in his analysis of auditory formulations, repeatedly points to the problem of indeterminacy in the linkage between his intervening variables and his final dependent variable as perhaps the most troublesome puzzle in his thinking.

b) Return of the repressed: Perhaps the single most conspicuous and significant change ushered in by neo-neobehaviorism is *the massive return to a concern with empirical problem areas long bypassed or only glancingly acknowledged because of their subjectivistic "odor"* (or, I would add, because of an entirely realistic appraisal of the difficulties of significant progress on these problems in an exclusively "objective" mode). A little of the more remote history here might be instructive. In his first publication on behaviorism (1913), Watson had said:

The situation is somewhat different when we come to a study of the more complex forms of behavior, such as imagination, judgment, reasoning, and conception. . . . Our minds have been so warped by the fifty-odd years which have been devoted to the study of states of consciousness that we can envisage these problems only in one way. We should meet the situation squarely and say that we are not able to carry forward investigations along all of these lines by the behavior methods which are in use at the present time. . . . The topics have become so threadbare from much handling that they may well be put away for a time (76, p. 468).

But Watson was able to pursue this policy only until the end of the paragraph in which it was proposed. In the very next paragraph, we find an adumbration of his motor theory of "the so-called 'higher thought' processes." And in his eagerness to write a behavior psychology, "and never go back upon our definition," we find Watson conspicuously concerned, during the rest of his career as a psychologist, with attempts to show that the problems of subjectivistic phychology could find an objective resolution. In his efforts toward dramatic conquests along these lines, he, in effect, did something worse than neglect the problems at issue: he *liquidated* them via a series of the most arbitrary, simplistic, and ontology-distorting solutions. The reaction during the period of neobehaviorism to this (and to similar tendencies on the part of other classical behaviorists) was, in effect, to eschew investigations of the "higher processes" and adopt a rationale which held that the laws of these would be forthcoming as secondary derivations from postulates asserting fundamental behavior principles based (typically) on learning data. In consonance with such a rationale, there is a shift from Watson's recommended tactic of extending conditioning methods to the analysis of *human* behavior, to the concentration upon determining general behavior laws via intensive application of conditioning methods to animals. But the point to stress is that with the exception of a few illustrative efforts made mainly by Hull in the earlier phases of the development of his theory (e.g., 30 and 31) the promised "derivations" of perceptual, cognitive, and other "complex phenomena" were not forthcoming.

It is of the first significance, then, that beginning (roughly) in the late forties, one can detect a markedly increased disposition, especially among younger behaviorists, to give analytic and sometimes research attention to such formerly eschewed areas as perception, language behavior, thinking, and so-called mediational processes in general. Evidence of the dramatic growth of such interests may be found in the three volumes of Study II of *Psychology: A Study of a Science* (39). In this study, devoted to the interrelations of major subject matter areas of psychology, the tactic was to invite representatives of various areas to pursue the analysis of bridging relations between the given area and any others that the contributor might be interested in considering. *All* authors selected to represent the field of learning chose to consider relations with *perception*. Of the six authors in this group (two were collaborators), five would define themselves with little equivocation as neobehaviorists. Other authors of neobehaviorist cast, who had been invited to represent (as their field of primary affiliation) fields as broadly disparate as sensory psychology, motivation, social psychology, and psycholinguistics, also chose perception and cognitive process as important termini of their bridging interests. The result is an extensive sub-anthology on extensions of neobehaviorist theory to the long-forbidden areas—a kind of massive study in the return of the repressed.

I leave this audience to interpret the preceding extraordinarily fragmentary rundown of history. To me it suggests the story of the gradual attenuation of a position that was never *seriously* tenable, never consistent, based on thin and shifting rationales, and adopted more to serve needs for comfort and security than a passion for knowledge. Does this story of attenuation, attrition, and compromise "refute" behaviorist epistemology? Here I can only revert to my earlier observation that in certain connections "refutation" is an (unsystematically) ambiguous notion. I think that our story begins to suggest the unfruitfulness of the position, its restrictive effects on problematic curiosity, its scholastic character, perhaps most of all, its basic ludicrousness. Perhaps it is the last, which, in the end, will be the most compelling. When the ludicrousness of the position is made sufficiently plain, perhaps it will be laughed out of existence. Behaviorists have themselves done a pretty good job in rendering this quality apparent. Perhaps the following lines of consideration, which presuppose, but further specify, certain aspects of our historical outline, will carry the *"argumentum ab ludicrum"* a bit further. For me, these considerations are reasons for proposing that the position be considered once and for all defunct.

2. BEHAVIORISM'S EVAPORATING METHODOLOGICAL SUPPORT

I return now to a theme suggested in the preamble to this paper—the few pages in which I tried to justify its ornate title.

General Changes in the Philosophy of Science

For more than thirty years, the central—I think it fair to say "entire"—defense of behaviorist epistemology has been on methodological grounds. The neobehaviorists have *wanted* it this way. But the picture of scientific method now beginning to emerge among physicists, other natural scientists, many philosophers of science, and others challenges the behaviorist conception of science and the imported methodological views on which it was based, at virtually every point. The idea of behaviorism was that replicability of findings, reliability of prediction, and so on, could be purchased only by use of fixed linkages with "objective indicators"; by conformity to schemata which assumed that elaboration, application, and verification of a theory must take place in something like a wholly articulate, wholly stated context of *rules*. But for some years now, physicists and biologists, philosophers of science and historians of science have been converging upon a view of science which emphasizes the extent to which the scientific process is, in principle and at all stages, *underdetermined by rule*. If one wishes defensively to fall back on the distinction between "context of discovery" and "context of justification," one falls back on a distinction that any empirically apt account of inquiry shows to be unsupportable and that, indeed, no longer receives support in many expert quarters. Any detailed analysis of the "justificatory" activities of scientists, for instance, will show justification at many points to depend as much on extra-rule-determined processes as does discovery.

Among the re-analyses of inquiry that are now shaping up there is no point-for-point consensus, but most agree in stressing the absurdity in principle of any notion of *full formalization,* in underlining the gap between any linguistic "system" of assertions and the unverbalized processes upon which its interpretation and application (not to mention its formulation) are contingent, in acknowledging the dependence of theory construction and use at every phase on individual sensibility, discrimination, insight, judgment, guess. The emerging re-definition of inquiry knocks away virtually every one of the props on which the strange caution-inspired epistemology of the behaviorist had leaned. Even the presumptive, borrowed prestige attaching to his views is gone.

If the behaviorist refuses to resonate to this emerging redefinition of inquiry (and I suspect that one or two will resist), he should then be reminded that he began to become bereft of his extracurricular methodological supports very shortly after he discovered them. Be-haviorism has stood pat on a few issues dissected out of the method-ology of science anywhere from twenty to thirty years ago. But philosophers and scientific methodologists have not stood pat. Debate, revision, and change have been continuous, and even among those philosophers and methodologists who in some residual sense hold on to a rule-saturated conception of science, not a single plank in the old positivist-neopragmatic scaffolding remains unaltered.

The traditional positivistic distinction between analytic and syn-thetic statements has been broadly questioned (by positivists among others). Continuing analysis of the nature of logical and mathematical systems has revealed new complexities; few would be content now with the view that regards formal statements as tautologies. Whatever can be meant by the "interpretation" of formal systems is now itself interpreted in markedly different ways than formerly. The veri-fiability theory of meaning (and cognate formulations) has long languished in dereliction. More generally, attempts to state criteria which establish the limits of cognitive meaningfulness are either given up as self-stultifying in principle or have been so liberalized [e.g., Carnap (11)] as to make them compatible with certain classes of metaphysical statements. As suggested in the preamble to this paper, even the analytic (or "ordinary language") philosophers, themselves in some ways a protest group to logical positivism, have for some time been defecting from the more positivistically flavored features of their program.

But even more directly relevant to the issues at hand, certain for-mer positivists (e.g., Carnap, Feigl) have decreed—if only guardedly —a re-legitimization of *introspection*. Thus Carnap, in 1956, rather grudgingly points out:

Although many of the alleged results of introspection were indeed ques-tionable, a person's awareness of his own state of imagining, feeling, etc., must be recognized as a kind of observation, in principle not different from external observation, and therefore as a legitimate source of knowl-edge, though limited by its subjective character (11, pp. 70–71).

But the Bridgman of *The Way Things Are* (5), a book that has yet received little mention in psychological literature, is far less grudging. There he takes an uncompromisingly anti-behaviorist position, insisting that "first-person report" is essential to significant operational analysis in principle and, in psychological and social contexts, mandatory in practice. The flavor of his general position may be sensed from the following quotations:

Insistence on the use of the first person, either explicitly or implicitly, will inevitably focus attention on the individual. This, it seems to me, is all to the good. The philosophical and scientific exposition of our age has been too much obsessed with the ideal of a coldly impersonal generality. . . . Neglect of the role of the individual, with resulting overemphasis on the social, may well be one of the fundamental difficulties in the way the human race handles its mind (5, p. 5).

Another word for which I believe the private aspect is much more important than ordinarily realized is "proof." . . . Here I shall only reiterate my opinion that a proper appreciation of this will alter the common picture of science as something essentially public into something essentially private (5, p. 237).

It might be pointed out in passing that a remarkable affinity exists between the position taken in this 1959 book and that of another book published at about the same time—Michael Polanyi's *Personal Knowledge* (55).

Despite such far-flung developments as I have just tried to sample, some behaviorists will perhaps try to find aid and comfort in the circumstance that certain of the "ordinary language" philosophers find support, in their interpretations of linguistic "use," for what has been called "logical behaviorism." To such I would reply that this position is, in my impression, currently far less popular than it once was [say, shortly after the appearance in 1949 of Ryle's *Concept of Mind* (57)].

Newer Conceptions of Definition and Meaning

One topic which I would much like to discuss in substance, rather than merely in terms of historical trend, is the implications of certain newer ideas concerning definition, meaning, and language for the assessment of behaviorist epistemology. This I will try to do, if only in the most summary way.

Modern *philosophical* meaning theory has taken the form mainly of a search for a criterion of the cognitive significance of statements. The "solutions" or proposed criteria—though sub-groups fall into certain family relationships—have been most varied. Thus, taking logical positivism alone (and only a few examples at that), at various phases it has put forward criteria of significance (for a statement) in terms of "truth conditions," "complete verifiability," "falsifiability," "weak verifiability," "method of verification," "practical feasibility of verification," "verifiability in principle," "testability," "confirmability," etc. This samples the development through 1937; after that the "criteria" become more complex and more difficult to identify in a catchphrase. Most such criteria were, of course, embedded in detailed technical analyses and became the subjects of much polemical writing.[2]

When, in the early thirties, the Age of Theory began its search for a set of decision procedures, it could have turned to any of the above criteria except the last two ("testability" and "confirmability," in the special senses defined by Carnap, did not become available until 1936–37) or, indeed, to many others. Instead, partly by historical accident, psychology focused on the early formulations of Bridgman's "operational criterion" of meaning, which, by phrasing the meaning of a scientific concept in terms of "corresponding" *experimental* and (ultimately) observational operations, offered attractive imagery to a science at once self-conscious of its newly won experimental status and eager to get experiment into tighter relation with theory. The historical accident was essentially that a few psychologists (*a*) happened to become apprised of Bridgman's work and (*b*) published on its implications for psychology. If they had done their outside reading in slightly different order, they might have focused on the proposals of Schlick, or of early mid-Carnap, or of the neopragmatist, C. I. Lewis, or, in fact, on a variety of other criteria having an intent similar to Bridgman's. In such a case the clang of the psychological literature re definition would today be different.

As I earlier indicated, the lore concerning operational definition soon began to fuse with the lore concerning logical positivism. Carnap (10) published, in "Testability and Meaning," what was quickly

---

2 Useful historically oriented analyses of positivist meaning criteria may be found in Hempel (1959) and Blanshard (1962, pp. 189–248). It might be noted in passing that the 1959 Hempel reference is a reprint of Hempel, 1950, and includes a section of author's "remarks" as of 1958: in these latter, Hempel suggests that the "idea of cognitive significance . . . has lost its promise and fertility as an explicandum" (p. 129).

Useful though the preceding references be, it is fair to say that no truly adequate history of modern philosophical meaning theories as yet exists. Such a history would have to start at least as early as the formulations of the pragmatism (James and Pierce) and the positivism (Mach, Avenarius, and Poincaré) of the late nineteenth and early twentieth centuries. Especially in recent decades, issues in this field have become so intricately ramified, and differences in position so subtly shaded, as to pose a formidable challenge to historical scholarship. Such a book as L. J. Cohen's *The Diversity of Meaning* (1962), though not essentially a historical study, considers meaning-conceptions over a sufficiently broad spectrum to suggest the magnitude of the problem.

to become the most influential analysis of meaningfulness in the history of logical positivism. I believe that I was the first author (34) to discuss this analysis in the psychological literature and to examine its relation to operationism—but note that this was not until 1941. No presentation in the literature—including mine—has done justice to the technical detail of Carnap's treatment. However, the notions of the "disposition concept," the "reduction sentence," and "chains" thereof, soon entered the jargon of psychological commerce.

I ask you to note an interesting circumstance. Since 1937, there has been the lushest proliferation of philosophical discussions of meaning in history. Not only have Carnap (11) and other positivists liberalized their meaning criteria out of all recognition, but analytic philosophers have uncovered new vistas of subtlety with their discriminations of such matters as "open-texture" and "language strata" [Waismann (74, 75)] and a previously unanticipated complexity of "utterance" types in natural languages [e.g., Austin (2)]. Yet very little of this has penetrated into psychology. The typical theoretically oriented psychologist, not excluding the behaviorist, still draws sustenance and security from a theory of definition (and more generally of science) over twenty years old, and moreover, one which its originators have largely abandoned.

Not only have the newer philosophical considerations of meaning made obsolete the older "supports" for behavioristic analyses of definition and, in general, the conditions of communication in our science, but they converge on a picture remarkably inconsonant with behaviorist views. I nevertheless have a feeling that there is a need for effective *psychological* analysis of the nature of language, especially such problems as those of definition, meaningfulness, and meaning. Treatment of these by the philosopher has perhaps been limited by the traditional problematic concerns and modes of analysis of epistemology. The linguist, to the best of my knowledge, has, at least until very recently, pretty much side-stepped these problems. The field called "psycholinguistics" in recent years *has* considered them, but in a mode predetermined by orienting attitudes and specialized theories of behaviorism. What I think necessary, at least as a preliminary, is relatively simple-minded *empirical* analysis of the conditions of communication and of actual definitional practice in the natural languages. If one believes, further, that scientific languages differentiate out of the natural language—and I do not see how this can be doubted—the conclusions could also be of interest from the point of view of science.

I have recently made a stab in such a direction and am impressed by what a bit of preliminary thinking seems to reveal. If we look at the problem of definition *psychologically*, we immediately see that a definition, if apprehended by a recipient, must result in a process of perceptual learning and that what is learned is the discrimination of the properties, relations, or system thereof that the definer wishes to designate by the term. This clearly means that definition, at bottom, is a *perceptual training process* and that everything that we know about the *conditions* of perceptual training and learning must apply to the analysis of definition. Adding to this a few obvious circumstances concerning the genesis and status of words of natural languages—circumstances that can be inferred from the study of sources no more esoteric than dictionaries—quite a few matters take on a new light. It emerges, for instance, that contrary to what we were once told by logical positivists and others, no natural language and no scientific one of any richness can be regarded as organized into logical levels such that all terms are reducible to, or definable upon, a common definition base [and indeed, as the usual story goes, an extremely restricted one, as e.g., the "observable predicates" of the "thing language"; cf. Carnap (10)]. On the contrary, if we want to pinpoint with a term any reasonably subtle, embedded, or delicately "contoured" relation or property, we must often, if using verbal means of definition, build up our defining expression from words that are *just as*, or even more, "rarefied" (remote from the presumptive definition base) as the one at issue. Moreover, for defining abstract or subtle concepts or concepts based on "new" discriminations, we will have to go outside language and relate the term to a carefully controlled "perceptual display" (as it were) far more often than any logical positivist, especially of an older day, would care to admit.

Such findings, if they are that, are related to others at considerable variance with our lore and strictures concerning our *own* definitions in psychological discourse. Thus, one thing that eventuates is the utter irrationality of expecting that all terms will be understood and used with equal nicety by all people in a scientific field (even with a "competent investigator" clause thrown in), depending only on the adequacy of the "operational" definitions.

For instance, a recently published glossary of terms used in the "objective science of behavior" (73) says of "operational" definitions: "They demand agreement; and they make it possible for anyone who is able to read to reconstruct the observations to which the terms apply." At another place, in a characterization of the "data language," the relevance of "training" is acknowledged, but in this way: "words . . . in the data language . . . must be defined so that anyone after a minimum of training can use them consistently." Now "*a minimum of training*" necessary for the consistent use of a word—

particularly if that word denotes a highly embedded property or relation of events—may necessitate a *very great deal* of training. Yet in the psychological literature re empirical definition, it is quite clear that the force of such expressions is more like "minimal training" (absolutely) than the minimum of training *necessary* for discriminating "so-and-so."

It is strange that the very individuals who have espoused or accepted such a conception of the observation base often acknowledge in other connections that the application-conditions for observation terms, and terms close to the observation base, can only be learned and "discriminated" with sensitivity by working face-to-face with individuals who are masters of certain experimental crafts. Thus, there is a large group of individuals much interested in delicate and dramatic "shapings" of behavior who are ready, even eager, to admit that the true subtleties of the art can be assimilated only by prolonged laboratory contact with one of its acknowledged masters. They are right! But they have failed to generalize upon this truly profound knowledge. Language is at best a feeble instrument, even among members of a highly trained language community having quite limited problematic interests. None of the currently institutionalized sciences form single, homogeneous language communities. Physicists in one empirical area do not necessarily fully understand physicists in another; pathologists do not necessarily understand electrophysiologists, etc. And within each scientific area, even when cut rather finely, there may be distinguished disorderly *hierarchies* of language communities. In the extreme case, there may be quite definite and unique observable properties and relations which only two men, perhaps working in the same laboratory, may be able to perceive and denote by some linguistic expression. Moreover, it should be stressed that the stratification of language communities within a science may reflect variations in *sensitivity* of observers just as much as differential levels or foci of *training*. There was a time when Einstein was apprised of certain invariant properties of the universe, yet could communicate these "discriminations" to few men.

Now a language community must obviously be specified on a *psychological* criterion—a complex one demanding a certain criterial overlap of learned discriminations and specialized discriminative capacities (sensitivities) among members. Say that this criterion defines a "discrimination pool." I think there are strong grounds to believe that the discrimination pool demanded for adequate communication in *any* area of science is far richer, more differentiated, and subtle than ordinarily supposed. One may, for instance, think of a "pointer-reading" as some ultimate verifying operation (or reductive symptom). But the pointer is hooked up, both materially and inferentially, to a complex system of events, and the physicist must be attuned to relationships of great subtlety in that system if he is to interpret the pointer-reading in a truly significant way.[3] If one thinks, say, in terms of a presumably "simple" reduction sentence, the "test-result" (pointer position) may be specified via a relatively crass discrimination; the "test-condition" part may involve a most elaborate system of events which are *assumed to realize* an elaborate lattice of theoretical relationships, and the job of the physicist is to "discriminate" whether this is so. *That* is not a crass discrimination. Yet, be all this as it may, there is little question that the discrimination pools presupposed for communication in physical science as a whole may be fewer in number and, in each case, less differentiated and "rich" than the discrimination pools presupposed in biological science as a whole and especially psychology. In other words, the domain of physical science is such as to necessitate fewer language communities than do the domains of biology or psychology. Moreover, physical science language communities may well be more stable and perhaps more readily enlarged.

There are many reasons for these differences. I shall mention only one. In psychology, problems concerning *any* range of human endeavor or experience can be the object of study. No definition of our science—however restrictive its heuristic effect may have been on problem selection—has ever called into question this awesome peculiarity of our subject matter. In recent decades we have sought security by addressing only small and rather unadventurous segments of our subject matter. But problems—*psychological* problems—of art and morality, of scientific creativity, of human sensibility in all manifestations, of language, problem solution, and, of course, society, personality, etc., *do* stand before us almost untouched. If psychology is to study the conditions of the phenomena in any of these areas, it must premise its research on "discrimination pools," each of which overlaps to some definite extent with the discrimination pools of all of those widely ranged human areas. That is not to say that, for example, the psychological student of art must be an artist. (It would not hurt!) But it is grotesque to suppose that someone totally devoid of the special discriminations and sensitivities of the artist could make contributions to the psychology of art—just as grotesque as to expect, say, that an illiterate could contribute to the psychology of language.

All this is shamefully obvious, but the consequences—if the history of psychology be evidence—are not. In psychology we must have

<hr>

[3] Karl Zener makes a similar point in the context of an important analysis of "The Significance of Experience of the Individual for the Science of Psychology" (1958; cf. pp. 358 ff.).

many language communities: many sub-groups of individuals equipped with diverse stocks of discriminations and differently specialized sensitivities. *By definition,* we must have a greater number of language communities in psychology than perhaps in any other field of inquiry currently institutionalized. We must also expect more variability, both in sensitivity and in achieved discriminations, than within other scientific language communities. Indeed, the present position suggests that the *minimal* acceptable size of a language community for psychology must be a community of no more than two persons. Any formulation of the meaning criterion demanding a wider consensus group for *admission* of a term as meaningful would eliminate much meaning either from our universe of approachable data, or from that of the scientifically sayable. Worse than the *amount* of meaning lost would be its altitude—for science is such that at any given time its best ideas are likely to reside in only a few of its towering sensibilities.

In the most general terms, the behaviorist has sought to insure intersubjectivity by fixed definitional linkages to simple "objective indicators." But such an analysis as the one just vaguely summarized makes it plain that much communication which in fact takes place could not be mediated by definition based on such a paradigm. Often the application of a term (and of course the initial learning of its sense) will depend on the perception of highly subtle or embedded relational constancies in event manifolds that are fleeting, that vary from occasion to occasion, that evade ostension in its primordial "finger-pointing" sense, etc. Such meanings cannot be conveyed with any sharpness by a stipulated linkage to the elements of a "definition base" (as usually conceived), by an enumeration of stable and crassly discriminable "observable properties" or "symptoms," or indeed, by any conjunction or disjunction of these, whatever their number. The behaviorist who wishes to universalize the language community by such definitional practice will either be thwarted or end up with an extraordinarily crass language community, an extraordinarily crass set of descriptive and/or systemic concepts, and an extraordinarily degraded formulation of the psychological questions of potential interest to human beings. If this be democracy, it is not the kind that has characterized the sciences that the behaviorist is most eager to emulate.

The behaviorist who can acknowledge these things (if such there be) will inevitably fall back upon the demand for definition in such a way as to insure *public* applicability of terms (two or more observers must be able to perceive the identical referent), and *public* verifiability of statements containing them. But once the inadequacies of the older reductionist paradigms of definition are seen, insistence on such "publicity" becomes an exceedingly arbitrary form of obstinacy. For if it be granted that the language community cannot always be *universalized* with respect to *all* significant terms, the question of whether the referent be located in direct experience or in the "public" world becomes a relatively minor matter. In both cases, the fact of communication (thus "checkability") will be contingent on relevant observer sensitivities—which latter are, in principle at least, open to specification. In both cases, communication will often not be all or none, but rather a matter of degree. For both cases, the history of mankind and of science gives overwhelming evidence that high degrees of inter-observer agreement are attainable. Moreover, terms having both "types" of referent *can and do* enter into stable predictive relationships. What can be at the basis of persisting behavioristic negativism in the face of such considerations other than a deep metaphysical bias?

3. Pragmatic Consequences of Behaviorism: Effect on Problem Selection and Treatment

Here we resume a thread developed toward the end of the historical outline. There three points concerning effects of behaviorism on problem selection were stressed: (1) After expressing a resolve in 1913 to "put away for a time" the "threadbare" topics (as, e.g., the higher thought processes) of subjectivist psychology, Watson immediately proceeded to break that resolve and paced a trend in the classical interval for verbalistic "solutions" of the germane problems. (2) Neobehaviorism reacted to this largely by side-stepping the "higher processes" in the hope that laws concerning these would be forthcoming as secondary derivations from primary principles of simple learning and (in some cases) motivation. (3) Such derivations not coming markedly into evidence in the interval 1930–50, neo-neobehaviorism returns to a concern with perception and central process toward the end of this interval.

In general, perhaps the most decisive indictment of the behaviorist position is its long-term restrictive impact on problem selection and (what in effect can amount to the same thing) on problem treatment. If Watson and other classical behaviorists gave attention to "complex" phenomena discriminated by the older psychologies and by human beings generally, it was certainly not to study them but to liquidate them by fiat. The attitude of neobehaviorism is perhaps a cleaner one; but, in its concern with *general* laws of behavior based on intensive analysis of animal learning in a few standard situations, it fled the subtler fluxions (not to mention certain obvious hard facts of human function) so vigorously that these matters were all but forgotten. A policy initially of "gradualism" soon congealed into one of evading, even denying, subject matter. For most of the past thirty years, psychologists have allowed the rat to pre-empt the human, have shied away from investigations even of "behavior" when it is under the control of complex or labile internal factors, have concentrated on dependent variable indicators of a type dictated more by methodological caution than problematic relevance, etc. These facts are patent.

But in the present period of neo-neobehaviorism it *looks* as if *S-R* analysis is finally addressing the long-neglected matters of human import, righting the historic balance. About this, I hate to be cynical. I certainly welcome the renewed interests in perception, cognition, language, etc. These interests are a reassuring sign that ultimately subject matter will assert itself, that the world will not be totally subdued by a solipsism, however aggressive. But I think that these newer interests are best interpreted as a fading of the behaviorist blinders rather than as a proof of the viability of the position. For if problematic concerns now seem less constricted, the character of the treatment given to formerly bypassed problems suggests that these are not really being joined: they are again—as in Watson's day—being exorcized. True, they are being exorcized in a more sophisticated way— but the sophistication derives from the disposition of neo-neobehaviorists to take the findings of other groups of psychologists more seriously than did Watson.

If I had time, I think the following kind of case could be made: Much of the current behaviorist concern with perception and central process is given to *S-R* explications and paraphrases of phenomena and lawful relations discriminated by Gestalt and other non-behavioristic perception psychologists, by non-behavioristic students of cognition, by developmental psychologists like Piaget, by physiological psychologists and neurophysiologists. An examination of such "liberalized" positions as that of Neal Miller will give many illustrations of this sort of thing (cf. 51). Here he orders his "functionally defined" notions of central stimulus and response (along with the subsidiary hypothesis that laws discovered at the periphery may hold within the center) to phenomena discovered by Ivo Kohler, Wolfgang Köhler, to analyses made by Norbert Wiener, to discoveries made within brain physiology. Miller has an *S-R* explanation of everything.

With respect to analyses of this sort, which, though sometimes ingenious, involve a cosmically flexible use of *S* and *R*, I should think a critical question would be this: What is the probability that the *empirical discoveries* now finally being given a loose paraphrase in *S-R*

terms would have ever been made via research efforts guided by an
S-R terminology or, more properly, a scientific sensibility wholly
grooved in that idiom? What do such *S-R* explications and translations prove with respect to the heuristic fruitfulness of *S-R* concepts
and the associated orienting attitudes? The point may be driven home
by an example. Another contributor to *Psychology: A Study of a
Science*, Fred Attneave—an information theorist of neo-neobehavior-
ist cast—shows in his contribution a remarkable grasp of current developments in perception, neurophysiology, informational analysis,
etc. (1). He is sympathetic to current attempts to extrapolate neobehavioristic periphery laws to the center and to the use of *S-R* language for phrasing central process. I think him above that sort of thing
and said as much to him in a letter. His reply was that he considered
the use of such a vocabulary helpful and that, though he himself took
such usage lightly, he condoned neo-neobehavioristic practice in this
regard. But he did not answer a more specific question that I had
raised. His own analysis had made use of many particulate findings of
recent neurophysiology like, for instance, Hernández-Péon's discovery of central feedback to the receptors. What I wanted to have was
his estimate of the probability that such a fact would have been *discovered* in the first instance by individuals who perceived the organismic universe through a homogeneously *S-R* screen.

More generally, I think there is something frightening about the
way neo-neobehaviorism is treating the newly reclaimed subject matters. It is not merely that proffered problem solutions are trivial and
limited in significant research consequences. That is bad enough. But
the *attitudes* toward subject matter and toward the nature of knowledge at once betokened by such "solutions" and spawned in the wake
of their acceptance seem to me as perverse as in the day of Watson.
Scientific knowledge is, of course, "selective"—but when ontology is
distorted, denied, or evaded past a certain point, one is no longer in
the context of serious scholarship.

This lack of respect for ontology, let us face it, has remained pretty
much constant throughout the history of behaviorism. I think people
have largely forgotten that the notions of *S* and *R* originally had
something to do with specific end-organ activities. Throughout the
history of behaviorism, these words have been extended in reference
in ways not even held together by the thinnest kind of metaphor. By
a point quite early in the progress of *classical* behaviorism, every mentalist category distinguished in the history of thought, including, I
think, the medieval cholers, had been phrased either as a stimulus or a
response or as both. These tendencies were not diminished but, instead, burgeoned during the phase of neobehaviorism—especially in

the hands of theorists committed to the study of man-pertinent processes but committed also, as we all perforce are, to the maintenance
of professional respectability. Neo-neobehaviorism is now upon us,
and the situation grows worse. In pursuit of the strategy of extending
periphery laws to the center, the brain must now be furbished with
stimuli and responses. The mildly refractory ontological circumstance
that the brain contains no sense organs or muscles is easily handled
by "functional definitions" of S and R.

Thus we get the present family of analyses which phrase central
events in terms of one or another so-called S-R mechanism (all of
them quite similar). The general idea is that a second S-R system, or,
more properly, an R-S system, is interpolated between the peripheral
stimulus and the response. The interpolated response corresponds to a
neural event, or a molar-perceptual or cognitive process which is
some function of neural events. This is controlled by the peripheral
stimulus and in turn controls the final overt response. Since present
neurophysiology makes it clear that neural impulses in the central
nervous system get implicated in complex interactive and reverbera-
tory circuits, the R's generously imputed to the gray matter are supposed also to give rise to correlated S's (on the analogy to response-
produced stimulation), while these S's, of course, can lead to further
R's. When, after making a typical analysis of this sort, Miller (50, p.
242) points out that his notion of central response leaves him free "to
exploit" such matters as "images . . . perceptual responses," etc., it
would seem that he uses the word "exploit" advisedly.

4. S-R Scholasticism

A feature of the behaviorist framework which by now is perhaps
apparent in painful detail is the almost incredibly undifferentiated and
crass character of its major analytical tools—its exclusive *end terms* of
analysis and, in some formulations, the only terms of analysis: S and
R. Karl Zener has recently pointed out that:

[I]n no other science is there a single, unqualified noun referring to
the totality of events studied by that science, comparable to the term
behavior. There are optical, mechanical, magnetic, intra-atomic events,
all of which are physical events; there are a variety of biological events—
metabolism, growth, reproduction, contraction, secretion; but no single,
unqualified term exists in either science comprehending all of the events
which constitute its subject matter. Furthermore, there are no biological
laws comparable in *generality* to stimulus-response laws—no such physical
or chemical laws. No other science handicaps itself with the incubus of
a term which so discourages analysis and encourages overgenerality of
interpretation of obtained functional relationships.

The overabstract character of the concept of behavior (and that of stimulus) tends finally to produce the illusion that a *conceptually homogeneous set of lawful relationships* has been achieved or is achievable in psychology (81, p. 541).

I heartily agree. I also agree with Zener's further contention that psychology cannot avoid the use of a conceptually heterogeneous language. I would add that it was the philosophical presuppositions of the Age of Theory that prompted the absurdities of this quest for conceptual homogeneity and unbridled generality.

What we have, in effect, is a form of scholasticism in which what passes for "theorizing" involves arbitrary combinations and permutations among a few simple conceptual counters. It is as if physics proceeded in terms of three concepts: "cause," "effect," and, say, the notion of an "associative connection" between the first two. (Some physicists might wish to discriminate also a special event, "delta," the presence of which produces a finite increment in the strength of the "associative connection.") What the *S-R* theorists have ended up with is not a set of genuine analytic concepts—these to have any "bite" must be sufficiently differentiated to register at least a few of the observable subject matter distinctions—but a kind of primitive thought mold necessarily presupposed in all "causal," or if one prefers, "functional" thinking. In effect they have given to us as the primary analytic concepts for the most ambitious science ever conceived a mildly camouflaged paradigm for Hume's analysis of causality.

III. PHENOMENOLOGY

I had hoped to consider certain of the problems and prospects that arise when experience is unembarrassedly acknowledged as a part of the psychological universe and addressed as an object of study. But my assigned task in this symposium was to consider behaviorism. That I have done—even if I have not exactly "represented" behaviorism. Others will no doubt fulfil this last function, and Drs. MacLeod and Rogers will give positive consideration to problems of experiential analysis. I feel impelled, however, to close with a few general points concerning what is called "phenomenology," if only to insure that the incidence of my analysis of behaviorism not be misinterpreted.

I want to make it plain that I think there to be an intense current need for particular analyses of many issues connected with the use of experiential variables in psychology. Experientialism—if I may substitute that word for the term "phenomenology," which I dislike—was driven underground in American psychology for almost forty years. Even those committed to the acknowledgment of experiential events and to the use of experiential variables in their systematic work tended, because of the climate prevailing in that interval, to avoid direct discussion of the many methodico-creative problems that must be joined for effective development of a psychology that takes experience seriously. The paucity of direct considerations of such issues, say in the writings of the classical Gestalt psychologists or of Lewin (at least the writings of these men while in America), is in a way astounding. There are, after all, open and important questions having to do with the relations between experience and "report," optimal techniques for experiential observation, prospects for methods of observer training which might increase the sharpness and reliability of experience-language (this in turn depending on more general issues in the psychology of language), the formulation of adequate independent and dependent (experiential) variable categories, optimal modes for integrating behavioral and experiential data, and many others. These are no simple problems; they are not "methodological" in the idle, role-playing sense: the fate of psychology must be very much bound up with progress toward their resolution.

Because of the weakening hegemony of behaviorism, experientialists are currently somewhat less furtive. And such people as Gibson, Zener and Gaffron, Rogers and his group, Murray, are making significant strides, both substantive and methodic. Yet many long-neglected problems of the sort just mentioned are, of course, *still* wide open. A significant psychology, that long-heralded entity, is contingent on massive and responsible attack on such problems.

Yet many of the new dissidents, instead of attacking the questions raised by their readiness to confront experience in terms adjusted to the indigenous requirements of psychology, turn to fashionable forms of philosophical obscurantism—notably existentialism. I consider this trend regrettable. At the risk of ending up without any friends at all, I should like to say why.

The current turn to existentialism has the earmarks of the least fruitful kind of escape from a set of traditional constraints—an escape to an *Answer* rather than to a *problem*. Behaviorism won its initial acceptance because of severe shortcomings in the methodic proposals and research practices of early "phenomenologistic" programs in psychology. And it continued to thrive because of the absence in our science of muscular efforts toward reconsideration of those issues in the strategy of experiential analysis which earlier experientialism had handled in such artificial and limited ways.

Nothing could more jeopardize the prospects of the current counter-behaviorist revolution than the embracing of ready-made "answers" to these questions framed within the tradition of a philosophic school which—however charitably one tries to be disposed—can only reveal itself to have a high tolerance, if not a positive appetite, for the opaque. To unearth whatever might be suggestive for scientific modes of analysis in existentialism would, to put it modestly, require a level of scholarship, self-determining critical insight, and analytic prowess that no current psychologist is likely to have. This is no insult to psychologists, for existentialism, perhaps more than any other trend in modern thought, requires, for any degree of comprehension that might transcend the content of a few identifying slogans, first-hand and long immersion in one of the nuclear language communities in which existentialist philosophy is practiced. And even were that condition satisfied, the outcome would perforce remain in doubt. Merleau-Ponty, who is regarded as one of the most technically competent philosophers among the French existentialists, opens his book on the *Phenomenology of Perception* (1962) in this way:

What is phenomenology? It may seem strange that this question has still to be asked half a century after the first works of Husserl. The fact remains that it has by no means been answered (49, p. vii).

An analogy may be useful. *Effective* scientific development of psychoanalytic theory would, in the opinion of many, require insightful and rigorous re-analysis of a vast body of doctrine that has been generated in *that* field. Yet—despite the fact that the communicative problem in the psychoanalytic literature (great though it be) is minuscule in comparison with that presented by existentialist writing—not a few decades have gone by without such a task having been accomplished.

In light of such considerations, one is somewhat worried by the style of the current interest in existentialism in American psychology. There are woolly revivalist overtones—a disposition to accept in advance an intellectual object the properties of which have hardly been cognized. And there are indications that existentialism is tending to be viewed, in some global sense, as an *external source of authority* for whatever ideas the viewer already owns that he feels to be unconventional. There is a marked parallelism here with the tendency of the neobehaviorists to seek support for attitudes which *they* had already embraced by a similarly global appeal to a prestigeful philosophical movement: in that instance, logical positivism. All of these tendencies are painfully apparent in a widely known symposium published under the title *Existential Psychology* (47) (it may be of interest that one of the contributions is entitled "Existential Psychology—What's in It for Us?") and in the introduction to a widely influential anthology entitled *Existence* (48).

If existential philosophy is to be of concrete significance for the problems of a psychology of experience, this remains to be *established*. The slogans per se (e.g., "existence precedes essence") are not especially illuminating, whatever comfort they may give. My guess, though limited by very slight contact with existentialist literature, is that even if the conditions for *responsible* exploitation were met, there might not be a great contribution to psychology forthcoming.

There is, I tend to think, a kind of kink in the communicative practices of existentialists which requires close study—however libertarian one tends to be about the conditions of meaningful communication. *Headlong assaults on the ineffable are commendable, but they are not pre-guaranteed to succeed.* One finds in reading, say, Sartre, a fluidity of discourse, a tendency to be only partially and variably constrained by the terms of posed problems, a love of paradox and of cryptic yet somehow pregnant slogans, and (especially in Sartre's case) a tendency toward public relations opportunism—all of which do not exactly make for pellucid discourse or a homogeneous distribution of profundity. These things must be faced: *scientists* especially cannot afford to ignore them. Some of these tendencies may not be incompatible with the purposes of literary discourse—though this can be questioned, and I, for one, would—but they certainly are incompatible with the purposes of scientific discourse.

Turning to certain more homely considerations, I have tended to note with true dismay that students with existentialist identifications (and one sees not a few these days), though often sensitive people with the best possible impulses, seem possessed of the same habit of thought and of communication that I have tried to reconstruct re Sartre. They simply are off in some realm of epigrammatic nuance, of ardent association-chasing, before a problem even gets stated, whether by themselves or others. They do not seem to think like scientists, however Dionysian one's conception thereof, nor do they, in my estimation, think like effective or able humanists. I think this unfortunate: they are often talented young men who hold values of the sort desperately needed in psychology.

I will spare this patient audience a summary. I merely wish to emphasize that, though it may not have seemed so at all points, we have been discussing grave matters. Modern society has provision for an ample margin of waste, especially of ideas. But nowhere can such "give" in the system lead to less happy consequences than in psychology. For if psychology does not influence man's image of himself, what branch of the scholarly community does? That modern psychology has projected an image of man which is as demeaning as it is simplistic, few intelligent and sensitive non-psychologists would deny.

To such men—whether they be scientist, humanist, or citizen—psychology has increasingly become an object of derision. *They* are safe, even when most despairing. But for the rest, the mass dehumanization process which characterizes our time—the simplification of sensibility, homogenization of taste, attenuation of the capacity for experience—continues apace. Of all fields in the community of scholarship, it should be psychology which combats this trend. Instead, we have played no small role in augmenting and supporting it. It should be a matter of embarrassment that the few who are effectively working against the deterioration of culture are the physicists, biologists, philosophers, historians, humanists, even administrators, participating in the redefinition of knowledge to which I referred in my opening paragraphs, but *not ourselves.* Is it not time that we raise the courage to relent?

BIBLIOGRAPHY

1. ATTNEAVE, F. "Perception and Related Areas." In *Psychology: A Study of a Science,* ed. S. KOCH, IV, 619–59. New York: McGraw-Hill, 1962.
2. AUSTIN, J. L. *How to Do Things with Words,* ed. J. O. URMSON. Oxford: Clarendon Press, 1962.
3. BLANSHARD, B. *Reason and Analysis.* London: Allen and Unwin, 1962.
4. BRIDGMAN, P. W. *The Logic of Modern Physics.* New York: Macmillan, 1927.
5. ———. *The Way Things Are.* Cambridge, Mass.: Harvard University Press, 1959.
6. BRONOWSKI, J. *The Common Sense of Science.* London: Heinemann, 1951.
7. ———. *Science and Human Values.* New York: Harper Torchbook, 1959 (first published 1956).
8. BRONOWSKI, J., and MAZLISH, B. *The Western Intellectual Tradition.* New York: Harper, 1960.
9. BUTTERFIELD, H. *The Origins of Modern Science.* London: Bell, 1949 (new edition 1957).
10. CARNAP, R. "Testability and Meaning," *Philosophy of Science,* III (1936): 410–71; IV (1937): 1–40.
11. ———. "The Methodological Character of Theoretical Concepts." In *Minnesota Studies in the Philosophy of Science,* ed. H. FEIGL and M. SCRIVEN, I, 38–76. Minneapolis: University of Minnesota Press, 1956.
12. CASSIDY, H. G. *The Sciences and the Arts.* New York: Harper, 1962.
13. COHEN, I. B. *Franklin and Newton.* Philadelphia: American Philosophical Society, 1956.
14. COHEN, L. J. *The Diversity of Meaning.* London: Methuen, 1962.
15. CONANT, J. B. *On Understanding Science.* New Haven: Yale University Press, 1947.

16. ———. *Science and Common Sense.* New Haven: Yale University Press, 1951.
17. DUBOS, R. *The Dreams of Reason.* New York and London: Columbia University Press, 1961.
18. EASTWOOD, W. *A Book of Science Verse.* London: Macmillan, 1961.
19. EISELEY, L. *The Immense Journey.* London: Gollancz, 1958.
20. ———. *Darwin's Century.* London: Gollancz, 1959.
21. ———. *The Firmament of Time.* London: Gollancz, 1961.
22. GELLNER, E. *Words and Things.* London: Gollancz, 1959.
23. GILLISPIE, C. C. *The Edge of Objectivity.* Princeton: Princeton University Press; London: Oxford University Press, 1960.
24. GUTHRIE, E. R. "Association by Contiguity." In *Psychology: A Study of a Science,* ed. S. KOCH, II, 158–95. New York: McGraw-Hill, 1959.
25. HANSON, N. R. *Patterns of Discovery.* Cambridge: Cambridge University Press, 1958.
26. HEMPEL, C. G. "Problems and Changes in the Empiricist Criterion of Meaning," *Revue Internationale de Philosophie,* XI (1950).
27. ———. "The Empiricist Criterion of Meaning." In *Logical Positivism,* ed. A. J. AYER, pp. 108–29. Glencoe, Ill.: Free Press, 1959.
28. HOLTON, G. *Introduction to Concepts and Theories in Physical Science.* Cambridge, Mass.: Harvard University Press, 1952.
29. ———. "Modern Science and the Intellectual Tradition," *Science,* CXXXI (1960), No. 3408, 1187–93.
30. HULL, C. L. "Knowledge and Purpose as Habit Mechanisms," *Psychological Review,* XXXVII (1930), 511–25.
31. ———. "The Mechanism of the Assembly of Behavior Segments in Novel Combinations Suitable for Problem Solution," *ibid.,* XLII (1935), 219–45.
32. ———. *Principles of Behavior.* New York: Appleton-Century, 1943.
33. JOHNSON, H. M. "Some Properties of Fechner's 'Intensity of Sensation,'" *Psychological Review,* XXXVII (1930), 113–23.
34. KOCH, S. "The Logical Character of the Motivation Concept. I," *Psychological Review,* XLVIII (1941), 15–38.
35. ———. "Clark L. Hull." In *Modern Learning Theory* (W. K. ESTES *et al.*), pp. 1–176. New York: Appleton-Century-Crofts, 1954.
36. ———. "Epilogue." In *Psychology: A Study of a Science,* ed. S. KOCH, III, 729–88. New York: McGraw-Hill, 1959.
37. ——— (ed.). *Psychology: A Study of a Science,* Study I, Vols. I–III. New York: McGraw-Hill, 1959.
38. ———. "Behaviourism," *Encyclopaedia Britannica* (1961), III, 326–29.
39. ——— (ed.). *Psychology: A Study of a Science,* Study II, Vols. IV–VI. New York: McGraw-Hill, 1962–63.
40. KOYRÉ, A. *Etudes Galiléennes.* 3 Vols. Paris: Herman & Company, 1939.
41. ———. *From the Closed World to the Infinite Universe.* Baltimore: John Hopkins Press, 1957.

42. KUHN, T. S. *The Structure of Scientific Revolutions*. Chicago: University of Chicago Press, 1962.

43. LAPAGE, G. *Art and the Scientist*. Bristol, England: John Wright, 1961.

44. LAZARSFELD, P. F. "Latent Structure Analysis." In *Psychology: A Study of a Science*, ed. S. KOCH, III, 476–543. New York: McGraw-Hill, 1959.

45. Leverhulme Study Group to the British Association for the Advancement of Science. Report. *The Complete Scientist*. London: Oxford University Press, 1961.

46. LICKLIDER, J. C. R. "Three Auditory Theories." In *Psychology: A Study of a Science*, ed. S. KOCH, I, 41–144. New York: McGraw-Hill, 1959.

47. MAY, R. (ed.). *Existential Psychology*. New York: Random House, 1961.

48. MAY, R., *et al.* (eds.). *Existence*. New York: Basic Books, 1958.

49. MERLEAU-PONTY, M. *Phenomenology of Perception*. Translated by COLIN SMITH. London: Routledge & Kegan Paul; New York: Humanities Press, 1962.

50. MILLER, N. E. "Comments on Theoretical Models Illustrated by the Development of a Theory of Conflict Behavior," *Journal of Personality*, XX (1951), 82–100.

51. ———. "Liberalization of Basic S-R Concepts: Extensions to Conflict Behavior, Motivation, and Social Learning." In *Psychology: A Study of a Science*, ed. S. KOCH, II, 196–292. New York: McGraw-Hill, 1959.

52. OPPENHEIMER, J. R. *Open Mind*. New York: Simon & Schuster, 1955.

53. ———. "Science and Culture," *Encounter*, XIX (1962), No. 4, 3–10.

54. POLANYI, M. *The Logic of Liberty*. Chicago: University of Chicago Press, 1951.

55. ———. *Personal Knowledge*. Chicago: University of Chicago Press, 1958.

56. ———. *The Study of Man*. Chicago: University of Chicago Press, 1959.

57. RYLE, G. *The Concept of Mind*. London: Hutchinson's University Library, 1949.

58. SKINNER, B. F. *Science and Human Behavior*. New York: Macmillan, 1953.

59. SMITH, S., and GUTHRIE, E. R. *General Psychology in Terms of Behavior*. New York: Appleton-Century, 1921.

60. SNOW, C. P. *The Two Cultures and the Scientific Revolution*. New York: Cambridge University Press, 1959.

61. SPENCE, K. W. "The Nature of Theory Construction in Contemporary Psychology," *Psychological Review*, LI (1944), 47–68.

62. THOMPSON, G. *The Inspiration of Science*. London: Oxford University Press, 1961.

63. TOLMAN, E. C. "A New Formula for Behaviorism," *Psychological Review*, XXIX (1922), 44–53.

64. ———. *Purposive Behavior in Animals and Men.* New York: Century, 1932.

65. ———. "Psychology vs. Immediate Experience," *Philosophy of Science*, II (1935), 356–80.

66. ———. "Operational Behaviorism and Current Trends in Psychology," *Proceedings of the 25th Anniversary Celebration Inaug. Grad. Stud.*, pp. 89–103. Los Angeles: University of Southern California Press, 1936.

67. ———. "An Operational Analysis of 'Demands,' " *Erkenntnis*, VI (1937), 383–90.

68. ———. "The Determiners of Behavior at a Choice Point," *Psychological Review*, XLV (1938), 1–41.

69. ———. "Principles of Purposive Behavior." In *Psychology: A Study of a Science*, ed. S. KOCH, II, 92–157. New York: McGraw-Hill, 1959.

70. TOULMIN, S. *The Philosophy of Science.* London: Hutchinson's University Library, 1953.

71. ———. *Foresight and Understanding.* London: Hutchinson, 1961.

72. TOULMIN, S., and GOODFIELD. J. *The Fabric of the Heavens.* London: Hutchinson, 1962.

73. VERPLANCK, W. "A Glossary of Some Terms Used in the Objective Science of Behavior," *Psychological Review*, LXIV (1957), Suppl. viii. Pp. 42.

74. WAISMANN, F. "Verifiability." In *Logic and Language*, ed. A. G. N. FLEW, pp. 117–144. Oxford: Blackwell, 1951.

75. ———. "Language Strata." In *Logic and Language* (second series), ed. A. G. N. FLEW, pp. 11–31. Oxford: Blackwell, 1953.

76. WATSON, J. B. "Psychology as the Behaviorist Views It," *Psychological Review*, XX (1913), 158–77. Reprinted in *Readings in the History of Psychology*, ed. W. DENNIS, pp. 457–71. New York: Appleton-Century-Crofts, 1948.

77. ———. "The Place of the Conditioned Reflex in Psychology," *Psychological Review*, XXIII (1916), 89–116.

78. ———. *Psychology from the Standpoint of a Behaviorist.* 2d ed. Philadelphia: Lippincott, 1924.

79. ———. *Psychology from the Standpoint of a Behaviorist.* 3d ed. Philadelphia: Lippincott, 1929.

80. ZENER, K. "The Significance of Experience of the Individual for the Science of Psychology." In *Minnesota Studies in the Philosophy of Science*, eds. H. FEIGL, M. SCRIVEN, and G. MAXWELL,II, 354–69. Minneapolis: University of Minnesota Press, 1958.

81. ZENER, K., and GAFFRON, M. "Perceptual Experience: An Analysis of Its Relations to the External World through Internal Processings." In *Psychology: A Study of a Science*, ed. S. KOCH, IV, 515–618. New York: McGraw-Hill, 1962.

PARAPHRASE OF DISCUSSION

COMMENTS OF PROFESSOR SKINNER

In commenting on Professor Koch's paper, Skinner spoke of his feeling of loneliness at the symposium. He had looked over the people on the symposium to see where he could find a little support and had "felt perhaps Sig Koch might be my man—but you see now how little I have to expect from him." Koch skillfully presented him as being on the "wrong side," which led Skinner to "the feeling of *déjà vu*." In the early thirties he had made the decision to spend his "life in the analysis of behavior." He knew his work would be "unfashionable for twenty-five years, perhaps. . . . Watson has had his day, all of the Titchnerians are still heads of departments everywhere throughout the country, and the social psychologists are coming up with all sorts of new mentalistic concepts. I must just cultivate my garden quietly and wait for a change of mood and a change of interests—and now I find the change is just beginning and it is still running away from me."

However, the stories of early behaviorists, in fact, Koch's history of the last thirty years of behaviorism seems "to be irrelevant." Skinner would make a distinction between "behaviorism as a philosophy of science and the science of behavior." He does not "subscribe to any of the stratagems of science" Koch described. He would "have nothing to do with hypothetico-deductive systems," had very early rejected the value of "drive as an intervening variable," and insists that "behaviorism is not to be identified with logical positivism." Behaviorism is concerned with "the basic subject matter of the science of psychology," and should not be confused with ways of going about studying it. A *science of behavior* is now flourishing, cumulative recorders throughout the country are gathering basic data, all without regard to arguments about concepts and methodology which are irrelevant to the scientist in the laboratory. "The science of behavior is moving very rapidly and very powerfully and it does not need this kind of philosophical justification. It justifies itself by its success in dealing with the subject matter. . . ." There is a science of behavior whether or not there is a "useful philosophy of science of behaviorism."

MEMBER OF THE AUDIENCE

What Professor Koch presented did not seem "truly representative of what Skinner has to say." Would Koch "talk specifically for a minute about the philosophical issues involved in Skinner's work?"

COMMENTS OF PROFESSOR KOCH

He had "necessarily to speak about behaviorism in a more or less abstract and generic way." While he has many specific things to say about Skinner's position, the fact that it is a "Pickwickian position" and that Skinner is "the most subtle individual who has in some sense shared certain of the orienting attitudes of the behaviorists' point of view," makes it "rather difficult to cover Skinner exhaustively and, at the same time, talk about behaviorism in general." He hopes "this kind of issue can be joined from time to time" if time allows as the symposium continues.

He would like to reply to Professor Skinner's "touchingly mild" comments. "I felt awfully badly that I could not be the one person in this group on his side. We all change, you know." Nevertheless, he was "disturbed" by Skinner's approach to the issues raised because it was somewhat "strange and equivocal." It is very difficult to know exactly what Skinner's position is on certain central areas. For example, "his position in connection with theory has always, it seems to me, been, shall we say, close to systematically ambiguous." In one article as late as 1950 "he will, in effect, say theories of learning are not possible, and then, in his concluding paragraph, he will talk about a descriptive approach to behavior and attribute features to it which are indistinguishable from conventional analysis of theory . . . as this term has been defined in stable methodological practice in psychology for some time."

While the analysis was not designed to handle Skinner in detail, many general features do apply. It is impossible in such a limited time to spell out its bearing on Skinner because, as has been indicated, he is ambiguous about certain of his attitudes, particularly in relationship to such matters as methodology and theory.

Skinner, "of all the behaviorists," has made "discriminations about the subject matter of psychology," which Koch "in a somewhat different way . . . would resonate to and which, in a somewhat different way" he would make. Skinner, "of all behaviorists," has "embraced in a serious fashion" certain of the "so-called complex psychological problems," but "the mode of his treatment is very seriously limited."

MEMBER OF THE AUDIENCE

Professor Koch was "able to dispose of behaviorism on the one hand and existentialism on the other." Would he care to comment on "Maslow's so-called third force within psychology"?

COMMENTS OF PROFESSOR KOCH

"I do not like to appear in the role as . . . a rejecter of everything, and I am not." He hopes to finish a book soon which will make this clear. Rather than rejecting existentialism he expressed concern "about the unfruitfulness of the way in which people are making a rapid identification with an object . . . the properties of which they do not quite understand." He is "worried" in somewhat the same way about the third force. It is a "metaphor that is becoming a little bit over-abused." Insofar as he can see, the third force "is an extraordinarily loose congeries of people who are very much concerned about the constriction of problematic interests in American psychology . . . who are eager to embrace some kind of alternative." To speak of "this as a force is the bad use of a metaphor . . . because it is *not* a third force, it is a group of a large number of individuals who . . . would have considerable difficulty communicating with each other and who stand for nothing focal other than a feeling of disaffection from the emphases of recent American psychology." While he does not reject it, he does not look on it as "some wave of the future" which can "rescue psychology."

MEMBER OF THE AUDIENCE

In speaking of "many language communities within psychology," is reference being made to the idea that, although there are different vocabularies in each community, "one individual who had sufficient capacity and sensitivity" could learn to "speak all of the languages," or, is reference being made to the idea that "the syntax and structure of the languages would be so radically different" that the "unitary human individual is fractured up into languages compatible for morals, languages compatible for a variety of subjects"?

COMMENTS OF PROFESSOR KOCH

In general, he was speaking of language communities in both senses. There is more than one language community in any field of science. The communities are defined in terms of learned discriminations on the one hand and discriminative capacities and perceptual sensitivities of the organism on the other. "One must expect *far* more language communities defined in these terms (in psychology) than in any other field of science" because of the "incredibly general" conception of the subject matter. The "discrimination pools which are definitive of such language communities" do "overlap," but one cannot make a commitment beforehand either "to the extent of overlapping" to be expected, or to the question, say, of whether an individual who has the capacity for "high level" specialization in the study of the psychology of art could, by virtue of this capacity, be a member of a language community specialized for the study of scientific inquiry. These are, to a large extent, empirical questions.

MEMBER OF THE AUDIENCE

While it is popular in philosophy today to "follow more or less the aspects approach to the totality of human nature following Wittgenstein," this does not seem to apply successfully to ordinary experience. For example in a court of law, people speak the languages of science, of theology, of morals from their theoretically independent logical bases; yet an unsophisticated jury "comes out with a language that apparently can encompass them all." "Now it seems to me it is not a question of whether one individual can speak all the languages . . . but whether there is a theoretical structure or theoretical definition of man in terms of which the comprehension of all of these languages can be understood without negating the understanding in one language as long as you are talking another."

COMMENTS OF PROFESSOR KOCH

No such theoretical structure exists for the language communities relevant to the subject matter of psychology. While "one could conceive of a language that could be constructed which would render discriminations which are expressed in a [limited] plurality of language communities relevant to psychology, one could not necessarily assume that one could construct a language which would render, as one might want it to, *all* languages generated by the language communities" of psychology. One cannot predetermine the limits, but it is most likely that there will be shown to exist universes of discourse in psychology dealing "with subject matter in ways so disparate and involving analysis of that subject matter in terms of categories so inconsonant" as to be incommensurable. "I think other sciences are, to a greater extent than is appreciated, that kind of science even now, and psychology is going to turn out to be very much that kind of science."

R. B. MacLEOD

Phenomenology: A Challenge to Experimental Psychology

By EXPERIMENTAL PSYCHOLOGY I choose to mean the traditional study, within the controlled and repeatable setting of the laboratory, of the psychological processes of normal, human adults. Thus, one regards as experimental psychologists such investigators as Helmholtz, Fechner, Wundt and his pupils, Ebbinghaus, Külpe, G. E. Müller and his pupils, modern gestalt psychologists and modern behaviorists, but not such people as James Mill, Brentano, and Freud. This is not to deny the use of the word "experimental" to the many fields of research, notably clinical and social psychology, in which answers are sought through controlled and quantified observation; it is merely to maintain a distinction which has been with us for some time. I admit that this distinction is gradually losing its usefulness.

Within this narrowly defined tradition of experimental psychology, however, there have been some important divergencies of opinion and approach. Let me first discuss a bit of the history behind these divergencies. Then I shall attempt to distinguish psychological phenomenology from some of the other movements which have been termed "phenomenological." Finally, I shall dwell on a few examples which I hope will demonstrate the usefulness of the phenomenological approach in experimental psychology.

HISTORICAL CONSIDERATIONS

A brief and superficial excursion into history will suffice. I shall resist the temptation to begin with Aristotle. I admit this omission is shocking, but I think that René Descartes and John Locke will serve our purposes better. Neither was original in his psychology, of course, but we look back on Descartes as the father of analytic introspection and on Locke as the father of analytic associationism. Nor was either

R. B. MacLeod, Professor, Department of Psychology, Cornell University.

an experimentalist in the modern sense of the term, although Descartes conducted some crude experiments which furthered the science of optics. What is important for psychology is the fact that, living at a time when the physical and biological sciences were steadily advancing, both men recognized the need for a science of the human mind. But they conceived of this science in two quite different ways. Descartes, while thoroughly mechanistic in his physiology, refused to identify mind with matter. He considered mind *res cogitans*, unextended and unlocalizable in space. The study of mind could be approached only through a scrutiny of the contents of consciousness.

Locke was also interested in the contents of consciousness, but in a different way. We usually list him, and rightly, as one of the great ancestors of modern empiricism. The term "empirical" has to do with experience, but the word has at least two meanings which are commonly confused. The Germans make a convenient distinction between *Erlebnis* and *Erfahrung*. *Erlebnis* refers to present experience, that which is immediately there for the observer without reference to its origin; *Erfahrung*, to the accumulation of past *Erlebnisse*. In the first sense, Descartes was at least as empirical as Locke, since, if we are to believe the account in the *Discours de la Méthode* (1637), he honestly tried to look without bias at the data of *Erlebnis*. (Let the historians quarrel about the validity of his conclusions.)

Locke, on the other hand, was empirical only in the sense that the facts of observation were to be accepted, in the physical sciences at least, as the final test of theory. Remember that Locke's *Essay* (1690) came only three years after Newton's *Principia* and that Newton had been depicting an impressive mechanical universe composed of particles of matter existing in space and time and impelled by force into motion or change of motion. Small wonder, then, that Locke's foray into psychology should be patterned after a science that was explaining the material world in terms of the interactions of simple material particles. Locke's central question was: How can we explain mind through the combination and interaction of its elements? This leads to an empiricism centered about *Erfahrung*.

Locke's system is thus atomistic and reductionistic. His primary qualities of sense are obviously related to Newton's particles of matter, and their combinations into complex states and processes similarly resemble the Newtonian analysis. We may overlook, for the moment, his distinction between primary and secondary qualities. This was an unfortunate distinction, and Berkeley efficiently demolished it in his *Three Dialogues Between Hylas and Philonous* (1713). At any rate, whether we follow Locke, Berkeley, or any of their successors, associationism was born of Newtonian physics and nurtured throughout the eighteenth and nineteenth centuries by the Newtonian philosophy. All mental life was explained away through the reduction of the complex to the simple; even when the term "idea" was replaced by elementary stimulus-response combinations, the ideal of a science of mind was still essentially Newtonian.

One may ask whether Darwin's revolution in biology did not represent a challenge to the Newtonian type of psychology. The answer is that Darwin was, in his early years at least, a Newtonian at heart. He tried, without invoking a teleology, to reduce the complex evidence of evolution to a few simple, almost mechanical, principles. His zealous admirers may be credited with picking up such a Darwinian metaphor as "the struggle for survival" and finding in it support for a renewed defense of religion. Darwin's revolution in biology had notable consequences for psychology. Although there was a period of enthusiastic anecdotalism, C. Lloyd Morgan's restatement of the law of parsimony was taken seriously, and the subject matter of psychology became the behavior of organisms, described and explained in terms as nearly mechanical as possible. Words like "mind" and "consciousness" were not immediately banished; in fact, William James could use both without embarrassment. They were employed more and more, however, to apply to the functions of adjusting organisms. In 1904 James Rowland Angell could write:

If the reflexes and the automatic acts were wholly competent to steer the organism through its course, there is no reason to suppose that consciousness would ever put in an appearance (1).

Thus "mind" was becoming, not a unique stuff, but a mode of organismic functioning not necessarily unique to man.

Long before Darwin, the term "original nature" was used to designate the vast unlearned repertory of acts and tendencies which contribute to the survival of the individual and the species. For the early functionalist, whatever his concept of original nature might be, one of the central problems of psychology became inevitably that of learning, the machinery whereby the adjustive behavior of organisms becomes modified. William James (11) referred to habit as "the enormous fly-wheel of society," a theme which was later to become central in Dewey's system (3). You will recall that in Thorndike's massive *Educational Psychology* (19), Volume I was devoted to original nature, Volume II to learning, and Volume III to individual differences. Since the beginning of this century, I think it is safe to say, and certainly since John B. Watson's ebullient response to the findings of the Russian reflexology, the ability of man and animal to acquire and retain modes of response which we call skill and knowledge has become the central preoccupation of American psychology. Hilgard's *Theories of Learning* (8) could almost be subtitled "a systematic survey of American psychological theory."

But what is the actual machinery of learning? This is the crucial question. I do not think I shall be offending anyone when I assert that the concept of learning has become reified. To say that an act has been learned is to say nothing more than that it has developed along lines which could not have been predicted in accordance with the classical principles derived from garden peas and fruit flies. Contemporary geneticists, as you know, are refreshingly open-minded about the so-called laws of genetic determination, especially so far as behavior is concerned. The question of what is genetically determined and what is learned is not as simple as it appeared even a few decades ago. If you will pardon me, I suggest that we banish "learning" from psychology as an explanatory construct and substitute some such purely descriptive term as "development," or even "change." Surely we and our animal friends are always undergoing developmental changes, only some of which become explicitly observable and even less frequently reportable.

And now for another quick look at Descartes and the beginnings of psychological phenomenology. Let me repeat, as in the case of Locke and the empiricist movement, that Descartes has no claim to historical priority; we could easily go back to the time of Saint Augustine or even earlier. We usually list Descartes among the rationalists, and this judgment can be easily defended. I consider it unfortunate, however, that he is so frequently associated with the doctrine of innate ideas. After all, the empiricist Locke found himself speaking of the "powers of the mind" as though the mind had its own inherent structure, and even David Hume, in his spirited battle against the rationalists, made skillful use of the immutable laws of logic. From our point of view, however, what is impressive about Descartes is not the *cogito ergo sum* and his logical derivation of God and a rational order but his presumably honest attempt to look, without predisposing biases about origins, at the sheer facts of experience (*Erlebnis*). It is interesting that one of Husserl's influential books was his *Cartesian Meditations* (9), published originally in French. Husserl went far beyond Descartes, of course, and in directions which need not concern us here; but both men shared the determination to place in brackets (*einklammern*) the biases of tradition and to ferret out from experience that which is essential and indubitable.

Husserl is, without question, the towering figure in modern phenomenology. Husserl was, however, a philosopher; he saw in phenomenology a bold way of reconstructing philosophy's method and content, and the bulk of his writing concerns itself with philosophical topics. Let me state emphatically that what we call psychological phenomenology is not to be confused with Husserl's philosophy. Husserl was deeply influenced by some of the psychologists, notably by Brentano, Stumpf, and William James, but he could not regard their work as "pure" phenomenology. In the work of the "new" psychology of the late nineteenth century—what James called the "brass instrument" psychology—he found little to challenge the philosopher. For him the beginning of a true philosophy rested on the intuition of essences in experience, and this was not the preoccupation of the psychologists who were his contemporaries. The fate of phenomenology as philosophy will have to be judged by the historian. The movement has certainly grown since Husserl's early years, and in directions which are now somewhat confusing. Herbert Spiegelberg, in *The Phenomenological Movement* (18), considers it the great modern alternative to the analytic philosophy of Wittgenstein. Martin Heidegger, especially in *Sein und Zeit* (6), emphasized the concept of *Existenz*, which we must translate as "existence"; and the existentialist movement has branched out into theology, literature, drama, the visual arts, psychiatry, and certain of the social sciences and even has had its influence on politics. Whether or not the various forms of existentialism can be intelligibly linked to Husserl's phenomenology I cannot say. To be quite frank, I must confess that I find Heidegger as deadly as Hegel and that many existentialist plays leave me merely uncomfortable. Fortunately we can leave this question to the historians too.

Phenomenology and Experimental Psychology

My task is to relate phenomenology to experimental psychology, and this in itself is not an easy undertaking. Let me emphasize four general points before proceeding to specific examples. First, the phenomenologist—psychological or philosophical—accepts, as the subject-matter of his inquiry, all data of experience (*Erlebnis*). I am using the word "datum" in its correct sense: "that which is given." Colors and sounds are data; so are impressions of distance and duration; so are feelings of attraction and repulsion; so are yearnings and fears, ecstasies and disillusionments; so are all the relations—ranging from the crude and obvious to the delicate and intangible—with which the world presents us. These are data, given in experience, to be accepted as such and to be wondered about. Many writers have distinguished between the raw data of sense as primary and the relations between sense-data as secondary. No phenomenologist can begin with such a distinction, although his very scrutiny of the phenomena may help him to understand why it is so easy to accept the notion that some data are more primary than others; but degree of primacy is just one way in which phenomenal data may be ordered. William James faced the question in his famous chapter on "The Stream of Thought." Criticizing both the Intellectualists and the Sensationalists, he said:

But from our point of view both Intellectualists and Sensationalists are wrong. If there be such things as feelings at all, *then so surely as relations between objects exist in rerum natura, so surely, and more surely, do feelings exist to which these relations are known.* There is not a conjunction or a preposition, and hardly an adverbial phrase, syntactic form, or inflection of voice, in human speech, that does not express some shading or other of relation which we at some moment actually feel to exist between the larger objects of our thought. If we speak objectively, it is the real relations that appear revealed; if we speak subjectively, it is the stream of consciousness that matches each of them by an inward coloring of its own. In either case the relations are numberless, and no existing language is capable of doing justice to all their shades.

We ought to say a feeling of *and*, a feeling of *if*, a feeling of *but*, and a feeling of *by*, quite as readily as we say a feeling of *blue* or a feeling of *cold*. Yet we do not: so inveterate has our habit become of recognizing the existence of the substantive parts alone, that language almost refuses to lend itself to any other use (11).

Forgive the long quotation, but it leads to the second point. Transitive states of consciousness, asserts James, are just as truly data as are substantive states; their relegation to a secondary status reveals a bias, a word which James did not use. If you dislike the word "bias," you may substitute something like "implicit assumption." The phenomenologist begins his observation of phenomena by suspending his biases, by putting his implicit assumptions in brackets. If your immediate comment is that it is impossible to observe anything without bias, all I can say is that I heartily agree. There is no observation without bias, but there can be a deliberate attempt to identify bias and temporarily suspend it or at least to shift observation systematically from one bias to another. I shall not weary you with a catalogue of observational biases. My examples will, I hope, bring a few into focus; but I cannot resist one illustration. Koffka, speaking about the study of perception, used to say that its central problem was to explain why it is that we see the world as we do. My colleague, J. J. Gibson, in spite of years of association with Koffka, rendered it as "why we see the world as it is." This reveals an epistemological bias, which Gibson cheerfully admits. Gibson stubbornly insists that there is a real world "out there" to which the phenomena world can be co-ordinated. Perhaps he is right, but it seems to me that the phenomenologist should first ask:

What are the properties of phenomena which invite a belief in the existence of an external world? What, for that matter, invites us to distinguish between external and internal?

The third point has to do with phenomenological observation as such. Please do not confuse psychological phenomenology, on the one hand, with the kind of introspection which Titchener so rigorously defined and practiced, or, on the other hand, with what is coming to be referred to more and more vaguely as empathy. "Introspection" is Titchener's rendering of Wundt's *Selbstbeobachtung*, literally, "observation of one's self." This is obviously a misleading expression; when one observes a color one is not observing oneself, unless one expands the meaning of self to a point at which it ceases to be meaningful, as Berkeley did. For Titchener, to introspect is to analyze, through disciplined observation, the data of experience into their irreducible elements—sensations, feelings, and images—and to specify their attributes—quality, intensity, extensity, protensity, and attensity. Take the experience of wetness as an example. You are doing a dissection in the laboratory and, before drawing on your rubber gloves, you dust your hands with talcum powder. At the end of the dissection, before you remove the gloves, you rinse your hands in cold water. Your hands, through the gloves, feel wet. The experience is so compelling that you are almost startled to discover later that the powder on your hands is completely dry. Is wetness a sensation? No, said Titchener, for it can be reduced to a combination of the elementary sensations of cold and pressure. We can demonstrate this experimentally by directing a stream of air at the surface of the skin, with pressure constant and temperature variable. When the air is cold you feel wetness; as temperature is increased you feel pure pressure, then dryness, then oiliness, and finally pain. If you are a sufficiently good introspectionist, i.e., if you were trained at Cornell University, you can perform the analysis directly, using the experimental devices primarily for duplication and quantification. When the students of thinking in Würzburg claimed to have found imageless-thought contents, Titchener rejected their *Bewusstseinslagen, Bewusstheiten,* and *Aha-Erlebnisse* as merely evidence of poor introspection. When the problem solver happily reports "Aha! I have it," his imagery, Titchener insisted, is being supported by a complex of kinesthetic sensations.

It is clear that introspection is not far removed from phenomenological observation and description. Both are directed at experience (*Erlebnis*). But there are two crucial differences. First, the introspectionist makes the initial assumption that experience is reducible to a finite number of conscious elements and attributes; this is a bias which the phenomenologist attempts to bracket. Secondly, and perhaps more important, there is no place in introspective analysis for meaning, except insofar as meanings can be reduced to elements and their attributes. For the phenomenologist, meaning is central and inescapable. To try to abstract or extract meaning from the phenomenal world is futile; all we achieve is a change of meaning. But I shall say more about meaning when we approach the phenomenology of communication.

About empathy I shall have more to say presently. It has become a very popular word and has already added considerably to our confusion. Theodore Lipps was probably the first to introduce *Einfühlung* into psychology, and I think it was Titchener who suggested "empathy" as an English equivalent. You see an unbalanced statue which stays erect even though it seems to defy the laws of physics, and you find yourself almost imperceptibly straining your muscles to restore the balance. This is *Einfühlung*, a form of projection. You see a weeping child and feel the impulse to weep yourself; you are experiencing sympathy (*Mitgefühl*). Max Scheler in *Die Wesen und Formen der Sympathie* (17) distinguishes empathy from the various forms of sympathy and adds a number of other categories, for example, *Einsfühlung, Nachfühlung, Nachahmung, Sichhineinversetzung,* and *Gefühlsansteckung.* To tease out the various ways in which the perceiver may be affectively related to the perceived is a proper task for the phenomenologist, but not the only task. Phenomenology is more than just sympathy or empathy, more than just putting oneself in the other person's shoes; it seeks, with all the discipline of Titchenerian introspection, to bring under scrutiny the very phenomena which Titchener so skillfully avoided.

The fourth and last point is little more than repetition. Psychological phenomenology is not psychology: it is propaedeutic to a science of psychology. To build a science of psychology one must begin with the phenomenal world, but then one must transcend it. Köhler makes this point in the chapter on "Beyond Phenomenology" in *The Place of Value in a World of Facts* (14). There are various ways of transcending the phenomenal world. The first, of course, is by building a metaphysics which says something about the non-phenomenal world. Every scientist is a metaphysician, whether or not he likes to admit it, at least to the extent that he asserts the existence of something which he does not fully understand but which he is determined to investigate. The transcendent reality may be a world of material things, a world of ideas, a world of values, or a world of spirits; all transcend the world of phenomena. I know of no writer, even Berkeley, who .has consistently maintained a solipsistic position. The phenomenological approach in psychology is likely to lead us into psychophysics, into psychophysiology, into social psychology, perhaps even—and I suggest this with great diffidence—into a sophisticated behaviorism. One is often asked whether phenomenology can be reconciled with Freudian psychoanalysis, which seems to be its absolute antithesis. I do not know whether the extreme Freudian position can be reconciled with anything in science. Certainly, however, the phenomenological approach has yielded rich rewards in psychodiagnosis and psychotherapy.

The approach, to be repetitious again, always represents a fascination with the world of experience (*Erlebnis*) as it is there for us. Once again the Germans have something of a linguistic jump on us. When we ask the question: What is there for me? we are tempted to distinguish between "there" and "here," between "me" and "not-me." The Germans can simply ask: *Was ist da?* and the reference can be to everything that appears, including the "I" or "me" which sometimes seems to have a unique status in the world of phenomena. The Germans can talk about the *Dasein* or the *Sosein* of the thing or of the "me" without sounding more than usually pedantic; whereas when we use terms like "thereness" and "thusness" we are immediately identified as professors. At any rate, there is a "thereness" or a "hereness" about the self, which makes it just as truly a part of the phenomenal world as is any perceived thing or event and consequently makes it equally worthy of phenomenological analysis. I shall have to say a little more presently about the dimensions of selfhood. For the time being, may I merely remind you that in the phenmenal world the dividing line between self and not-self is not always a clear one and that such distinctions as those between internal and external, introjection and projection, private and public may sometimes lead to unnecessary confusion. When we speak of the internalization of values, for instance, or the projection of guilt, we imply that something has moved from the outside to the inside or from the inside to the outside. But outside what and inside what? It is certainly not the skin or the brain or some part of the brain. Both the tree I am looking at, which is out there, and the headache I feel, which is in here, presumably have similar neurophysiological correlates; yet one is apprehended as objective, the other as subjective. It is clear that we cannot speak lightly of internalization or projection without having first explored the phenomenology of subjectivity and objectivity.

And now for a few examples of phenomenology as it is related to specific psychological problems, I have agreed to limit myself to problems or problem areas which may be broadly termed "experimental." This is going to be difficult because with almost every advance in theory one feels a need to look again at the phenomena that the theory attempts to explain. Similarly, with almost every advance in methodology one finds certain crucially important phenomena slipping out of focus. A good example is the psychology of the expressive arts, with which we have done so little. If you have not already done so, you might look at Gaffron's study of Rembrandt's etchings (5). Gaffron presents an array of observations which invite the psychophysicist to return to experimental aesthetics. Staying within the realm of aesthetics, how many of us have taken a close look at the phenomena of disgust? Certainly we can quantify rejection or avoidance behavior or specify the stimuli which evoke regurgitation. This gives us some crude information, but it does not tell us what it actually feels like to be disgusted. In one of the early volumes of Husserl's *Jahrbuch* (10) there is an article on *Die Phänomenologie des Ekels* that is quite interesting. I shall not embarrass you by giving gruesome details, but we are all familiar with the disgusting odor that changes its character radically as soon as we apprehend it as the odor of a particularly delectable cheese. Just a little phenomenology, even in an armchair, will reveal subtle dimensions of the experience of disgust that will challenge not only the psychophysiologist but also the social psychologist.

The problems of aesthetics are entrancing, but let me spend the rest of my time on three experimental areas in which psychological phenomenology has already demonstrated its relevance or at least shows promise of being able to do so. These are: (*a*) phenomenal constancy, (*b*) the phenomenology of the other person, and (*c*) the phenomenology of communication.

PHENOMENAL CONSTANCY

Phenomenal constancy is a familiar problem, and I apologize for selecting it. To put it briefly, the structures and properties of the phenomenal world tend to remain constant in spite of variations in stimulation. Why? Most of our information comes from visual studies of size, shape, color (including the black-white series), and orientation, but there have also been important pioneer studies of the constancy of loudness, of speech patterns, of the properties of tactually perceived surfaces, and even of temperature. It explains nothing to say that were it not for phenomenal constancy we would be living in a chaotic world in which we could not survive. What we must understand is the machinery whereby this constancy is maintained. Let me begin by asserting, as others have done before, but for varying reasons, that phenomenal constancy is not a legitimate problem at all; it is rather a pseudo-problem thrust upon us because of our traditional confusion of the phenomenal with the physical.

The story goes back to Sir Isaac Newton. Early in the eighteenth century Newton (*Opticks*, 1704) demonstrated how passing "white" light through a prism broke it down into its spectral components, the familiar colors of the rainbow, and that these, when judiciously re-combined, produced white. It might consequently be argued, as it was, that white is not a true sensation, but merely a combination of sensa-tions, and that black is not a sensation at all but merely the absence of visual stimulation. This is an argument from the properties of the physical to the properties of the phenomenal, an argument which caused no trouble in the early eighteenth century. In fact it was not until much later, when the laws of contrast were more fully under-stood, that the blackest of all blacks was found to be dependent, not merely on the absence of stimulation, but rather on the presentation of a stimulus-free area surrounded by brilliant white. About a century after Newton, Goethe attempted a rebuttal. His massive book on color, *Zur Farbenlehre* (1810), has received a rather poor press, but his obvious failure to upset Newton's physics should not lead us to undervalue his contribution to psychology. Thinking of colors as phenomena and not as wave lengths, there is no reason at all to con-clude, from the fusion of lights which normally produce yellow with lights which normally produce blue into a combination which pro-duces white, that therefore the color white is a combination of the colors yellow and blue. White is a color in its own right.

So great was Newton's prestige in the early nineteenth century that Goethe's phenomenological protest went largely unheeded. Even today in moments of laziness, and with an even lazier language, we catch ourselves referring to wave lengths in the neighborhood of seven hundred millimicrons as though there were something intrinsi-cally red about them. Wave lengths as such have no color. This was quickly recognized, notably by the physiologists who pointed out that a physical process does not really become a stimulus until it has activated a specialized receptor substance with sufficient strength to send an impulse charging through the nerve fibers to the brain. Only in the brain can we find the structures or the activities immediately responsible for the difference between yellow and blue. According to the law of specific energies, anticipated by Bell and Magendie, de-veloped by Johannes Müller, and refined by Helmholtz, the unique-ness of any sensory quality is ultimately to be explained in terms of the neuroanatomy and neurophysiology of the nervous system, the anatomy and physiology of the selecting receptors, and the physics of the stimuli themselves. The nineteenth century witnessed enor-mous advances in all these fields. The physics of stimulation was being clarified; there was an avid search for specialized sensory receptors; the machinery of conduction was beginning to be understood; and, by the end of the century, notable advances were being made toward a theory of cortical localization. The outlook was promising: it looked as though the problem of sensation would soon be solved.

And what were the experimental psychologists doing all the while? The psychologists were meekly following in the footsteps of their colleagues in the natural sciences, accepting and refining their methods, adding a new fact here and there, but never challenging their fundamental assumptions. They did not challenge the assumption that consciousness is composed of elements for each of which there must exist an equally elementary process of stimulation, reception, and conduction. Few psychologists raised the questions, except above a whisper: Has anyone ever really observed a pure sensation? Does a strictly psychological analysis require us to believe in sensations as elements? William James asked these questions, but he was not really an experimentalist. The loyal experimentalists did not dare to say to their colleagues in physiology and neurology, "We are grateful to you for your discoveries, but we cannot in good conscience allow your assumptions to dictate our science. Let us look at our own phenomena for a while, and then perhaps we shall be able to suggest some new directions for your research." Perhaps this challenge was not laid down for the simple reason that most of the early experimental psychologists were themselves physicists, physiologists, and neurologists, with their own appropriate biases. One of the best illustrations is to be found in the search for receptors. It was assumed that for every differentiable quality of sensation there must be a correspondingly differentiated sensory structure. We know, intuitively perhaps, the difference between yellow and blue. We have not yet found corresponding brain processes; but they must be there. We are still quarreling about retinal receptors, but we are sure that there must be some that give us yellow and others that give us blue. Why? It is simply an article of our faith. The search for cutaneous end-organs is even more instructive. We can all recognize pain, pressure, warm, and cold; so there must be receptors for each. Free nerve endings and Meissner's corpuscles seemed to be responsible for the first two, and for a while it looked as though Ruffini corpuscles and Krause's end-bulbs might take care of the others. But now, at least in the field of temperature sensation, the question of cutaneous receptors is again wide open: quite a new type of theory may be on the way. What is amusing is that throughout this frustrated search for receptors we have known all along what it is we are looking for: the correlates of sensory quality. And where do we find the qualities to which we are trying to match the as yet undiscovered receptors? We find them simply "there" in our own immediate experience. Had the voice of Goethe rung out a little more clearly, the experimentalists might have been saved a good deal of time.

What has this little historical detour to do with phenomenal constancy? The answer is simple. Helmholtz, the best of the experimentalists, knew perfectly well that we do not in the naïve sense see sensations; we see objects, and these objects as we see them do not change in appearance with every change in stimulation. Yet Helmholtz's faith in the point-for-point correspondence between stimulus and sensation was such that he simply had to retain the sensations as elements, even if we are not directly aware of them, and to look elsewhere for an explanation of phenomenal constancy. Writing a century ago, he found his answer in the concept of unconscious inference. Stimulus changes do in fact produce corresponding changes in sensation, but, because of our past experience, we unconsciously and with lightning speed re-interpret these changes in such a way as to maintain the apparent constancy of the object. This is, of course, an unassailable position, as is any retreat into the unconscious. I do not think we can say that Helmholtz has been fully refuted. If he were writing today, I suspect that he would long since have scrapped the terminology of unconscious inference and would be now excitedly constructing brain models and testing them with electronic computers. As a matter of fact, the best perceptrons of today are more or less Helmholtzian in their design, and they have replicated in a very modest way some of the phenomena of constancy.

Helmholtz was attacked in his own day, notably by Ewald Hering, who attacked almost everything Helmholtzian. The real challenge did not come, however, until early in this century, and the basis of it was essentially phenomenological. In 1911 David Katz published *Die Erscheinungsweisen der Farben* (12) (the modes of appearance of color). The challenge was at first a little cautious, for he appended in the subtitle, *und ihre Beinflüssung durch die individuelle Erfährung* (and the ways in which these are influenced through individual experience). Katz was a pupil of G. E. Müller, but he also had direct contact with Hering and Husserl. Katz's approach to color was somewhat as follows: If we are to understand the world of color, we must first look carefully at the colors themselves, not just at their qualities, but at all the ways in which they appear. They usually appear as surfaces with particular shapes and particular orientations in space; but they may also have a filmy quality devoid of surface characteristics (*Flächenfarbe*), or they may be seen as tridimensional or as lustrous or glowing. These are all different modes of appearance of the same color. When a change in stimulus intensity is introduced, as in the shadowing of a white surface, the surface may continue to look white, but as a white seen through a darker medium. Viewed through a reduction screen, it becomes a gray filmy color. The same stimulus applied in different contexts may produce radically different perceptions of color. As long as a color appears as a surface it will tend within limits to maintain its constancy. The surface appearance is not a simple function of the wave length or intensity of incoming light; it is a complex function of many variables which contribute to the structuring of the visual world. By inverting the traditional problem, by beginning with phenomena rather than with stimuli or hypothetical sensation elements, Katz helped to free the psychology of perception for tasks which it could not otherwise have undertaken.

About the same time as Katz was working with colors, Wertheimer was doing his classic experiments with the phenomena of apparent movement. The details are familiar to everyone, so I shall not repeat them. Suffice it to say that apparent movement had been traditionally an illusion, to be explained away because the orthodox theory had no place for sensations of movement. Wertheimer simply accepted movement as a valid phenomenon, studied the conditions under which it occurs or does not occur, and then developed a theory of perception which accorded primary explanatory significance to properties of organization rather than to properties of elements. Gestalt theory went beyond perception into the psychology of learning, thinking, and motivation, and it even made some forays into neurophysiology. The heat of the battle may now have died down, but the Gestaltists have opened up for exploration a world which is structured and meaningful. Our question about phenomenal constancy must consequently be replaced by a whole series of questions: How does the phenomenal world become structured? What factors contribute to the strength and stability of a given structure? How do structures support one another or come into conflict? And, inevitably, how is phenomenal structuring to be related to the physical and physiological processes of the organism?

THE "OTHER PERSON"

Let me switch now to the phenomenology of the other person. Since this topic really belongs to Dr. Rogers, I shall do nothing more than try to relate it to experimental psychology. Too often the experimentalists have dismissed the problem as mere philosophy, with which no true scientist should dirty his fingers. You will not find many papers on "the self" or the "other self" delivered at meetings of experimental psychologists. Fortunately, our clinical colleagues have found the problem staring them in the face, and the clinical literature is steadily growing richer. Both experimentalists and clini-

cians are aware, sometimes only dimly, that there is always an epistemologist lurking around the corner ready to jump on us when-
ever we use words like "self" and "other self." My impulse, of course,
is to plunge in and see what happens; the epistemologist might even
turn out to be a friend.

To put our question in colloquial language, can we, as psychologists or even as human beings, ever fully understand what is going on
in someone else's head? I suspect that most philosophers are bored
with that one; they have discussed it for centuries. But it would do no
harm if psychologists were to take another look at it, not—heaven
forbid!—with the thought that a final answer will be found, but possibly with the hope that here and there a relevant observation might
be made.

If you do not mind, I shall disregard the old question of solipsism.
At one time or another every schoolboy discovers the problem. I see
something as red, and you say it looks red to you; but how do I know
that what you call red is not what I see as blue? This is, of course, a
pseudo-problem which can be disposed of in various ways; but if we
wish to consider it as a problem we see at once that it is not peculiar
to the phenomenologist. The *ipse solus*, the self alone, could equally
well be an astronomer or a poet, each watching his own lonely stars
or dreaming his own lonely dreams.

Much more embarrassing than the solipsistic riddle is a series of
difficulties created for us by, or at least reflected in, our language. It
is easy enough to say we are interested in things, events, and relations
as they appear to us. Accordingly, we direct our attention toward
certain aspects of the phenomenal world, we refine our questions, set
up our experimental controls, record our observations, test these for
significance, and so forth, just as any other experimenter would. This
is pretty much what Katz and Wertheimer did in their early experiments. But note that in their very experimental procedures they accepted as trustworthy their timing devices, their illuminometers, their
meter sticks, and all the other measuring instruments necessary for the
stabilizing of conditions of observation. Every experimental phenomenologist must, of necessity, anchor his observations to certain non-
phenomenal controls. In the cases I have mentioned the controls are
supplied by the techniques of physics. This is probably why the early
experimenters found it easiest to concentrate on problems of perception and, particularly, of visual perception. As we move from simple
perceptual phenomena, which can be physically anchored, to the
more complex forms of cognition or to the delicate interactions in social behavior, we find it increasingly difficult to find independent
variables against which we can plot our psychological dependent

variables. In a problem-solving experiment, for instance, we like to think that the problem as presented in the instruction is an independent variable; we may hold the instruction constant or we may deliberately vary it to observe the effects of a changed instruction on problem-solving. What we discover, of course, is that what we think is the same instruction may turn out to be quite different instructions to different people. How then are we to understand what is really "there" for the other person? If plotting the characteristics of our own world sometimes seems like pulling ourselves up with our own bootstraps, then doing the same for someone else's world might seem to be about as easy as taking the measurements of a room with a whimsical snake as one's yardstick. Should we concede that everything is relative to everything else and give up our hope of ever understanding another person? Or should we simply don our emperor's new clothes and pretend that we are measuring with yardsticks and not with snakes? The relativists, particularly some of our anthropological friends, take an almost sadistic pleasure in pointing out exceptions to everything we psychologists dare to say about people. Our more pragmatic friends seem to be content with the belief that any instrument that predicts, to our satisfaction, what other people will do is a good instrument. Perhaps we should resign as psychologists and become mathematicians or engineers.

Before we take such a step, let me confuse the situation still a little further. Throughout this discussion I have been using such words as "I," "me," "my," "we," "our," "you," and "yours," as though we knew what they meant. English is rich in personal pronouns; yet if we had a separate word for every personal reference we make, we would choke before we could say anything. I do not propose to introduce a new jargon, but let me occasionally use the word "self" where we need something more or less neutral. In the earlier phenomenological studies I have mentioned, the role of the self is relatively inconsequential. The observer says, "I see the color on the left as brighter." The "I" in "I see" is nothing more than a reference point for the judgment; he might just as well have signaled it by pressing a key. In a Sherif-type of experiment with autokinetic movement the observer may say, "You may see the spot moving upward, but I see it moving to the right." The "I" in this case may be somewhat more prominent, and it can become very prominent indeed if you keep challenging the observer; but you will not find him talking about "my spot." He is more likely to say, "You're crazy." The "I" is still a reference point for a judgment of movement. In this experiment, as you know, the spot is physically stationary, and many writers have placed autokinetic movement, along with afterimages, optical illusions, phantom limbs, and the like, in the category of subjective phenomena. If by subjective we mean related to a variable state of the organism, then of course these are subjective phenomena; but so is every other phenomenon observed by the psychologist or, for that matter, by any other scientist. If we wish to follow this line we shall find our psychology hopelessly confused with epistemology.

In a quandary like this the best thing to do is to take another look at the phenomena. You will pardon me, I hope, if I continue to use words like "I" and "my"; but there is no way of avoiding them. I have no right, as a matter of fact, to speak of "my" or "your" or "his" phenomenal world. The world of phenomena is simply there. It is easy to blame the confusion on our language; but, if we are good phenomenologists, we must concede that language in its clumsy way keeps reminding us of distinctions which are worth closer scrutiny. Granted that the afterimage is phenomenally objective, just as this table is phenomenally objective, it is nevertheless just a little less objective than is the table, for it moves and changes size as I change my fixation; it is just a little more closely related to me. There are degrees of phenomenal objectivity which must be specified in relation to the phenomenal self.

The phenomenal self, or subject, is just as truly a datum of experience as is the phenomenal object, and there are degrees of subjectivity just as there are degrees of objectivity. As phenomenal datum the self can be studied, not as easily, but as legitimately as we study the phenomenal object. I am not going to say anything about the psychology of selfhood other than to point out that, like the object, the self is localized and bounded; it possesses the identity of continuity, but it can change in time; it can be active or passive, strongly or weakly organized, and so forth. In our empirical studies of the self we usually begin with the body-percept, but we quickly realize, as James and McDougall did, that the boundaries of the body are not necessarily the boundaries of selfhood. The self may be the final flicker of consciousness that precedes total anesthesia, or it may become so broad that the mystic can say with conviction, "I and the world are one."

States and activities of the self can be studied empirically. How about those of the "other self"? If we can continue to curb the impulse to charge into a discussion of epistemology, I think, again, that we have a set of researchable problems. To begin with a commonplace observation, we are constantly being confronted with things and events that are phenomenally not me, i.e., they are objective. Some of these we call "things," others "persons." What differentiates a person from a thing? Not as simple a question as it may appear, yet we all behave as though we knew the answer. Our modest experimental approach is to transform persons into things and things into persons, observing what has been gained or lost in the process. A simple way of transforming a person into a thing is by the skillful use of a gun, but this technique is frowned upon as unscientific. An easier and safer experiment is to begin with a thing and then change it judiciously until it appears as a person. The skilled painter is doing this in part when he transforms some impersonal colors, lines, and smudges into a lifelike portrait. Mona Lisa is not exactly a complete person, but at least *she*, and not *it*, has an enigmatic smile. In Michotte's experiments on the perception of causality (15) we have the compelling impression that one little square is pushing or dragging another little square. A few years before Michotte's experiments, Heider and Simmel (7) made a movie in which a big triangle, a little triangle, and five straight lines are moved about in rather unsystematic fashion. Only the most stubbornly sophisticated observer fails to see a touching little drama being played out, with the triangles and the circle as almost real persons. Add a few sound effects, and we might almost be convinced. But not quite; even the best Hollywood technicians and the best puppeteers have never fully succeeded. Mona Lisa smiles at us or at something, but she is still a portrait on a canvas; Michotte's and Heider's little figures push and pull each other about in frenzies of emotion, producing all sorts of empathy and sympathy in us, but we are never really fooled. What is missing? I do not know the answer, but I am sure that some day we shall find it. Perhaps we miss in the thing the ability to respond to us in a way that makes sense to us or, perhaps better, in a way that bewilders us at first and then makes sense. I have never yet played chess with a computer. When I do and he beats me, as I am assured he will, I hope I shall accept the defeat gracefully. Shall I feel like taking off my hat to the man who made the computer? Or to the computer himself? I think the latter. I might even find myself, in a sour mood, resenting his game as unethical.

Suppose we discover all the conditions necessary for the creation of the impression of personality and then hire a clever engineer to build a machine that looks and behaves exactly like a human. Will this disturb us? This is an old question, and a silly one. Of course it will not disturb us any more than we are disturbed when the anatomist and the physiologist explain the structure and functioning of the body. The very perception of something as a person includes the perception of responsiveness, animation, emotion, and probably many other properties that we have not yet identified. I am not suggesting that this sort of perception is something instantaneous, for every percept is a process in time. What I do suggest is that the other self as a percept, albeit more difficult to deal with, presents no problems that are, in principle, different from those of impersonal objects.

Are we then justified in speaking of the phenomenal world of the other person? I think we are, and I think we may legitimately ask about the phenomenal world of the dog, the rat, or even the earthworm; although I grant that the farther down the scale we go the more difficult it is to be sure of our answers. I have already indicated my impatience with the loose use of the word "projection." When we try to understand the other person (or the other earthworm), we are not thrusting something from ourselves into him. We are looking and listening, as it were, trying to let what is there speak to us. Insight is seeing into, and it is not always sudden and dramatic. It takes little or no insight to see that the bus is approaching, a little more to see the figure concealed in a jumble of lines, much more to see, behind that poker face, the almost imperceptible gleam that signifies four aces.

Reconstructing the world of the other person involves an opening of the self to the other self. This is where empathy as an enriched and disciplined form of perception can be so important; sympathy may be a hindrance rather than a help; identification in some of the Freudian senses may be quite destructive of understanding, but in Scheler's sense (*Sichhineinversetzung*) it may provide a useful test. I confess that when it comes to reconstructing the world of the earthworm or the honeybee I feel safer when I have a hard-boiled behaviorist with me to keep me from mistaking anthropomorphism for empathy. You may or may not have agreed with the late Edward Tolman, but I think you will concede that he knew his rats. He liked to be classed as a behaviorist, but one time he made a slip. In the heat of one of the controversies (20) he declared his intention "to go ahead imagining how, *if I were a rat*, I would behave. . . ." I accused him of being a phenomenologist, but he did not fully appreciate this as a compliment.

COMMUNICATION

My third, and final, example comes from the psychological study of communication; and I shall have to limit myself drastically. It is strange that experimental psychology, while always recognizing the significance of language, has until recently done very little about it. James devoted only a few pages to the topic, and Wundt's two volumes in the *Völkerpsychologie* (1900–1920) are frankly non-experimental. In addition, there were a number of valuable contributions from animal psychologists, child psychologists, students of the abnormal, and linguists with a psychological orientation. The experimental study of language did not really "catch on" until World War II stimulated certain mathematicians and engineers to attempt the streamlining of procedures of communication. Out of the practical problem there emerged some suggestive theory, and what we now know as "information theory" was born. We are all familiar with the vocabulary of information theory—encoding, transmission, decoding, bits of information, noise, redundancy, feedback, and the like—and we find such terms cropping up in all sorts of contexts. The theoretical simplicity of information theory had an immediate appeal to many linguists and experimental psychologists. In 1951 a summer seminar was held at Cornell University to explore common problems of psychology and linguistics, one of the outcomes of which was a bulky monograph entitled *Psycholinguistics* (2). This has added a new word to our vocabulary and has stimulated an impressive quantity of research.

I have no particular objection to the word "psycholinguistics," except that it gives us still another word beginning with "psycho"; nor have I anything but admiration for some of the things the information theorists are doing, granted that they have not given us a theory and that the word "information" may be a little misleading. What tires one is the thought of all the translating we shall have to do if we are finally to adopt the new language. Nevertheless, although linguists and philosophers have fought a losing battle to preserve the purity of the word "semantics," they have not, apart from the waste of time and energy, suffered very great pain. What I shall now try to point out is that we may be deriving spurious comfort from the methods of analysis offered by information theory. There is still a place for phenomenology in the study of communication.

The information theory paradigm is simple and appealing. It is based on the analogy of the telegraph wire along which pulses of energy can pass. These pulses are separated by varying time intervals, as in the Morse code. Add a few more variables, such as intensity and pitch, and we have a more efficient instrument like the telephone. It can be argued that this is precisely what happens in vocal communication. At the input end certain disturbances are produced which are transmitted through the medium and then registered at the output end, distortions in transmission being taken care of by feedback, redundancy, and similar devices. There is nothing in this transmission which cannot be specified physically and mathematically. Add to the oral-aural system not only the machinery of vision, as we are now doing in television, but also machinery appropriate to the other sensory modalities, and there is theoretically no limit to the complexity of the messages which will eventually be encoded and subsequently decoded. Many years ago Bertrand Russell remarked, perhaps wistfully, perhaps wryly, that the time will come when any one person anywhere will be able to be completely present to any other person anywhere else.

As I have intimated already, I have nothing but admiration for the present and prospective achievements of this kind of engineering; and if psychologists wish to become engineers they will have an exciting time, and they will undoubtedly make more money than they do now. But this is not psychology. What the communications engineers frankly and explicitly ignore is the *meaning* of the message; they are interested primarily in the techniques of encoding, transmitting, and decoding. Behind the encoding machine, however, is someone with a message, and what is decoded must be understood by someone else. Until communication is taken over by electronic thinkers at both ends of the transmission wire, I think there will still be a place for a few of us who are interested in the content of communication. In the psychology of language we have tended in the past to be concerned more about the machinery of output and input, i.e., in the psychophysics and psychophysiology of sound production and sound perception, than with the meanings that are being conveyed.

Let me suggest schematically a phenomenological paradigm. This is less elegant than that of the telegraph wire, but I think it comes closer to communication as we ordinarily encounter it. Communication involves minimally a speaker, a medium, and a hearer. In the best examples, speaker and hearer are human beings whose roles are regularly reversed, with the consequence that there is usually feedback in both directions. The medium is usually a language, in the conventional sense of the term, either spoken or written, but it may include gestures, postures, facial expressions, and a host of other variables. In very old-fashioned terminology we say that the speaker has some ideas which he conveys to the hearer. If we approach the whole problem phenomenologically we must try to find out what is there for speaker and hearer and what role the medium plays in the interaction between the two. The parallel to the information theory paradigm is obvious, but in this case we have re-introduced meaning. Psychologists have contorted themselves in ridiculous ways to avoid the use of the term "meaning." Granted that it is not a very precise term, it pops up in our communication so irresistibly that I think we might just as well live with it:

"I am sure you know what I mean."

"What's the meaning of 'serendipity'?"

"That poem is nonsense? Certainly not. It's meaning is simply too deep for you to grasp."

"Was heisst das?"

"Ich meine, es wird bald regnen."

"Jeder Traum hat seine besondere Bedeutung."

"Qu'est ce que ça signifie?"

"C'est le symbole de la jeunesse."

"Qu'est ce que ça veut dire?"

One could run on indefinitely. Meaning is with us in every conversation.

Let me say again, quite dogmatically, that no experience is devoid of meaning. Even a pinpoint of light in a dark room has meaning in that it is white and not red, small and not large, out there in space and not in here in me. A branch of a tree for Köhler's ape may be "something to swing from" and then "something with which to pull in a banana." That piece of modern music may be for me a jumble of sounds, for you a delicately ordered composition. To say that it is a jumble is not to say that it has no meaning, merely that it has a different meaning. Meaning is literally what is there for you when you confront the world; but there are various levels of meaning, and here is where a bit of phenomenology can help us with our experimental psychology of communication. I shall have to content myself with a few illustrations, and my earlier apologies about the use of personal pronouns still stand.

When we say, "What I mean is . . ." and, "The bell means that I ought to stop talking," we are using the word "mean" in two rather different ways. In the first case I am struggling with an inadequate language to say something to you; in the second case something other than me is saying something to me and to other people as well. Both are intentional, the first in the everyday sense, the second in a sense closer to Brentano's, namely, something pointing beyond itself to something that is not itself. I like particularly the French expression, "Qu'est que ça veut dire?"; "What does that wish to say?" not necessarily "What does that wish to say to me?"

The phenomenal world of the speaker contains at least the phenomenal speaker, the phenomenal hearer, and the phenomenal medium, but also a great many other structures, properties of structures, and relations, which may or may not be relevant to the act of communication. The speaker as a self may dominate the field almost to the exclusion of the medium and the hearer. In a violent state of emotion the self may loom so large that the words spoken and the person to whom they are spoken slip into insignificance. One might say that this is sheer expression, communication without message or intended recipient. This may be characteristic of much animal communication, and there is undoubtedly a great deal of human communication that is quite unintentional, e.g., the accent or pronunciation which reveals things about the speaker of which he is totally unaware. By contrast, the speaker may become so engrossed in his message and in its relation to the medium that he ceases to be aware of the hearer. The cognitive content of a message may be clear, but the problem of putting it into satisfactory language is so great that he loses contact with the hearer for whom it is intended. This is a common characteristic of professors. In the standard act of communication, however, there is the phenomenal hearer, i.e., not necessarily the hypothetical real hearer, but the hearer to whom the speaker thinks he is speaking. The actor on the stage may be speaking to his audience or to his opposite number on the stage, and the critic is likely to note the difference. We pray to an invisible God; we write with the specter of the reader peering over our shoulder. Whoever the phenomenal hearer may be, he helps to govern what the speaker says and how he says it.

The world of the hearer may be analyzed in the same way as that of the speaker. There is the phenomenal speaker, who may or may not bear some relation to the actual speaker and who may or may not be listened to, and there is the phenomenal medium, which may or may not convey to the hearer what was intended by the speaker. The hearer hears what is there for him.

Studies of personality and social behavior have contributed richly to our understanding of the uniqueness of the individual's world. I shall pass these by reluctantly and dwell briefly on problems connected with the medium itself, for here, I think, is where experimental psychology needs a little more challenging. We can have perfect communication, hypothetically, when the phenomenal worlds of speaker and hearer are identical, including identical representations of the medium. This, of course, never happens. We can have adequate communication when the message has to do with relatively sequestered concerns. Thus two mathematicians of widely different temperament and background and little knowledge of each other's language can collaborate happily, because the language of mathematics is almost universal. You point to an article in a French shop and say "Comme bien?" "Cent francs," the shopkeeper answers. "C'est trop," you say, and leave the shop. Your limited French was quite adequate, and you saved one hundred francs; but you would not have dared to talk politics with the shopkeeper. When we appreciate the enormous difference between the world of the speaker and that of the hearer, and especially when we have been reading Benjamin Lee Whorf, we are tempted to think that, except on the most superficial of levels, no adequate communication can ever be established, even when linguistic backgrounds are similar, much less when the cultures are widely different. Yet the fact is, and this is what keeps one from total despair, that in spite of all these differences we seem to succeed reasonably well. Why?

One answer is rather simple-minded, but it can help us to formulate some more precise questions. We, as organisms, the answer states, live in physical environments which possess more commonalities than they do differences; during the course of evolution we have developed similar structures and similar modes of adjustment to the common features of these environments; during this evolutionary process, we have developed more flexible modes of adjustment to these, and eventually the ability to respond selectively by means of behavior surrogates, i.e., words, to which other organisms can learn to respond appropriately even in the absence of the original stimuli. This involves some assumptions which philosophers may wish to challenge, but I do not see any harm in such a quasi-biological approach.

As a phenomenologist, my inclination of course is to bracket provisionally the evolutionary hypothesis and to focus on what seems to be the central psychological problem, namely, similarity. This is crucial in the psychology of perception, and I think it is crucial in the psychological study of language. For speaker and hearer to understand each other adequately, the medium must convey similarities between the two worlds. It would be convenient if every word resembled its referent. Most linguists will tell us, however, in spite of the temptations of onomatopoeia, that the linkage of a word to a thing is either arbitrary or accidental. "Horse" and *Pferd* do not look or sound alike. If this were all there were to it, the psychologist would have no problems except those of perception and learning. How do we associate the percept of the animal with the word "horse," and then this, with *Pferd?*

Our basic handicap is the tradition that language is composed of words, especially nouns and verbs, which is not at all the case. True, there are words in every spoken language and also phones, phonemes, morphemes, etc., and in non-spoken languages there are still other units of analysis. But every linguist knows, and so does anyone who has tried his hand at translation, that word-for-word translation is seldom possible, even between languages that are very closely related. The good translator tries to grasp the intended meaning of the speaker and then to use all the devices of the second language to render that meaning intelligible. This sometimes requires ingenuity. The marvelous thing about human languages, as compared with the severely impoverished telegraph wire, is the almost limitless number of ways in which messages can be conveyed. The rich inflections of Latin have been largely replaced in modern French by prepositions, articles, and word order; yet it is easy to translate from one to the other. Gaps in vocabulary can be overcome through the judicious use of circumlocution, and we have a host of other variables, such as intonation, stress, the pause for emphasis, and even the supplementary gesture. All these variables may eventually be reducible to a single efficient code which can be fed to a computer. But before we do this, if we wish to do it, we must first find out exactly how one person uses the linguistic medium to communicate with another person—a challenge to psychology as well as to linguistics.

May I close this topic with a three-level classification of meaning that I do not like especially but find useful. The first is the *symbolic* level, symbolization being restricted to the arbritray connection of one thing with another. The cleanest symbols are found in mathematics and logic, but the psychologist is also interested in symbol acquisition, especially in the practical context of learning. On the second level we have *significative* or sign meaning (in German, *Bedeutung*). The word or expression points beyond itself to something else, another word or an action or a situation. A chair is something to sit on, a pencil something to write with, an adjective signals the approach of a noun, and so forth. Here we are obviously coming closer to language as behavior. Whereas pure symbolization has never been satisfactorily demonstrated in sub-human species, there is ample evidence of signaling in many animals, and virtually all human communication is characterized by significative meaning. On the third level we have what might loosely be called *perceptual* meaning, which must include expressive or physiognomic meaning. To delve into the problems of this field would take more time than I can afford, but I should like to stress the fact that the elementary perceptual properties of language help to determine the nature of the meaning communicated. Köhler (13) gave, as an illustration, two nonsense designs, one composed of jagged lines, the other of smooth, curved lines. One, he said, is *takete*, the other *moluma*. Which is which? Obviously the jagged one is *takete* and the smooth one *moluma*, but not, as Fox (4) demonstrated experimentally, because of what Sapir called phonetic symbolism. Percepts have physiognomic properties, and we can apprehend physiognomic similarities and differences just as we apprehend similarities and differences in shape and size. I do not care for the moment whether physiognomic meanings are learned or unlearned, whether or not a baby's smile in response to a friendly face is a product of some sort of conditioning. The fact is that they are there as essential components of communication which can be investigated. When we know a little more about them we may venture as psychologists into the even more entrancing fields of literature, poetry, and drama. But we had better hurry, because the electronic computer is gaining on us.

A Final Comment

In presenting psychological phenomenology, may I repeat that I am not presenting a psychological system, much less a philosophy. I am not even sure I am offering an alternative to behaviorism. I am merely insisting that what, in the old, prescientific days, we used to call "consciousness" still can and should be studied. Whether or not this kind of study may be called a science depends on our definition of the term. To be a scientist, in my opinion, is to have boundless curiosity tempered by discipline. Curiosity transforms every unknown into an inviting problem; methodology provides the necessary discipline. There have been times in the history of the sciences when weakness in methodology has permitted irresponsible speculation; there have been other times when concern for rigor of method has become so passionate as to rule out problems to which existing methods cannot be readily applied. Titchener and Watson belong, I think, in the latter category. Psychologists in their time were terribly concerned about wiping away the stains of philosophy and making their subject look and sound like physics or biology. They were successful to some extent, and perhaps it was a good thing. Today, a half century later, I do not find myself worried about psychology's status as a science; there are too many problems which strain our present methods and too many inviting phenomena for which we have not discovered an adequate language.

The final proposition in Wittgenstein's *Tractatus* (21) reads like a passage from Holy Scripture. It is the logical conclusion to a rigorous philosophical argument. Plucking it out of context, however, as I am doing, and addressing it to psychology today, it seems to me to offer just about the worst possible advice. "Wovon man nicht sprechen kann, darüber muss man schweigen." (Whereof one cannot speak, thereof one must be silent.)

Bibliography

1. Angell, J. R. Psychology. New York: Holt and Company, 1904.
2. Cornell University Seminar, 1951. *Psycholinguistics.* Baltimore: Waverly Press, 1954.
3. Dewey, John. *Human Nature and Conduct.* New York: Holt and Company, 1922.
4. Fox, C. W. "An Experimental Study of Naming," *American Journal of Psychology,* XLVII (1935), 545–79.
5. Gaffron, M. *Die Radierungen Rembrandts, Originale und Drucke.* Mainz: Kupferverlag, 1950.
6. Heidegger, Martin. *Sein und Zeit.* Halle: Max Niemeyer, 1931.
7. Heider, F., and Simmel, M. "An Experimental Study of Apparent Behavior," *American Journal of Psychology,* LVII (1944).
8. Hilgard, E. R. *Theories of Learning.* 2d ed.; New York: Appleton-Century-Crofts, 1956.
9. Husserl, E. *Cartesian Meditations.* The Hague: M. Nijhoff, 1960 (first published in 1931).

10. ———. *Jahrbuch für Philosophie und phänomenologische Forschung.* Halle: Max Niemeyer, 1916.
11. James, W. *Principles of Psychology,* I, II. New York: Holt and Company, 1890.
12. Katz, D. *Die Erscheinungsweisen der Farben.* Leipzig: J. A. Barth, 1911.
13. Köhler, W. *Gestalt Psychology.* New York: Liveright Publishing Company, 1929.
14. ———. *The Place of Value in a World of Facts.* New York: Liveright Publishing Company, 1938.
15. Michotte, A. *La Perception de la Causalité.* Louvain: Institut Supérieur de Philosophie; also Paris: Vrin, 1946.
16. Osgood, C. E., and Sebeok, T. A. *Psycholinguistics,* IV (1954) (Supplement to *American Journal of Psychology*).
17. Scheler, M. *Die Wesen und Formen der Sympathie.* 2d ed.; Bonn: Verlag von Friedrich Cohen, 1923.
18. Spiegelberg, H. *The Phenomenological Movement.* The Hague: M. Nijhoff, 1960.
19. Thorndike, E. L. *Educational Psychology,* Vols. I–III. New York: Teachers College, Columbia University, 1913–14.
20. Tolman, E. C. "Determiners of Behavior at a Choice Point," *Psychological Review,* LVII (1938), 243–59.
21. Wittgenstein, L. *Tractatus Logico-Philosophicus.* New York: Harcourt, Brace and Co., 1922.

Bibliographical Note

The literature on phenomenology and existentialism has grown enormously during recent years. The following suggestions reveal personal preferences and are intended explicitly for the reader with a psychological interest.

Husserl's most relevant contributions are to be found in the *Logische Untersuchungen* (1900–1901) rather than in his later, more technically philosophical, works. Husserl's *Jahrbuch für Philosophie und phänomenologische Forschung* contains many contributions to phenomenological psychology, as does its sequel, edited by Marvin Farber, *Philosophy and Phenomenological Research.* The Husserl Archives, lodged at the University of Louvain, have yielded a steady stream of valuable publications. Perhaps the best critical exposition of Husserl in English is still Farber's *The Foundation of Phenomenology* (1942). The whole movement, including the more strictly existentialist writers, is brilliantly surveyed and annotated in Herbert Spiegelberg's *The Phenomenological Movement* (1960). Of great influence among European philosophers and worthy of psychologists' attention is Merleau-Ponty's *Phénoménologie de la Perception* (1945; Eng. trans., 1962). Among Sartre's numerous publications, perhaps the most relevant are *Esquisse d'une Théorie des Émotions* (1939; Eng. trans., 1948) and *L'Imaginaire: Psychologie phénoménologique de l'imagination* (1940; Eng. trans., 1948). Closely related to phenomenology is the German *verstehende Psychologie*, represented in the writings of Dilthey, Scheler, Spranger, and, especially, Jaspers.

The pioneer work in experimental phenomenology stems primarily from the Göttingen group, best represented by Katz's *Aufbau der Farbwelt* (rev. ed., 1930; Eng. trans., 1935) and *Aufbau der Tastwelt* (1925), and from the Gestalt group, many of whose studies are to be found in the volumes of the *Psychologische Forschung*. The earlier Gestalt work is reviewed in Koffka's *Principles of Gestalt Psychology* (1935), and many of the most important studies appear in condensed form in Ellis' *A Source Book of Gestalt Psychology* (1936). In *Documents of Gestalt Psychology* (1961) Mary Henle has made a good selection of the more recent Gestalt contributions. It must be remembered, however, that nearly all German experimental psychology since the beginning of this century has been influenced, to some extent at least, by phenomenology.

American psychologists have been particularly interested in the phenomenological approach to clinical and social psychology and to psychopathology. Selections from these fields are to be found in *The Phenomenological Problem* (1959), edited by A. E. Kuenzli, and *Existence* (1958), edited by R. May, E. Angel, and H. F. Ellenberger. A comprehensive bibliography of English language contributions, prepared by Joseph Lyons, appeared in *Psychological Reports* (1959, 5, 613–31) and is reprinted in part in *Existential Psychology* (1961), edited by Rollo May.

PARAPHRASE OF DISCUSSION

MEMBER OF THE AUDIENCE

The study of communication and of meaning has been going on for a long time. Why do "you people act as if it has just been discovered?"

COMMENTS OF PROFESSOR MacLEOD

He was speaking, primarily, about experimental psychology. It is to be hoped that experimental methods, especially in the psychology of perception, will be able to make contributions to the study of, for example, metaphor in communication. While earlier workers have written on the psychology of language, "they did it without any real appreciation of what was going on at that time in the psychology of perception, which has led us into the experimental approach to the study of expression in its various forms and which, I hope, will lead us into a study of metaphor as a psychological problem." While "it is a very, very old problem, it is a problem in which we have not, until fairly recently, attempted to use experimental procedures."

MEMBER OF THE AUDIENCE

Comment on the value of "computing machines that exhibit animal behavior to experimental psychology."

COMMENTS OF PROFESSOR MACLEOD

"This is a delightful topic to speculate on." The Cornell Perceptron "has begun in a very modest way to replicate some of the phenomena of constancy." Some years ago Simon and Newell programmed a machine to operate as a logician would and trained people skilled in symbolic logic to report to the experimenter what they were doing at each stage in solving problems. On comparing what the logicians did with what they "knew had been built into the machine," they found "that the logicians, though they were much slower in coming to the conclusions, were going through pretty much the same procedures which the machine is going through."

However, even if one could build a machine that could replicate emotions, percepts, and sequences of thought, one must remember the machines could not be built so, if "we did not have a decent psychology to begin with." The Perceptron was built on a somewhat Helmholtzian model and is adequate for rather simple constancy problems like constancy of size and shape. For "more elaborate forms of constancy," one will "need better psychological theory." "What we are really doing is replicating the *outcome* of a set of processes," not the processes themselves.

A particularly interesting possibility for the future is to "take a full array of theories of learning—everything from a very simple association model on up to the theory which involves the assumption of different patterns, strategies, . . . feed in different kinds of learning theory to different computers and find out which of these . . . works best." One can, incidentally, look forward to the time when the Yale machine plays the Harvard machine in chess.

MEMBER OF THE AUDIENCE

Comment on the distinction between psychological phenomenology and philosophical phenomenology "or, more exactly, [on] a general distinction between what we call science or scientific method on the one hand and philosophy on the other."

COMMENTS OF PROFESSOR MACLEOD

He would prefer to suspend the question until the papers of the two philosophers have been delivered. He is not "concerned . . . about whether or not psychology is a science." He has no definition of science, but, "for practical purposes in psychology," the two essentials of science can be "referred to as attitudes of an individual . . . who is willing to bracket certain assumptions, whose curiosity is aroused by what he saw, and who has a passionate concern with self-critical ways." Galileo, not Newton, is the ideal here; he confronted tradition. Galileo questioned the assumption of inherent properties but "curbed and disciplined" his curiosity with experimental methods. We find in Newton and in his "grand synthesis of physics" the same "curiosity and discipline."

"Any phenomena that you observe and can order in a disciplined sort of way can become a *Wissenschaft* in German. . . . *Wissenschaft*, in the broadest sense, I think, is capable of including a great deal more than what is in the tradition of English and French science, which are limited pretty much to physics, chemistry, biology, and related disciplines." Although psychology might not be a science as Newton would have defined it, "it is a *Wissenschaft*."

COMMENTS OF PROFESSOR MALCOLM

Concerning the remarks about the experiments with computers and logicians, it was said that "the same processes occur in the computer as occur in the logician." "What could you mean by the same processes occurring? . . . If we are very phenomenological, we could think of some process that might occur in the mind of a logician when he was trying to solve a difficult problem in mathematical logic. He might think of a certain formula or he might have an image of it. . . . He might feel a certain tension or strain. . . . He might say something to himself. All of these are processes that could occur in the case of the logician. Now I would not have thought . . . it would make any sense to say that they took place in the electronic computer, so I was somewhat puzzled as to what sort of processes you had in mind."

COMMENTS OF PROFESSOR MACLEOD

This is just a manner of speaking. When the logicians report their strategies, they report encountering blind alleys, backing up, trying different paths. The experimenters can tell from its actions that the machine is doing somewhat the same. Simon, in conversation, has described activities of the machine that might be called "slight emotional upheaval."

COMMENTS OF PROFESSOR KOCH

The computer under discussion was programmed to perform simple derivations in the sentential calculus, which is the most highly mechanized of the calculi. "The fact that you can get the machine to make derivations in this calculus is more a tribute to Whitehead and Russell in the first instance and to the other logicians who have further simplified this calculus than it is to the machine or whoever designed the machine." Further, to speak of "emotion" and "nervousness" is to use "a very, very distant metaphor."

COMMENTS OF PROFESSOR MACLEOD

". . . [T]he point you make is quite well taken." The designers of the machine could not have produced it had they not first studied the process of logical inference. Further, to repeat, replication of the outcome of an operation does not necessarily indicate a replication of the operation itself.

MEMBER OF THE AUDIENCE

"What sort of technique can be used to reach an agreement with the person who disagrees with you about the content of *Erlebnis?*" What happens to "the ideal of consensus in scientific theory" if one cannot achieve agreement on what is given? "Without consensus on a given, it is hard to see how one can get consensus on a theory."

COMMENTS OF PROFESSOR MACLEOD

"It may be that you could push me into an objective idealism here. I think I would resist a little bit, but perhaps not very efficiently." Experience in the training of "psychological observing," which is "not a training in seeing what [one] ought to see but more or less a training in just seeing over and over and over again," suggests that the "observer begins to see things . . . that he never would have dreamed of seeing before. There, then, you are approaching consensus."

Concerning values, "a good many of those people who are inclined toward a relativistic theory of value come pretty close to a projectionist theory of perception." One usual, though "not satisfactory," way of approaching value judgment is to examine the personal and cultural history of individuals, to find events and circumstances which seem to account for particular value judgments. "But in the phenomenological approach we do distinguish between the value judgment which is more nearly rooted in our own impulses, inclinations, and so on, and the value judgment which seems to be a judgment of something that is of value quite apart from what I think of it." It is difficult to be experimental in this area, "but if you go into . . . settings in which value judgments are made, it seems to me that, phenomenologically, a great deal of what we characterize as value is that which we apprehend as good or bad, desirable or undesirable, quite apart from the state of our own motivation."

MEMBER OF THE AUDIENCE

[For the most part, the comment and question were inaudible. They seemed to have to do with phenomenology as a "method" to get "rid of the biases," "irrespective of the philosophy."]

COMMENTS OF PROFESSOR MACLEOD

The phenomenological approach to psychology involves curiosity about experience—*Erlebnis*. Any good scientist tries to bracket his biases. The history of physics offers many fine examples of this. Einstein and others raised questions about the assumptions of Newtonian physics. "This was a matter of becoming aware of a subtle bias that had been there." But the physicist is not interested in experience as such. Ernst Mach, who was a physicist and psychologist, "tried to describe what was there, particularly in the visual world," but physicists as such do not.

Titchener, in *Systematic Psychology*, used the term "existential experience" in comparing the physicist, the biologist, and the psychologist. According to Titchener, they all begin with existential experience, but while the biologist and physicist are interested in "what is revealed through that experience about something that is not directly experienced," the psychologist is interested in experience as experience. "I would see no excuse for a psychology unless we, as psychologists, . . . look at what we think of as almost uniquely characteristic of human beings."

MEMBER OF THE AUDIENCE

"Can you, experimentally or rationally, point the direction from which philosophical psychology might consider" the question of "the meaning of man for man?"

COMMENTS OF PROFESSOR MACLEOD

"The sort of meaning that we can bring into the laboratory is still a very modest meaning. The sort of meaning you were talking about does lead us into a metaphysics. It certainly leads us into ethical theory. I should be the last person to assert that any experimental psychologists, or even any empirical psychologists, can, through empirical investigation alone, solve these problems. We can work toward a self-consistent philosophy which will give us a definition of meaning we find acceptable."

B. F. SKINNER

Behaviorism at Fifty

Behaviorism, with an accent on the last syllable, is not the scientific study of behavior but a philosophy of science concerned with the subject matter and methods of psychology. If psychology is a science of mental life—of the mind, of conscious experience—then it must develop and defend a special methodology, which it has not yet done successfully. If it is, on the other hand, a science of the behavior of organisms, human or otherwise, then it is part of biology, a natural science for which tested and highly successful methods are available. The basic issue is not the nature of the stuff of which the world is made or whether it is made of one stuff or two but rather the dimensions of the things studied by psychology and the methods relevant to them.

THE INNER MAN

Mentalistic or psychic explanations of human behavior almost certainly originated in primitive animism. When a man dreamed of being at a distant place in spite of incontrovertible evidence that he had stayed in his bed, it was easy to conclude that some part of him had actually left his body. A particularly vivid memory or a hallucination could be explained in the same way. The theory of an invisible, detachable self eventually proved useful for other purposes. It seemed to explain unexpected or abnormal episodes, even to the person behaving in an exceptional way because he was thus "possessed." It also served to explain the inexplicable. An organism as complex as man often seems to behave capriciously. It is tempting to attribute the visible behavior to another organism inside—to a little man or homunculus. The wishes of the little man become the acts of the man observed by his fellows. The inner idea is put into outer words. Inner

B. F. SKINNER, Professor, Department of Psychology, Harvard University.

This paper has been published also in *Science* (CXL [1963], 951–58) with permission of the University of Chicago Press.

feelings find outward expression. The explanation is successful, of course, only so long as the behavior of the homunculus can be neglected.

Primitive origins are not necessarily to be held against an explanatory principle, but the little man is still with us in relatively primitive form. He was recently the hero of a television program called "Gateways to the Mind," one of a series of educational films sponsored by the Bell Telephone Laboratories and written with the help of a distinguished panel of scientists. The viewer learned, from animated cartoons, that when a man's finger is pricked, electrical impulses resembling flashes of lightning run up the afferent nerves and appear on a television screen in the brain. The little man wakes up, sees the flashing screen, reaches out, and pulls a lever. More flashes of lightning go down the nerves to the muscles, which then contract, as the finger is pulled away from the threatening stimulus. The behavior of the homunculus was, of course, not explained. An explanation would presumably require another film. And it, in turn, another.

The same pattern of explanation is invoked when we are told that the behavior of a delinquent is the result of a disordered personality or that the vagaries of a man under analysis are due to conflicts among his superego, ego, and id. Nor can we escape from the primitive features by breaking the little man into pieces and dealing with his wishes, cognitions, motives, and so on, bit by bit. The objection is not that these things are mental but that they offer no real explanation and stand in the way of a more effective analysis.

It has been about fifty years since the behavioristic objection to this practice was first clearly stated, and it has been about thirty years since it has been very much discussed. A whole generation of psychologists has grown up without really coming into contact with the issue. Almost all current textbooks compromise: rather than risk a loss of adoptions, they define psychology as the science of behavior *and* mental life. Meanwhile the older view has continued to receive strong support from areas in which there has been no comparable attempt at methodological reform. During this period, however, an effective experimental science of behavior has emerged. Much of what it has discovered bears on the basic issue. A restatement of radical behaviorism would therefore seem to be in order.

Explaining the Mind

A rough history of the idea is not hard to trace. An occasional phrase in classic Greek writings that seemed to foreshadow the point of view need not be taken seriously. We may also pass over the early bravado of a La Mettrie who could shock the philosophical bourgeoisie by asserting that man was only a machine. Nor were those who simply preferred, for practical reasons, to deal with behavior rather than with less accessible, but nevertheless acknowledged, mental activities close to what is meant by behaviorism today.

The entering wedge appears to have been Darwin's preoccupation with the continuity of species. In supporting the theory of evolution, it was important to show that man was not essentially different from the lower animals—that every human characteristic, including consciousness and reasoning powers, could be found in other species. Naturalists like Romanes began to collect stories which seemed to show that dogs, cats, elephants, and many other species were conscious and showed signs of reasoning. It was Lloyd Morgan, of course, who questioned this evidence with his Canon of Parsimony. Were there not other ways of accounting for what looked like signs of consciousness or rational powers? Thorndike's experiments at the end of the nineteenth century were in this vein. He showed that the behavior of a cat in escaping from a puzzle-box might seem to show reasoning but could be explained instead as the result of simpler processes. Thorndike remained a mentalist, but he greatly advanced the objective study of behavior which had been attributed to mental processes.

The next step was inevitable: if evidence of consciousness and reasoning could be explained in other ways in animals, why not also in man? And if this was the case, what became of psychology as a science of mental life? It was John B. Watson who made the first clear, if rather noisy, proposal that psychology should be regarded simply as a science of behavior. He was not in a very good position to defend it. He had little scientific material to use in his reconstruction. He was forced to pad his textbook with discussions of the physiology of receptor systems and muscles and with physiological theories which were at the time no more susceptible to proof than the mentalistic theories they were intended to replace. A need for "mediators" of behavior that might serve as objective alternatives to thought processes led him to emphasize sub-audible speech. The notion was intriguing, because one can usually observe oneself thinking in this way; but it was by no means an adequate or comprehensive explanation. He tangled with introspective psychologists by denying the existence of images. He may well have been acting in good faith, for it has been said that he himself did not have visual imagery; but his arguments caused unnecessary trouble. The relative importance of a genetic endowment in explaining behavior proved to be another disturbing digression.

All this made it easy to lose sight of the central argument—that behavior which seemed to be the product of mental activity could be explained in other ways. Moreover, the introspectionists were prepared to challenge it. As late as 1883 Francis Galton could write: "Many persons, especially women and intelligent children, take pleasure in introspection, and strive their very best to explain their mental processes" (5). But introspection was already being taken seriously. The concept of a science of mind in which mental events obeyed mental laws had led to the development of psychophysical methods and to the accumulation of facts which seemed to bar the extension of the principle of parsimony. What might hold for animals did not hold for men, because men could see their mental processes.

Curiously enough, part of the answer was supplied by the psychoanalysts, who insisted that, although a man might be able to see some of his mental life, he could not see all of it. The kind of thoughts Freud called "unconscious" took place without the knowledge of the thinker. From an association, verbal slip, or dream it could be shown that a person must have responded to a passing stimulus, although he could not tell you that he had done so. More complex thought processes, including problem-solving and verbal play, could also go on without the thinker's knowledge. Freud had devised, and never abandoned faith in, one of the most elaborate mental apparatuses of all time. He nevertheless contributed to the behavioristic argument by showing that mental activity did not, at least, *require* consciousness. His proofs that thinking had occurred without introspective recognition were, indeed, clearly in the spirit of Lloyd Morgan. They were operational analyses of mental life—even though, for Freud, only the unconscious part of it. Experimental evidence pointing in the same direction soon began to accumulate.

But that was not the whole answer. What about the part of mental life which a man can see? It is a difficult question, no matter what one's point of view, partly because it raises the question of what seeing means and partly because the events seen are private. The fact of privacy cannot, of course, be questioned. Each person is in special contact with a small part of the universe enclosed within his own skin. To take a non-controversial example, he is uniquely subject to certain kinds of proprioceptive and interoceptive stimulation. Though two people may in some sense be said to see the same light or hear the same sound, they cannot feel the same distention of a bile duct or the same bruised muscle. (When privacy is invaded with scientific instruments, the form of stimulation is changed; the scales read by the scientist are not the private events themselves.)

Mentalistic psychologists insist that there are other kinds of events that are uniquely accessible to the owner of the skin within which they occur but which lack the physical dimensions of proprioceptive or interoceptive stimuli. They are as different from physical events as colors are from wave lengths of light. There are even better reasons, therefore, why two people cannot suffer each other's toothaches, recall each other's memories, or share each other's happinesses. The importance assigned to this kind of world varies. For some, it is the only world there is. For others, it is the only part of the world which can be directly known. For still others, it is a special part of what can be known. In any case, the problem of how one knows about the subjective world of another must be faced. Apart from the question of what "knowing" means, the problem is one of accessibility.

PUBLIC AND PRIVATE EVENTS

One solution, often regarded as behavioristic, is to grant the distinction between public and private events and rule the latter out of scientific consideration. This is a congenial solution for those to whom scientific truth is a matter of convention or agreement among observers. It is essentially the line taken by logical positivism and physical operationism. Hogben (7) has recently redefined "behaviorist" in this spirit. The subtitle of his *Statistical Theory* is "an examination of the contemporary crises in statistical theory from a behaviorist viewpoint," and this is amplified in the following way:

The behaviourist, as I here use the term, does not deny the convenience of classifying *processes* as mental or material. He recognizes the distinction between personality and corpse: but he has not yet had the privilege of attending an identity parade in which human minds without bodies are by common recognition distinguishable from living human bodies without minds. Till then, he is content to discuss probability in the vocabulary of *events*, including audible or visibly recorded assertions of human beings as such. . . .

The behavioristic position, so defined, is simply that of the publicist and "has no concern with structure and mechanism."

The point of view is often called operational, and it is significant that P. W. Bridgman's physical operationism could not save him from an extreme solipsism even within physical science itself. Though he insisted that he was not a solipsist, he was never able to reconcile seemingly public physical knowledge with the private world of the scientist (3). Applied to psychological problems, operationism has been no more successful. We may recognize the restrictions imposed by the operations through which we can know of the existence of properties of subjective events, but the operations cannot be identified with the events themselves. S. S. Stevens has applied Bridgman's principle to psychology, not to decide whether subjective events exist, but to determine the extent to which we can deal with them scientifically (9).

Behaviorists have, from time to time, examined the problem of privacy, and some of them have excluded so-called sensations, images, thought processes, and so on from their deliberations. When they have done so not because such things do not exist but because they are out of reach of their methods, the charge is justified that they have neglected the facts of consciousness. The strategy is, however, quite unwise. It is particularly important that a science of behavior face the problem of privacy. It may do so without abandoning the basic position of behaviorism. Science often talks about things it cannot see or measure. When a man tosses a penny into the air, it must be assumed that he tosses the earth beneath him downward. It is quite out of the question to see or measure the effect on the earth, but it must be assumed for the sake of a consistent account. An adequate science of behavior must consider events taking place within the skin of the organism, not as physiological mediators of behavior, but as part of behavior itself. It can deal with these events without assuming that they have any special nature or must be known in any special way. The skin is not that important as a boundary. Private and public events have the same kinds of physical dimensions.

SELF-DESCRIPTIVE BEHAVIOR

In the fifty years since a behavioristic philosophy was first stated, facts and principles bearing on the basic issues have steadily accumulated. For one thing, a scientific analysis of behavior has yielded a sort of empirical epistemology. The subject matter of a science of behavior includes the behavior of scientists and other knowers. The techniques available to such a science give an empirical theory of knowledge certain advantages over theories derived from philosophy and logic. The problem of privacy may be approached in a fresh direction by starting with behavior rather than with immediate experience. The strategy is certainly no more arbitrary or circular than the earlier practice, and it has a surprising result. Instead of concluding that man can know only his subjective experiences—that he is bound forever to his private world and that the external world is only a construct—a behavioral theory of knowledge suggests that it is the private world which, if not entirely unknowable, is at least not likely to be known well. The relations between organism and environment involved in knowing are of such a sort that the privacy of the world within the skin imposes more serious limitations on personal knowledge than on scientific accessibility.

An organism learns to react discriminatively to the world around it under certain contingencies of reinforcement. Thus, a child learns to name a color correctly when a given response is reinforced in the presence of the color and extinguished in its absence. The verbal community may make the reinforcement of an extensive repertory of responses contingent on subtle properties of colored stimuli. We have reason to believe that the child will not discriminate among colors—that he will not see two colors as different—until exposed to such contingencies. So far as we know, the same process of differential reinforcement is required if a child is to distinguish among the events occurring within his own skin.

Many contingencies involving private stimuli need not be arranged by a verbal community, for they follow from simple mechanical relations among stimuli, responses, and reinforcing consequences. The various motions which comprise turning a handspring, for example, are under the control of external and internal stimuli and subject to external and internal reinforcing consequences. But the performer is not necessarily "aware" of the stimuli controlling his behavior, no matter how appropriate and skillful it may be. "Knowing" or "being aware of" what is happening in turning a handspring involves discriminative responses, such as naming or describing, which arise from contingencies necessarily arranged by a verbal environment. Such environments are common. The community is generally interested in what a man is doing, has done, or is planning to do and why, and it arranges contingencies which generate verbal responses which name and describe the external and internal stimuli associated with these events. It challenges his verbal behavior by asking, "How do you know?" and the speaker answers, if at all, by describing some of the variables of which his verbal behavior was a function. The "awareness" resulting from all this is a social product.

In attempting to set up such a repertory, however, the verbal community works under a severe handicap. It cannot always arrange the contingencies required for subtle discriminations. It cannot teach a child to call one pattern of private stimuli "diffidence" and another "embarrassment" as effectively as it teaches him to call one stimulus "red" and another "orange," for it cannot be sure of the presence or absence of the private patterns of stimuli appropriate to reinforcement or lack of reinforcement. Privacy thus causes trouble, first of all, *for the verbal community*. The individual suffers in turn. Because the community cannot reinforce self-descriptive responses consistently, a person cannot describe or otherwise "know" events occurring within his own skin as subtly and precisely as he knows events in the world at large.

There are, of course, differences between external and internal stimuli which are not mere differences in location. Proprioceptive and interoceptive stimuli may have a certain intimacy. They are likely to be especially familiar. They are very much with us: we cannot escape from a toothache as easily as from a deafening noise. They may well be of a special kind: the stimuli we feel in pride or sorrow may not closely resemble those we feel in sandpaper or satin. But this does not mean that they differ in physical status. In particular, it does not mean that they can be more easily or more directly known. What is particularly clear and familiar to the potential knower may be strange and distant to the verbal community responsible for his knowing.

Conscious Content

What *are* the private events which, at least in a limited way, a man may come to respond to in ways we call "knowing"? Let us begin with the oldest, and in many ways the most difficult, kind, represented by "the stubborn fact of consciousness." What is happening when a person observes the conscious content of his mind, when he looks at his sensations or images? Western philosophy and science have been handicapped in answering these questions by an unfortunate metaphor. The Greeks could not explain how a man could have knowledge of something with which he was not in immediate contact. How could he know an object on the other side of the room, for example? Did he reach out and touch it with some sort of invisible probe? Or did he never actually come in contact with the object at all but only with a copy of it inside his body? Plato supported the copy theory with his metaphor of the cave. Perhaps a man never sees the real world at all but only shadows of it on the wall of the cave in which he is imprisoned. (The "shadows" may well have been the much more accurate copies of the outside world in a *camera obscura*. Did Plato know of a cave, at the entrance of which a happy superposition of objects admitted only the thin pencils of light needed for a *camera obscura?*) Copies of the real world projected into the body could compose the experience which a man directly knows. A similar theory could also explain how one can see objects which are "not really there," as in hallucinations, afterimages, and memories. Neither explanation is, of course, satisfactory. How a copy may arise at a distance is at least as puzzling as how a man may know an object at a distance. Seeing things which are not really there is no harder to explain than the occurrence of copies of things not there to be copied.

The search for copies of the world within the body, particularly in the nervous system, still goes on, but with discouraging results. If the retina could suddenly be developed, like a photographic plate, it would yield a poor picture. The nerve impulses in the optic tract must have an even more tenuous resemblance to "what is seen." The patterns of vibrations which strike our ear when we listen to music are quickly lost in transmission. The bodily reactions to substances tasted, smelled, and touched would scarcely qualify as faithful reproductions. These facts are discouraging for those who are looking for copies of the real world within the body, but they are fortunate for psychophysiology as a whole. At some point the organism must do more than create duplicates. It must see, hear, smell, and so on, as forms of *action* rather than of *reproduction. It must do some of the things it is differentially reinforced for doing when it learns to respond discriminatively*. The sooner the pattern of the external world disappears after impinging on the organism, the sooner the organism may get on with these other functions.

The need for something beyond, and quite different from, copying is not widely understood. Suppose someone were to coat the occipital lobes of the brain with a special photographic emulsion which, when developed, yielded a reasonable copy of a current visual stimulus. In many quarters this would be regarded as a triumph in the physiology of vision. Yet nothing could be more disastrous, for we should have to start all over again and ask how the organism sees a picture in its occipital cortex, and we should now have much less of the brain available in which to seek an answer. It adds nothing to an explanation of how an organism reacts to a stimulus to trace the pattern of the stimulus into the body. It is most convenient, for both organism and psychophysiologist, if the external world is never copied—if the world we know is simply the world around us. The same may be said of theories according to which the brain interprets signals sent to it and in some sense reconstructs external stimuli. If the real world is, indeed, scrambled in transmission but later reconstructed in the brain, we must then start all over again and explain how the organism sees the reconstruction.

An adequate treatment of this point would require a thorough analysis of the behavior of seeing and of the conditions under which we see (to continue with vision as a convenient modality). It would be unwise to exaggerate our success to date. Discriminative visual behavior arises from contingencies involving external stimuli and overt responses, but possible private accompaniments must not be overlooked. Some of the consequences of such contingencies seem well established. It is usually easiest for us to see a friend when we are looking at him, because visual stimuli similar to those present when the behavior was acquired exert maximal control over the response. But mere visual stimulation is not enough; even after having been exposed to the necessary reinforcement, we may not see a friend who is present unless we have reason to do so. On the other hand, if the reasons are strong enough, we may see him in someone bearing only a superficial resemblance or when no one like him is present at all. If conditions favor seeing something else, we may behave accordingly. If, on a hunting trip, it is important to see a deer, we may glance toward our friend at a distance, see him as a deer, and shoot.

It is not, however, seeing our friend which raises the question of conscious content but "seeing that we are seeing him." There are no natural contingencies for such behavior. We learn to see that we are seeing only because a verbal community arranges for us to do so. We usually acquire the behavior when we are under appropriate visual stimulation, but it does not follow that the thing seen must be present when we see that we are seeing it. The contingencies arranged by the verbal environment may set up self-descriptive responses describing the *behavior* of seeing even when the thing seen is not present.

If seeing does not require the presence of things seen, we need not be concerned about certain mental processes said to be involved in the construction of such things—images, memories, and dreams, for example. We may regard a dream, not as a display of things seen by the dreamer, but simply as the behavior of seeing. At no time during a daydream, for example, should we expect to find within the organism anything that corresponds to the external stimuli present when the dreamer first acquired the behavior in which he is now engaged. In simple recall we need not suppose that we wander through some storehouse of memory until we find an object which we then contemplate. Instead of assuming that we begin with a tendency to *recognize* such an object once it is found, it is simpler to assume that we begin with a tendency to *see* it. Techniques of self-management which facilitate recall—for example, the use of mnemonic devices—can be formulated as ways of strengthening behavior rather than of creating objects to be seen. Freud dramatized the issue with respect to dreaming when asleep in his concept of dreamwork—an activity in which some part of the dreamer played the role of a theatrical producer while another part sat in the audience. If a dream is, indeed, something seen, then we must suppose that it is wrought as such; but if it is simply the behavior of seeing, the dreamwork may be dropped from the analysis. It took man a long time to understand that when he dreamed of a wolf, no wolf was actually there. It has taken him much longer to understand that not even a representation of a wolf is there.

Eye movements which appear to be associated with dreaming are in accord with this interpretation, since it is not likely that the dreamer is actually watching a dream on the undersides of his eyelids. When memories are aroused by electrical stimulation of the brain, as in the work of Wilder Penfield, it is also simpler to assume that it is the behavior of seeing, hearing, and so on, which is aroused rather than some copy of early environmental events which the subject then looks at or listens to. Behavior similar to the responses to the original events must be assumed in both cases—the subject sees or hears—but the reproduction of the events seen or heard is a needless complication. The familiar process of response chaining is available to account for the serial character of the behavior of remembering, but the serial linkage of stored experiences (suggesting engrams in the form of sound films) demands a new mechanism.

The heart of the behavioristic position on conscious experience may be summed up in this way: seeing does not imply something seen. We acquire the behavior of seeing under stimulation from actual objects, but it may occur in the absence of these objects under the control of other variables. (So far as the world within the skin is concerned, it always occurs in the absence of such objects.) We also acquire the behavior of seeing-that-we-are-seeing when we are seeing actual objects, but it may also occur in their absence.

To question the reality or the nature of the things seen in conscious experience is not to question the value of introspective psychology or its methods. Current problems in sensation are mainly concerned with the physiological function of receptors and associated neural mechanisms. Problems in perception are, at the moment, less intimately related to specific mechanisms, but the trend appears to be in the same direction. So far as behavior is concerned, both sensation and perception may be analyzed as forms of stimulus control. The subject need not be regarded as observing or evaluating conscious experiences. Apparent anomalies of stimulus control, which are now explained by appealing to a psychophysical relation or to the laws of perception, may be studied in their own right. It is, after all, no real solution to attribute them to the slippage inherent in converting a physical stimulus into a subjective experience.

The experimental analysis of behavior has a little more to say on this subject. Its techniques have recently been extended to what might be called the psychophysics of lower organisms. Blough's adaptation of the Békésy technique—for example, in determining the spectral sensitivity of pigeons and monkeys—yields sensory data comparable with the reports of a trained observer (1, 2). Herrnstein and van Sommers have recently developed a procedure in which pigeons "bisect sensory intervals" (6). It is tempting to describe these procedures by saying that investigators have found ways to get non-verbal organisms to describe their sensations. The fact is that a form of stimulus control has been investigated without using a repertory of self-observation or, rather, by constructing a special repertory the nature and origin of which are clearly understood. Rather than describe such experiments with the terminology of introspection, we may formulate them in their proper place in an experimental analysis. The behavior of the observer in the traditional psychophysical experiment may then be reinterpreted accordingly.

Mental Way Stations

So much for "conscious content," the classical problem in mentalistic philosophies. There are other mental states or processes to be taken into account. Moods, cognitions, and expectancies, for example, are also examined introspectively, and descriptions are used in psychological formulations. The conditions under which descriptive repertories are set up are much less successfully controlled. Terms describing sensations and images are taught by manipulating discriminative stimuli—a relatively amenable class of variables. The remaining kinds of mental events are related to such operations as deprivation and satiation, emotional stimulation, and various schedules of reinforcement. The difficulties they present to the verbal community are suggested by the fact that there is no psychophysics of mental states of this sort. That fact has not inhibited their use in explanatory systems.

In an experimental analysis, the relation between a property of behavior and an operation performed upon the organism is studied directly. Traditional mentalistic formulations, however, emphasize certain way stations. Where an experimental analysis might examine the effect of punishment on behavior, a mentalistic psychology will be concerned first with the effect of punishment in generating feelings of anxiety and then with the effect of anxiety on behavior. The mental state seems to bridge the gap between dependent and independent variables and is particularly attractive when these are separated by long periods of time—when, for example, the punishment occurs in childhood and the effect appears in the behavior of the adult.

The practice is widespread. In a demonstration experiment, a hungry pigeon was conditioned to turn around in a clockwise direction. A final, smoothly executed pattern of behavior was shaped by reinforcing successive approximations with food. Students who had watched the demonstration were asked to write an account of what they had seen. Their responses included the following: (1) The organism was conditioned to *expect* reinforcement for the right kind of behavior. (2) The pigeon walked around, *hoping* that something would bring the food back again. (3) The pigeon *observed* that a certain behavior seemed to produce a particular result. (4) The pigeon *felt* that food would be given it because of its action; and (5) the bird came to *associate* his action with the click of the food-dispenser. The observed facts could be stated respectively as follows: (1) The organism was reinforced *when* it emitted a given kind of behavior. (2) The pigeon walked around *until* the food container again appeared. (3) A certain behavior *produced* a particular result. (4) Food was given to the pigeon *when* it acted in a given way; and (5) the click of the food-dispenser *was temporally related* to the bird's action. These statements describe the contingencies of reinforcement. The expressions "expect," "hope," "observe," "feel," and "associate" go beyond them to identify effects on the pigeon. The effect actually observed was clear enough: the pigeon turned more skillfully and more frequently; but that was not the effect reported by the students. (If pressed, they would doubtless have said that the pigeon turned more skillfully and more frequently *because* it expected, hoped, and felt that if it did so food would appear.)

The events reported by the students were observed, if at all, in their own behavior. They were describing what they would have expected, felt, and hoped for under similar circumstances. But they were able to do so only because a verbal community had brought relevant terms under the control of certain stimuli, and this was done *when the community had access only to the kinds of public information available to the students in the demonstration.* Whatever the students knew about themselves which permitted them to infer comparable events in the pigeon must have been learned from a verbal community which saw no more of their behavior than they had seen of the pigeon's. Private stimuli may have entered into the control of their self-descriptive repertories, but the readiness with which they applied them to the pigeon indicates that external stimuli had remained important. The extraordinary strength of a mentalistic interpretation is really a sort of proof that in describing a private way station one is, to a considerable extent, making use of public information.

The mental way station is often accepted as a terminal datum, however. When a man must be trained to discriminate between different planes, ships, and so on, it is tempting to stop at the point at which he can be said to *identify* such objects. It is implied that if he can identify an object, he can name it, label it, describe it, or act appropriately in some other way. In the training process he always behaves in one of these ways; no way station called "identification" appears in practice or need appear in theory. (Any discussion of the discriminative behavior generated by the verbal environment to permit a person to examine his conscious content must be qualified accordingly.)

Cognitive theories stop at way stations where the mental action is usually somewhat more complex than identification. For example, a subject is said to *know* who and where he is, what something is, or what has happened or is going to happen—regardless of the forms of behavior through which this knowledge was set up or which may now testify to its existence. Similarly, in accounting for verbal behavior, a listener or reader is said to understand the *meaning* of a passage, although the actual changes brought about by listening to, or reading, the passage are not specified. In the same way, schedules of reinforcement are sometimes studied simply for their effects on the *expectations* of the organism exposed to them, without discussing the implied relation between expectation and action. Recall, inference, and reasoning may be formulated only to the point at which *an experience is remembered or a conclusion reached,* behavioral manifestations being ignored. In practice, the investigator always carries through to some response, if only a response of self-description.

On the other hand, mental states are often studied as causes of action. A speaker thinks of something to say before saying it, and this explains what he says, although the sources of his thoughts cannot be examined. An unusual act is called "impulsive," without inquiring further into the origin of the unusual impulse. A behavioral maladjustment shows anxiety, but the source of the anxiety is neglected. One salivates upon seeing a lemon because it reminds one of a sour taste, but why it does so is not specified. The formulation leads directly to a technology based on the manipulation of mental states. To change a man's voting behavior, we change his opinions; to induce him to act, we strengthen his beliefs; to make him eat, we make him feel hungry; to prevent wars, we reduce warlike tensions in the minds of men; to effect psychotherapy, we alter troublesome mental states; and so on. In practice all these ways of changing a man's mind reduce to manipulating his environment, verbal or otherwise.

In many cases we can reconstruct a complete causal chain by identifying the mental state which is the effect of an environmental variable with the mental state which is the cause of action. But this is not always enough. In traditional mentalistic philosophies various things happen at the way station which alter the relation between the terminal events. The effect of the psychophysical function and the laws of perception in distorting the physical stimulus before it reaches the way station has already been mentioned. Once the mental stage is reached, other effects are said to occur. Mental states alter one another. A painful memory may never affect behavior or may affect it in a different way, if another mental state succeeds in repressing it. Conflicting variables may be reconciled before reaching behavior if the subject engages in mental action called "making a decision." Dissonant cognitions generated by conflicting conditions of reinforcement will not be reflected in behavior if the subject can "persuade himself" that one condition was actually of a different magnitude or kind. These disturbances in simple causal linkages between environment and behavior can be formulated and studied experimentally as interactions among variables; but the possibility has not been fully exploited, and the effects still provide a formidable stronghold for mentalistic theories designed to bridge the gap between dependent and independent variables in the analysis of behavior.

METHODOLOGICAL OBJECTIONS

The behavioristic argument is nevertheless still valid. We may object, first, to the predilection for unfinished causal sequences. A disturbance in behavior is not explained by relating it to felt anxiety until the anxiety has in turn been explained. An action is not explained by attributing it to expectations until the expectations have in turn been accounted for. Complete causal sequences might, of course, include references to way stations, but the fact is that the way station generally interrupts the account in one direction or the other. For example, there must be thousands of instances in the psychoanalytic literature in which a thought or memory is said to have been relegated to the unconscious because it was painful or intolerable, but the percentage of those offering even the most casual suggestion as to why it was painful or intolerable must be very small. Perhaps explanations could have been offered, but the practice has discouraged the completion of the causal sequence.

A second objection is that a preoccupation with mental way stations burdens a science of behavior with all the problems raised by the limitations and inaccuracies of self-descriptive repertories. We need not take the extreme position that mediating events or any data about them obtained through introspection must be ruled out of consideration, but we should certainly welcome other ways of treating the data more satisfactorily. Independent variables change the behaving organism, often in ways which survive for many years, and such changes affect subsequent behavior. The subject may be able to describe some of these intervening states in useful ways, either before or after they have affected behavior. On the other hand, behavior may be extensively modified by variables of which, and of the effect of which, the subject is never aware. So far as we know, self-descriptive responses do not alter controlling relationships. If a severe punishment is less effective than a mild one, it is not because it cannot be "kept in mind." (Certain behaviors involved in self-management, such as reviewing a history of punishment, may alter behavior, but they do so by introducing other variables, rather than by changing a given relation.)

Perhaps the most serious objection concerns the order of events. Observation of one's own behavior necessarily follows the behavior. Responses which seem to be describing intervening states alone may embrace behavioral effects. "I am hungry" may describe, in part, the strength of the speaker's on-going ingestive behavior. "I was hungrier than I thought" seems particularly to describe behavior rather than an intervening, possibly causal, state. More serious examples of a possibly mistaken order are to be found in theories of psychotherapy. Before asserting that the release of a repressed wish has a therapeutic effect on behavior, or that when one knows why he is neurotically ill he will recover, we should consider the plausible alternative that a change in behavior resulting from therapy has made it possible for the subject to recall a repressed wish or to understand his illness.

A final objection is that way stations are so often simply invented. It is too easy to say that someone does something "because he likes to do it," or that he does one thing rather than another "because he has made a choice."

The importance of behaviorism as a philosophy of science naturally declines as a scientific analysis becomes more powerful, because there is then less need to use data in the form of self-description. The mentalism that survives in the fields of sensation and perception will disappear as alternative techniques are proved valuable in analyzing stimulus control, and similar changes may be anticipated elsewhere. Cognitive psychologists and others still try to circumvent the explicit control of variables by describing contingencies of reinforcement to their subjects in "instructions." They also try to dispense with recording behavior in a form from which probability of response can be estimated by asking their subjects to evaluate their tendencies to respond. But a person rarely responds to a description of contingencies as he would under direct exposure to them, nor can he accurately predict his rate of responding, particularly the course of the subtle changes in rate which are a commonplace in the experimental analysis of behavior. These attempts to short-circuit an experimental analysis can no longer be justified on grounds of expedience, and there are many reasons for abandoning them. Much remains to be done, however, before the facts to which they are currently applied can be said to be adequately understood.

BEHAVIORISM AND BIOLOGY

Elsewhere, the scientific study of man has scarcely recognized the need for reform. The biologist, for example, begins with a certain advantage in studying the behaving organism, for the structures he analyzes have an evident physical status. The nervous system is somehow earthier than the behavior for which it is largely responsible. Philosophers and psychologists alike have, from time to time, sought escape from mentalism in physiology. When a man sees red, he may be seeing the physiological effect of a red stimulus; when he merely imagines red, he may be seeing the same effect re-aroused. Pyschophysical and perceptual distortions may be wrought by physiological processes. What a man feels as anxiety may be antonomic reactions to threatening stimuli. And so on. This may solve the minor problem of the nature of subjective experience, but it does not solve any of the methodological problems with which behaviorism is most seriously concerned. A physiological translation of mentalistic terms may reassure those who want to avoid dualism, but inadequacies in the formulation survive translation.

When writing about the behavior of organisms, biologists tend to be more mentalistic than psychologists. Adrian could not understand how a nerve impulse could cause a thought. A recent article on the visual space sense in *Science* (8) asserts that "the final event in the chain from the retina to the brain is a psychic experience." Another investigator reports research on "the brain and its contained mind." Pharmacologists study the "psychotropic" drugs. Psychosomatic medicine insists on the influence of mind over matter. And psychologists join their physiological colleagues in looking for feelings, emotions, drives, and pleasurable aspects of positive reinforcement in the brain.

The facts uncovered in such research are important, both for their own sake and for their bearing on behavior. The physiologist studies structures and processes without which behavior could not occur. He is in a position to supply a "reductionist" explanation beyond the reach of an analysis which confines itself to terminal variables. He cannot do this well, however, so long as he accepts traditional mentalistic formulations. Only an experimental analysis of behavior will define his task in optimal terms. The point is demonstrated by recent research in psychopharmacology. When the behavioral drugs first began to attract attention, they were studied with impromptu techniques based on self-observation, usually designed to quantify subjective reports. Eventually the methods of an experimental analysis proved their value in generating reproducible segments of behavior upon which effects of drugs could be observed and in terms of which they could be effectively defined and classified. For the same reasons, brain physiology will move forward more rapidly when it recognizes that its role is to account for the mediation of behavior rather than of mind.

Behaviorism in the Social Sciences

There is also still a need for behaviorism in the social sciences, where psychology has long been used for explanatory purposes. Economics has had its economic man. Political science has considered man as a political animal. Parts of anthropology and sociology have found a place for psychoanalysis. The relevance of psychology to linguistics has been debated for more than half a century. Studies of scientific method have oscillated between logical and empirical analyses. In all these fields, "psychologizing" has often had disappointing results and has frequently been rejected by turning to an extreme formalism emphasizing objective facts. Economics confines itself to its own abundant data. Political scientists limit themselves to whatever may be studied with a few empirical tools and techniques and confine themselves, when they deal with theory, to formalistic analyses of political structures. A strong structuralist movement is evident in sociology. Linguistics emphasizes formal analyses of semantics and grammar.

Strait-laced commitments to pure description and formal analysis appear to leave no place for explanatory principles, and the short-coming is often blamed on the exclusion of mental activities. For example, a recent symposium on "The Limits of Behavioralism in Political Science" (4) complains of a neglect of subjective experience, ideas, motives, feelings, attitudes, values, and so on. This is reminiscent of attacks on behaviorism. In any case, it shows the same misunderstanding of the scope of a behavioral analysis. In its extension to the social sciences, as in psychology proper, behaviorism means more than a commitment to objective measurement. No entity or process which has any useful explanatory force is to be rejected on the ground that it is subjective or mental. The data which have made it important must, however, be studied and formulated in effective ways. The assignment is well within the scope of an experimental analysis of behavior, which thus offers a promising alternative to a commitment to pure description on the one hand and an appeal to mentalistic theories on the other. To extend behaviorism as a philosophy of science to the study of political and economic behavior, of the behavior of people in groups, of people speaking and listening, teaching and learning—this is not "psychologizing" in the traditional sense. It is simply the application of a tested formulation to important parts of the field of human behavior.

BIBLIOGRAPHY

1. BLOUGH, D. S. "Dark Adaptation in the Pigeon," *Journal of Comparative and Physiological Psychology*, XLIX (1956), 425–30.
2. BLOUGH, D. S., and SCHIRER, A. M. "Scotopic Spectral Sensitivity in the Monkey," *Science*, CXXXIX (1963), 493–94.
3. BRIDGMAN, P. W. *The Way Things Are.* Cambridge: Harvard University Press, 1959.
4. CHARLESWORTH, J. C. (ed.). *The Limits of Behavioralism in Political Science.* Philadelphia: American Academy of Political and Social Sciences, 1962.
5. GALTON, F. *Inquiries into Human Faculty.* London: J. M. Dent and Company, 1883.
6. HERRNSTEIN, R. J., and SOMMERS, PETER VAN. "Method for Sensory Scaling with Animals," *Science*, CXXXV (1962), 40–41.
7. HOGBEN, L. *Statistical Theory.* London: Allen and Unwin, 1957.
8. OGLE, K. N. "The Visual Space Sense," *Science*, CXXXV (1962), 763–71.
9. STEVENS, S. S. "The Operational Basis of Psychology," *The American Journal of Psychology*, XLVII (1935), 323–30.

PARAPHRASE OF DISCUSSION

COMMENTS OF PROFESSOR SKINNER

Much of what Professor Koch had to say the day before concerned "failures of various approaches to the study of behavior rather than [failure in] the basic behavioristic philosophy." Koch tried "to convince you all that behaviorism is dead." If one distinguishes, as Skinner does, between the philosophy of science, "behaviorism," and the science of behavior, one cannot say "that the scientific study of behavior is dead."

". . . [T]he exponential growth curve of . . . very important work in the field of the behavior of infrahuman organisms, . . . studies using children, normal and retarded, and human adults, retarded, psychotic and . . . normal," is "a kind of natural growth" in "a science which does not begin by trying to solve all the difficult problems first" but "is content to wait until it has solved some of the simpler ones, so that it can then move on." He is "often shocked to discover that important figures in psychology . . . are scarcely aware of what *is* going on."

While the volumes Professor Koch has been "brilliantly" editing will stand as "a great tribute to his appreciation of the role of scientific method in the development of a science," it is possible they have encouraged psychologists to become too "method-conscious." There is a kind of science developing that does not make any great use of methodology. Until this science of behavior has gone further, "we cannot be sure that the behavioristic alternative to a mentalistic formulation is adequate." However, while "everything" has not yet "been proved," "to say that a behaviorism as a philosophy of science is dead, pending the ultimate achievement of a science of behavior, which is . . . by no means dead, is . . . a little rash, because we cannot tell the extent to which a science of behavior will be able to offer an alternative to mentalistic formulations."

"I am not in the least discouraged by being told that the phenomenologists will bury us."

COMMENTS OF PROFESSOR KOCH

"If behaviorism were an absolute, unambiguous corpse, I would not waste my time in the prodigal way I did. . . ." The point is that "if one traces through the history of behaviorism from approximately 1913, . . . one finds a story of progressive attenuation of the position from within and, more recently, . . . increasing and very strong attrition from without."

". . . [B]ehaviorism, in some form, had almost an absolute hegemony in . . . fundamental experimental psychology" from, approximately, the late twenties to the early fifties. Since then, "there has been a diversification of strategies with respect to research and systematic action in psychology," which has broadened the range of both the "orienting attitudes" and the "substantive ideas" with which psychology now works.

Professor Skinner's formulation in the paper presented is so "extraordinarily libertarian . . . that one begins to wonder what the actual defining characteristics of the behaviorist thesis or the behaviorist method might be in his particular case." Koch feels that Skinner uses such terms as "behavior," "operation," and "stimulus variables" with a "flexibility" and "undifferentiated" spread comparable to "other liberalized behavioristic writers." He questions the "fruitfulness of a science, the analytic tools of which are . . . variables that are so extraordinarily comprehensive and crassly defined."

Far from Project A's showing an "appreciation" for the methodology of psychology, one of its major aims was to "force . . . a massive test of the methodological premises of what was called 'The Age of Theory.'" These premises, "a scattering of methodological prescriptions imported . . . from logical positivism, of neo-pragmatism and operationism," were almost "canon law" in psychology. Even those who departed from this canon were "constrained" in their departure by its terminology, so that we had an "absolutely regulative" model of science. Project A contrasted this kind of law "with inquiring practice in the field," and, as was pointed out in the epilogue to the first study, a "strong stress against this canon law" is developing.

COMMENTS OF PROFESSOR SKINNER

He does not agree that American psychology was as "restrained by the strictures imposed by behaviorism" as Koch argues it was. Gestalt psychology, the demonstrations of Ames at Dartmouth, the "mentalistic" work of social psychology, flourishing work in audition and vision—all were going on at that time.

In the early fifties, "a *methodology* of the study of behavior began to collapse." This was a methodology with which he has never been identified—the Hullian *S-R* theory and Tolman's cognitive purposive psychology. The change in the fifties was "due to the fact that the study of behavior under the aegis of the Hullians" disappeared.

In the same decade, the *Journal for the Experimental Analysis of Behavior* was founded. Data are being gathered which are a part of a very consistent, coherent, reproducible, and vital science of behavior. He is not concerned, here, in justifying the methodology of this science would take time supposed to be given to the discussion of "behaviorism as a philosophy of science."

MEMBER OF THE AUDIENCE

What is Professor Skinner's "behavioristic account of the high intellectual activities" reflected in his paper?

COMMENTS OF PROFESSOR SKINNER

"May I say first that psychology needs to learn one very important lesson, and that is that it cannot answer every question which is asked of it." We cannot, now, give "a very adequate account" of intellectual activity—"probably the most complex behavior of the most complex organism which has yet appeared on the face of the earth. . . ."

His work on verbal behavior is an attempt to give such an account. He applies this to his own work, practicing "a behavioral form of self-management which permits [him] eventually to find out what [he] has to say." A reconstructive account of the preparation of the paper just given would show a process of emitted verbal responses being read and reread, leading to changes and modifications, the emitted changes and modifications leading, in turn, to further changes. By a cumulative graphing of time spent in working, his "verbal behavior" is reinforced. He has found it "useful" to regard himself exactly as he regards "the pigeons, rats, and other people" he studies.

Similar behavioral analysis of instruction should "work great changes." As such analysis proceeds, more of "what verbal behavior is about" will be understood, and "an improvement in thinking, an improvement in getting out one's own verbal behavior will come about."

Member of the Audience

The conceptual systems we use for explaining behavior would seem to be largely a matter of social reinforcements. Why is it that "mentalistic, molar concepts" seem to receive more reinforcements, or are more resistant to extinction, than behavioral concepts when dealing with therapy, prognosis, and the like?

Comments of Professor Skinner

This is "the course of any science." "Chemistry went through a period of this sort. . . ." The science of chemistry began when people were willing to disregard the very obvious and easily manipulated properties of compounds and substances and pay attention to the less obvious property of combining weight. One must turn one's back on the "dramatic things."

The "dramatic things in human behavior are tied up with our everyday experience" with people. Accounts of this experience are cast in a dualism that has become a part of our language. We are taught to think of human behavior in mentalistic terms. Questions about "what kinds of stimuli" are being presented, "what kinds of changes" can these stimuli bring about in behavior, are well worth asking, while attending to less dramatic aspects of everyday experience.

Member of the Audience

In speaking about "managing his own activities, arranging the re-inforcements and so on," Professor Skinner seems to be implying "that he *chooses* to do this, he *chooses* to do that." While he avoids talking about "choice," is there room in the behavioristic view "for the concept of choice as one of the determinants of behavior?"

Comments of Professor Skinner

"You can conceptualize a response system—if you like, personify it —but you gain nothing from that." To speak of "self-management" is to speak of a conceptualization for purposes of discussion, not for purposes of explanation.

The "activity called making a choice" occurs in situations "in which there is no single clear-cut response, but several responses" available. Such activity involves "more than just doing one or the other." It involves stimuli, "verbal and non-verbal activities which hasten the emergence of one response and hence release you from the aversive position of being faced with two—with no response actually coming out." It is possible to analyze "problem," "self," "behavior," and "making choices" in these terms.

In studying the "technology of teaching," if one decides not only "to analyze choosing but to teach effective choice behavior, you force yourself to consider the objective activity."

MEMBER OF THE AUDIENCE

Does the statement in the paper that problems of sensation and perception are problems of stimulus control imply that studies of perception must use a psychophysical approach?

COMMENTS OF PROFESSOR SKINNER

Through suitable scheduling of reinforcements one can get data on light sensitivity, dark adaptation, and color sensitivity in monkeys and pigeons "as precise as the data obtained with human subjects in a psychophysical experiment."

When it comes to perception, things are "much more difficult than this." "In general, the reason people get interested in perception is that what *appears* to be there is not what you know to be there [through] some other way" of observing. In studying perception one is "actually investigating the stimulus conditions under which people" report appearances that are at variance with information obtained by other means. "You never get to the way it *really* is. You do find different ways of presenting stimuli. . . ." The "business of perception" is to investigate the relationship between the ways the stimuli are presented and the appearance. Here, also, a functional behavioral analysis is applicable.

One cannot say "there are laws of perception which modify the physical stimulus into the subjective experience" and that that is what is being studied. The facts of perception cannot be explained by "a slippage between the physical stimulus and the subjective psychological stimulus." That names a problem. It does not explain it.

MEMBER OF THE AUDIENCE

The experimental analysis of behavior was described as falling between pure description and mentalistic explanations. ". . . Apparently you do not use the term 'explanation' in the usual logical-positivist sense of the term. Is the term 'explanation' a meaningful term as it relates to the experimental analysis of behavior?"

COMMENTS OF PROFESSOR SKINNER

"When I said 'explanation' I simply meant the causal account." An explanation is the demonstration of a functional relationship between behavior and manipulable or controllable variables.

A different kind of explanation will arise when a physiology of behavior becomes available. "It will fill in the gaps between terminal events. . . ." It must be arrived at by "independent observation and not by inference, or not by mentalistic constructions. . . ."

COMMENTS OF PROFESSOR MALCOLM

The remark in Professor Skinner's paper that seeing does not imply something seen is puzzling, not so much because he was not using the word "see" in a normal way, but, more importantly, because he says that this statement is the heart of behaviorism as a philosophy of psychology.

COMMENTS OF PROFESSOR SKINNER

It is "the heart *only* of the behavioristic understanding of conscious content." It applies to behavioristic interpretations of seeing, sensations, images, and the like. It does not apply to behavioristic interpretations of such "explanatory" mental activities as expectancies, expectations, etc.

A genetic view of "seeing" would regard it "as something which must be learned under differential reinforcements." This is "an extremely difficult subject" and our understanding of what is involved is incomplete. What it is that "gets reinforced by the community when it teaches the child to be aware of" something as distinct from teaching it to act "appropriately" to something is not yet clear. It must be some kind of socially reinforced behavior, verbal or otherwise, for which there are "no natural contingencies. . . . [I]t must be something that comes about when what you do about [seeing] does get differentially reinforced. . . . I suspect that it could, very well, be private stimulation which is a concomitant of the public stimuli used by the verbal community in such reinforcement."

MEMBER OF THE AUDIENCE

Who is it "that really arranges the schedules of reinforcement" so that a person "ends up thinking he is doing it himself?"

COMMENTS OF PROFESSOR SKINNER

"I do not end up thinking I am doing it myself." We learn to engage in "ethical and intellectual managing activities" in a particular cultural setting. Behavior is not a function of a person "stepping outside the stream of history and altering" his own actions but a function of differential reinforcement from the culture. How cultures evolve toward these forms of "self-control" is a separate issue which he has discussed elsewhere.

MEMBER OF THE AUDIENCE

Discuss self-management as it applies to creative, artistic activities. In painting, for example, how does one "evoke a mood?"

COMMENTS OF PROFESSOR SKINNER

Painting is an example from "a great family of skilled activities" in which one is responding, primarily, to his own previous actions. The question is how one can "arrive at something which is maximally reinforcing" to one's own actions. Research is now going on in an attempt to find some answers to that kind of question. "Devices which will shape . . . [the] fundamental activities . . . involved in artistic" activities are being investigated. He is engaged now in research attempting to teach children to "think musically," that is, "to give an objective behavioral base for acting out pitches, intervals, melodic line, and so on."

COMMENTS OF PROFESSOR SCRIVEN

Could not many of Professor Skinner's remarks be construed "as a procedure for giving a sympathetic analysis of mentalistic and psychic explanations?" Did he not "show that these [explanations] can be legitimately construed as references to a state of the organism in which all of the dispositions do produce behavior of certain kinds?" Does not the analysis argue that these states ought, properly, be referred to in behavioral terms and—"a crucial point"—should a state induced by an earlier exposure persist in an organism and modify later behavior, it must be referred to in these terms?

COMMENTS OF PROFESSOR SKINNER

"I do feel, in a way, that I am offering a reinterpretation of a mentalistic analysis—that you can redefine if you like—but that [redefinition] is always a dangerous kind of thing. . . ." It is preferable "to use terms which come out of an analysis" rather than apply terms from some other source.

There exists, at present, a gap between terminal events in our behavioral analysis. "Mentalistic explanations, physiological explanations, and conceptual inner events as explanations" are all "on a par" in their attempts to fill this gap. Some day the gap will be filled. The conceptual formulation is not helpful and the "mental properties added on to the conceptual are a distraction." It is most likely that the physiological explanation will "win out." Whatever it will be, it seems "reasonable" to carry out the "original decision" to "get on with the functional analysis of terminal events," rather than wait for the gap to be filled.

MEMBER OF THE AUDIENCE

One criticism of behaviorism is that it has not "captured" the "richness of human" life—it has "impoverished" the account of human behavior, especially with regard to "meaning."

COMMENTS OF PROFESSOR SKINNER

In his book on verbal behavior he did not use the concept of meaning or "any recognizable substitute for it." A "fundamental mistake" is made in assuming "the richness of, the meaning of, experience" are to be "found in the response rather than in the variables controlling the response."

No scientific analysis of behavior "will be as rich as *The Brothers Karamazov*," nor will the physicist's analysis of the world be as rich as walking around the campus. They are "not there to be rich." Whatever view of human nature emerges from the science of behavior will be different from any we now have, but "I cannot imagine anything which is less likely to be regarded as poverty-stricken than a genuinely effective understanding of human behavior."

MEMBER OF THE AUDIENCE

"Do you care to comment on just what you believe a reinforcement is?"

COMMENTS OF PROFESSOR SKINNER

"I am *not* interested in explaining why something *is* reinforcing. I identify a reinforcing stimulus only in terms of its observed effect. . . . I cannot explain why food is reinforcing to a hungry animal. . . . I have a good idea why it probably has become so, but I do not know why it is and I do not care. . . . This is a question about the science of behavior and not about the issue of behaviorism."

MEMBER OF THE AUDIENCE

The positions of Professors Koch and Skinner are in such contrast "that they both could not be right." "To what degree should our students be trained to still consider" alternatives to behaviorism as possibilities?

COMMENTS OF PROFESSOR SKINNER

"My impression is that we give them too much of" this "kind of doctrine," not only in psychology, but in many other areas of life. It is helpful to reject inner state terms, e.g., "drive," even though it is difficult to do. To say the animal has been deprived of food rather than to say its drive has been raised may be "embarrassingly paraphrastic," but it is valuable to do this consistently. By doing so, one is repeatedly reminded of what has been done to the animal.

"I would not be involved in this if I did not think that mentalistic ways of thinking about human behavior stand in the way of much more effective ways. . . . The notion of 'knowledge' and 'mental skills' and 'rational powers' which is still dominating the field of education is keeping us from teaching."

COMMENTS OF PROFESSOR KOCH

"I think that Dr. Skinner's answer was quite characteristic of the kind of attitude associated historically with behaviorists in general. It was an intolerant answer."

MEMBER OF THE AUDIENCE

"Would you be kind enough to clarify the term 'verbal community' a little bit further?"

COMMENTS OF PROFESSOR SKINNER

"I was referring to all those people in the environment of a child or adult who do actually respond to verbal behavior in ways which shape the behavior and maintain it and keep it going. This would include the speaker himself. He is a part of his own community when he talks to himself, as one does in writing a paper."

MEMBER OF THE AUDIENCE

"Do we have a listening community . . . or just a verbal community?"

COMMENTS OF PROFESSOR SKINNER

"The verbal community is either a listening or reading community . . . provided [we] were talking about ordinary linguistic verbal behavior. If it is the language of flowers, you will get a different reinforcing community, and so on."

COMMENTS OF PROFESSOR SCRIVEN

To follow up on the answer given to Scriven's earlier question, it appears to be the case that (1) mentalistic concepts can legitimately be interpreted as referring to a state of the organism which can alter future dispositions to behave and which can be explained in terms of earlier reinforcement schedules and (2) introspection is allowed in the sense that there are some parts of the universe to which an individual has direct access but to which no other individual has direct access.

"Can't we put these two together and say that organisms are sometimes able to detect their own states in a way which others are not able to detect and that, moreover, these states which they detect can also be regarded as giving a guide to future behavior, though not a perfect one because of . . . the language community's inadequacies in establishing constancy of labeling here? . . . Where have we got with a behaviorism that allows us on the one hand a legitimate interpretation of mentalistic language and [on the other] a direct access to 'mental' states, with 'mental' here meaning . . . a state of the organism which can be directly perceived and which . . . is an indicator of subsequent changes in behavior? . . . Why do you feel that you are, in fact, still in some sense a radical behaviorist rather than someone who is making an extremely useful recommendation about the way in which we should prune the surplus out of mentalistic language?"

COMMENTS OF PROFESSOR SKINNER

"I am a radical behaviorist simply in the sense that I find no place in the formulation for anything which is mental." This is a minor issue, the major reason for his position being his certainty that the reports about the "internal states" are not adequate. "They [the internal states] exist—we can create a vocabulary for talking about them and part of human progress has been the improvement of our description of these things." But this does not increase our "introspective clarity," rather, it helps us "understand the relevance of forces in our lives and in our history and in the current environment." If "behaviorism" means "simply the issue of the stuff of which the mental event is composed" then he is a radical behaviorist. Otherwise, he is a "methodological one, arguing [that] there are better ways of formulating relations than by setting up so-called intervening variables."

COMMENTS OF PROFESSOR MACLEOD

The data on color blindness and von Frisch's data on the "color spectrum" of honey bees suggest that "the distinction between public and private, when we approach it phenomenologically, becomes a much less clear-cut distinction than when we, more or less arbitrarily, consider the skin as the dividing line between what is public and what is private."

COMMENTS OF PROFESSOR SKINNER

While "the skin *is* an anatomical definition of a space," it is not the "boundary" Skinner uses in the distinction between public and private. By "private" he does not mean "events within the organism" that are accessible to "the individual himself," but events within the organism that are not, or are very inadequately, accessible to the "reinforcing community."

With the color blind, no matter how the reinforcing community "manipulates reds and greens," it "gets nowhere and so it stops, and the individual never does see red or green." Manipulations of certain wavelengths of light will have no effect with humans but noticeable effect with bees. These facts illustrate what he means by the public-private distinction, namely, "what the verbal community faces by way of problems in arranging the contingencies which lead to fine distinctions." The "boundary" for public-private is not the skin, but the line between the verbal community's being able to reinforce behavior differentially and its not being able to, or able to only with great difficulty.

COMMENTS OF PROFESSOR KOCH

An extremely important problem is raised by Professor Skinner's insistence on the all-pervading role of the verbal community in experience. The range of the "private" (Koch would prefer the term "experiential process" to "private stimulation") even as it is defined in Skinner's terms can be reduced "by building up discriminations which, in fact, attach verbal labels, verbal tags to . . . properties of experience . . . which have not, in general, been discriminated and tagged . . . in the previous history of civilization." It is the "tremendous emphasis" which Skinner places on the role of the verbal community in the development of this discrimination and tagging that is disturbing.

While is is "perfectly valid to maintain that the early learning of language necessarily depends on differential reinforcement ('differential guidance' is preferable) by the verbal community and that, initially, language has an external reference, . . . sensitive analysis of language will show that, ultimately, the individual is, to some extent, freed from the controls . . . [of] differential reinforcement by the verbal community."

"Ultimately, the individual, if he strives to establish verbal contact with his experience," will use the "relational properties" of language with "a considerable degree of precision" to "exhibit . . . aspects of experience which are subtle, are elusive and which may, perhaps, never before have been mapped in the previous history of discrimination, in the previous history of language." He will be able to do this through "devices like metaphor, devices like what is implicit in Peirce's notion of the 'icon,' namely, a kind of relational map," in general, through the use of the relational properties of language.

It is not possible, here, to develop these ideas in the detail that they must be developed in order to evaluate Professor Skinner's position. "The problem . . . is a very subtle and difficult one but one of considerable import."

COMMENTS OF PROFESSOR SKINNER

"In my operationism paper in 1945, I listed metaphor as one of the three or four ways in which, to some extent, the verbal community can transcend the problems posed by privacy and lead to terms descriptive of private stimuli. Almost all the language of emotion is metaphorical, as has often been pointed out, and, to a greater extent than we often realize, . . . a great part of our other mentalistic language is metaphorical. I only raise the question of the possible limits of accuracy of metaphorical extensions."

CARL R. ROGERS

Toward a Science of the Person

I SHARE with Maslow and others the view that there are three broad emphases in American psychology. These resemble three ocean currents flowing side by side, mingling, with no clear line of demarcation, yet definitely different. Like the flotsam and jetsam which float on each ocean current, certain words and phrases identify, even though they do not define, these separate flowing trends. Associated with the first trend are such terms as "behaviorism," "objective," "experimental," "impersonal," "logical-positivistic," "operational," "laboratory." Associated with the second current are terms such as "Freudian," "Neo-Freudian," "psychoanalytic," "psychology of the unconscious," "instinctual," "ego-psychology," "id-psychology," "dynamic psychology." Associated with the third are terms such as "phenomenological," "existential," "self-theory," "self-actualization," "health-and-growth psychology," "being and becoming," "science of inner experience."

What I wish to do in this paper is to consider the question: What are the consequences, for psychological theory and research, of the third stream of thought—the phenomenological, existential, self-theory stream? In considering this question there will doubtless be occasional comparative glances at each of the other currents of thought, yet the primary emphasis will be upon the third.

I would like to make it clear at the outset that I am speaking only for myself, from the perspective which my own experience has given me. I am certainly not attempting to speak for psychology as a whole. And, though I consider myself a part of this third trend, I am not attempting to speak for it. It is too diversified, its boundaries too vague, for me to endeavor to be a spokesman. Rather, as a member of

CARL R. ROGERS, Professor, Departments of Psychology and Psychiatry, University of Wisconsin. Professor Rogers would like to acknowledge his indebtedness to Allen Bergin and Eugene Gendlin for very helpful suggestions and criticisms of this manuscript.

this group, I shall be concerned with the meaning that this current has in modern psychological life as I perceive it. Toward what shores, what islands, what vastnesses of the deep is its compelling current carrying us? What will it mean for psychology as a science that this current has become a part of our profession?

THREE WAYS OF KNOWING

In order to lay a groundwork for what I wish to say, I should like to comment upon our process of "knowing." All knowing consists essentially of hypotheses, which we check in different ways. These hypotheses may be regarded as proven beyond question, or they may be held very tentatively. They may be concerned with any content whatsoever, from "2 plus 2 equals 4," to "I *am* beginning to love her"; from "She hates her mother" to "I am six feet tall"; from "He is an untrustworthy person" to "e equals mc²."

Sometimes we endeavor to divide such hypotheses as I have given, such examples of knowing, into objective and subjective knowledge. Perhaps this is not a helpful dichotomy, since every instance of knowing involves coming to terms in some way with the subjective and phenomenological. To me it has been helpful to think of three ways of knowing, ways which differ primarily in the manner in which we check our hypotheses. Let me describe these three approaches, though I would stress the fact that there are also other ways in which we may view this process of knowing. The threefold perspective I shall describe seems to me especially relevant to psychology and other behavioral sciences.[1]

SUBJECTIVE KNOWING

Within myself—from within my own internal frame of reference—I may "know" that I love or hate, sense, perceive, comprehend. I may believe or disbelieve, enjoy or dislike, be interested in or bored by. These are all hypotheses, which we often check, as Gendlin (9) has shown, by using the ongoing flow of our preconceptual experiencing as a referent. So I may check my hypothesis by asking, "Do I really hate him?" As I refer to my experiencing I realize that it is envy rather than hate which I feel. Or I may wonder, "Do I love her?" It is only by reference to the flow of feelings in me that I can begin to conceptualize an answer. In respect to another situation, I am placed by a psychologist in a dark room in which there is a pin point of light. I am asked if the light moves, or if it is stationary. I consult my experi-

---

[1] These three ways of knowing are not directly related to the three currents in psychology. Rather, this discussion of "knowing" is an attempt to look at some of the fundamental problems underlying all three trends in psychology.

encing of the situation, and I say that it is moving. (The fact that "objectively" it is stationary, will be dealt with later.) I form an inner hypothesis from the experiencing going on in me.

Let me take other examples. I taste a foreign dish. Do I like it? It is only by referring to the flow of my experiencing that I can sense the implicit meanings and conclude, "I like its flavor but not its consistency." Or in a very different situation, after studying a large body of data I ask, "What is the unity, the central principle, which I sense in all these varied and seemingly disparate events?" Again I turn to my experiencing to try to determine what it *is* that gives me this sense of a commonality.

I hope these fragmentary subjective examples will give some sense of the fashion in which a person tests, within his own skin, the inner hypotheses which he forms. These hypotheses are corrected by being more sharply differentiated, by becoming more precise and accurate. Any one who has experienced psychotherapy will have lived through this way of sharpening or of contradicting previously held inner hypotheses. Often an example of it in psychotherapy is the way in which the client searches and searches for the word that will more accurately describe what he is experiencing, feeling, or perceiving. There is a sense of real relief when he discovers a term which "matches" his experiencing, which provides a more sharply differentiated meaning for the vague knowing which has been present, which permits him to be more congruent within himself (9, chap. 1, 7).

The person who has tackled a complex new job, or who is faced with complicated data in a research, has also experienced this same process within himself. At first his "knowledge" of the task is global, imprecise, undifferentiated. Then he begins to sense pattern—that these events or these facts seem to go together, that these other events or facts, while they loom large on the surface, are probably not important. He acts tentatively to test these inner hypotheses, moving forward when the pattern is sensed as becoming stronger or correcting his direction when his sense of the pattern fades. Polanyi (21, chap. 3) has given an excellent description of the compelling pull which an inner sense of the significance of pattern has upon the scientist.

Thus one important way of knowing is through the formation of inner hypotheses, which are checked by referring to our inward flow of experiencing as we live in our subjective interaction with inner or outer events. This type of knowing is fundamental to everyday living. Note that though external cues and stimuli may be involved in this type of hypothesis formation, it is not the external situation against which we test our hypotheses. It is our inner experiencing to which we refer to check and sharpen and further differentiate the conceptual hypotheses we are forming from the implicit meanings.

Since this mode of knowing is not infallible and does not lead to publicly validated knowledge, little attention is given to it today. Yet this seems to me our most basic way of knowing, a deeply rooted organismic sensing, from which we form and differentiate our conscious symbolizations and conceptions.

I would voice the opinion that even the most rigorous science has its origin in this mode of knowing. Without the creative inner hypothesis, all the machinery of outward verification would be sterile. As Einstein said in regard to his search for the principle of relativity:

During all those years there was a feeling of direction, of going straight toward something concrete. It is, of course, very hard to express that feeling in words; but it was decidedly the case, and clearly to be distinguished from later considerations about the rational form of the solution (32, pp. 183–84).

This aspect of science—the creative inner hypothesis, which is checked and rechecked against the relevant aspects of one's experiencing and which may then eventuate as the formal hypothesis to be operationally tested—has been greatly ignored in American science. Especially has it been ignored in American psychology, where it has been considered slightly obscene to admit that psychologists feel, have hunches, or passionately pursue unformulated directions. Curiously enough, we are indebted to a strict behaviorist for a case history of his research development which freely describes this all-important subjective phase (26, pp. 76–99). Here the account of the development of his investigative directions is studded with such phrases as, "This was, of course, the kind of thing I was looking for"; "I was bothered by"; "I can easily recall the excitement of"; "Of course I was working on a basic assumption." Such phrases point up a sorely needed emphasis—that science always has its *beginning* as an inner subjective hypothesis, highly valued by the investigator because it makes patterned sense out of his experiencing.

It may be mentioned in passing that if I try to test these inner hypotheses by checking with others or with the external environment, then we have passed to the "objective" way of knowing. If I ask you, "*Am* I falling in love?" or "*Is* this light moving?" then I am using intersubjective verification, and this is part of another way of knowing.

OBJECTIVE KNOWING

Let us turn to this way of knowing, which has been so highly regarded as "objectivity." In this type of knowing, the hypotheses are based upon an external frame of reference, and the hypotheses are checked both by externally observable operations and by making empathic inferences regarding the reactions of a trusted reference group, usually a group of one's colleagues. Thus, if a physicist says that he "knows" that the speed of a freely falling object is expressed by the formula, $v = 32t$ (where $v =$ velocity in feet per second, and $t =$ time in seconds), what he means is that various individuals whom he trusts have each gone through similar operations, which can be precisely described, and have observed similar results; and each has arrived at a similar subjective conviction, which is expressed in the formula, which is understood in a similar manner by all. The physicist believes the convictions are similar because he has exercised his own empathic ability in understanding the communications and the internal frame of reference of these others. This psychological process is the basis of all logical positivism, operationalism, and the vast structure of science as we know it. Its achievements have been most impressive.

There are certain characteristics of this approach that have not been sufficiently understood. Since it deals only with observable objects, the elements of any problem studied by such an approach must be treated only as publicly observable objects. Thus if I wish to study the effect upon myself of a fever-inducing drug, I observe myself as an object. The rise of temperature in degrees upon the thermometer, the observable flush which ensues—these are the kinds of qualities which can be a part of this objective knowing, since these are observable by others, and my observations can be checked by another. Objectivity can only be concerned with objects, whether these are animate or inanimate. Conversely, this way of knowing transforms everything it studies into an object, or perceives it only in its object aspects.

There is another characteristic of this approach, which is concerned with the direction of the empathy of the knower. In the first mode of knowing, the subjective mode, it would be accurate to say that the knower is directing his capacity for empathy toward himself, trying to understand more deeply the implicit meanings of his own experiencing and to make those meanings more explicit. In the objective mode of knowing, empathic understanding is directed solely toward the reference group. Perhaps an illustration will help here.

Suppose a psychologist wishes to introduce an event into his experiment which will be a stimulus to his experimental animal. What is a stimulus? If he is to be objective, there are, I believe, only two possible and related criteria. The event must be one which is understood to be, and accepted as, a stimulus by his psychological colleagues. Or if he wishes to be even more precise, then others, as well as himself, must see the later behavior of the animal as a response to this event, which therefore defines it for each observer as a stimulus, and this conclusion is known to the experimenter through his capacity for understanding the internal frame of reference of these others. This matter is well discussed by Jessor (12, 13). It should be clear that a stimulus is not a simple objective event, but a mutually understood, and mutually agreed upon, subjective perception by qualified colleagues. The same reasoning applies as well to such terms as "response" and "reinforcer."

It must be evident that the choice of a reference group is extremely important in this type of knowing. Polanyi (21, pp. 216–22) has pointed out the intricate web of overlapping appraisals which functions for the scientist in choosing, more or less consciously, a respected group, the members of which, in some sense, confirm one another as careful observers, and whose communications, properly understood, are the mechanism of intersubjective verification.

The importance of the reference group is perhaps best shown by mentioning some reference groups which are too narrow. In any closed system, intersubjective verification can be obtained by admitting to the group only those who have agreed in advance to a series of observations or beliefs which will *not* be questioned. Thus many religions, the Communist party, orthodox psychoanalysis—to mention a few—obtain intersubjective verification of knowledge by admitting to their groups only those who have agreed in advance not to question core elements of the structure. Most of us regard the knowledge which emerges in these systems as having a pseudo-objectivity rather than a true objectivity. In general, the broader the range of individuals who are regarded as a competent reference group, the surer the basis of the beliefs obtained through this way of knowing.

There is still another point to be made about this objective way of knowing. Since it has had such vast importance and led to such incredible technological advances, it is often forgotten that it is not necessarily superior to the first, subjective way of knowing and that in crucial instances it bows to it. For example, the evidence for extrasensory perception is better than, or certainly as good as, the evidence for many of the principles which psychologists believe. Yet, with very few exceptions, psychologists reject this evidence with vehemence. It is not easy to impugn the methods which have been used in studying ESP, for they are the same as those used in any field of psychology. But the psychologist falls back on his subjective knowing. The evidence does not fit with the pattern of knowledge as he expects to find it, does not fit with his experiencing of the world. Therefore he rejects it.

There are many instances of this sort in the history of science. Sometimes the intuitive knowledge of scientists as a group has proven more valid than the seemingly "hard evidence" from a research investigation. Perhaps just as frequently the rejection by scientists of some new finding, on an intuitive basis, has proved in the long run to be erroneous, and it is the radical research finding of a Pasteur or van't Hoff which is upheld. Polanyi (21, pp. 150–60) gives a fascinating account of some of these controversies. The point is that neither the new research finding *nor* the subjective wisdom of scientists viewing that finding is infallible. The reason for pointing out these crucial uncertainties is to indicate the error of the widespread notion that objective knowledge is "out there," firm, impersonal, and secure. Quite the contrary, it is a very human invention—one of enormous value, to be sure, and containing some of the best safeguards man has devised against deceiving himself—but it is nonetheless a fallible and human way of knowing, depending basically upon an intelligently intuitive personal selection of the hypothesis, adequate operations for testing it, the wise selection of a reference group, and the empathic understanding of the experiences of that reference group when they actually (or more often in imagination) repeat the operations of the experimenter.

INTERPERSONAL KNOWING OR PHENOMENOLOGICAL KNOWLEDGE

Logically, somewhere between the two types of knowing I have discussed, is a third mode which applies primarily to knowledge of human beings and the higher organisms, and which, for lack of a better term, I am calling "interpersonal knowing." Here I "know" that you feel hurt by my remark or that you despise yourself or that you have a strong desire to get "to the top of the heap" or that you believe the Republican Party to be an excellent organization or that you are concerned about thermonuclear war. These knowings, like those described before, are all hypotheses. But in these instances, the way of checking these hypotheses is to use whatever skill and empathic understanding is at my command to get at the relevant aspect of your phenomenological field, to get inside your private world of meanings, and see whether my understanding is correct. I may simply ask you bluntly if my hypothesis is correct, but this is often a very inadequate method of inferring your private world. I may observe your gestures, words, and inflections and base my inferences on these. Or I may—and here is the essence of my experience in psychotherapy— create a climate which makes it psychologically safe and rewarding for you to reveal your internal frame of reference. Then you find that you can share with me your unsatisfied ambition, the disgust you feel with yourself, your pattern of beliefs, or any other aspect of your world of personal meanings. In psychotherapy we have found this way of knowing to be most fruitful. Utilizing empathic inference to the fullest, checking our hypotheses against the phenomenal world of the client, we have gained knowledge which has led to the formulation of psychological principles related to personality change.

In this interpersonal or phenomenological way of knowing, then, the direction of the empathy is toward the other individual. Our hypotheses are tested by relating them to the most accurate picture we can obtain of the internal frame of reference of this individual. The knowledge it gives is of a particular individual, but from this knowledge generalizations can be formed which can be tested in the same manner. It provides us scientific leverage in getting at the non-observable events which go on within the individual.

It may have seemed surprising that I did not limit this way of knowing to knowledge of other human beings. I believe that this way of knowing is limited only by the limits of our capacity for empathy, and the degree of our ingenuity in getting at the internal frame of reference of the organism. Classic studies by Snygg (27) and Krechevsky (15) indicate that it is possible to check a hypothesis against the inferred internal frame of reference of the rat. I am sure that such studies could be extended. Nevertheless, this mode of knowing is obviously of most significance in promoting our knowledge of the human being.

What are the criteria for this type of knowing? When am I justified in feeling that I "know" something in this interpersonal sense? I believe the criteria are twofold: either my hypothesis about the internal frame of reference of this individual is confirmed by the individual himself, or the inferences made about his internal frame of reference are confirmed by a concensual validation. For example, I sense that you are feeling unhappy this morning. If I say, "Looks as though your world is pretty dark this morning," and you by word or nod show your agreement, then I have checked my hypothesis and found that it has some validity. Another method of checking would be that if I kept to myself my empathic sensing of your unhappiness, but during the morning three other individuals came to me independently to speak of their concern over what seemed to them as your sadness, your depression, and the like, then the probability of the correctness of the inference as to your internal state would be greatly increased. In some instances, as in the animal experiments cited, the inference as to the phenomenological field is supported by the fact that it is the most reasonable and most parsimonious explanation of the behavior.

THE RELATEDNESS OF WAYS OF KNOWING

Here, then, are three ways by which we extend knowledge, by which we confirm or disconfirm the hypotheses which we are continuously forming, both as a part of our everyday living and as a part of our psychological science. I would advance the view that any mature psychological science uses each of these ways of knowing in appropriate relationship to the other two and that it is only as these three modes of knowing are adequately and appropriately interwoven that a satisfactory behavioral science can emerge.

If I may be permitted a slight digression into analogy, I would point out that the psychologically mature person, like the mature science, uses these three modes of knowing in an integrated fashion. The mature person trusts his experiencing, and the meanings and hypotheses which he formulates from this inner flow. He forms and tests extremely significant hypotheses for living in his empathic relationships to the significant others in his life. He recognizes that all hypotheses are put to their most severe test in the objective world, and he, like the good scientist, remains open and receptive to the experiences which confirm or disconfirm his tentatively held hypotheses. Thus the psychologically healthy person is open to the finer differentiations of meaning in his inner experience which check and sharpen his hypotheses; to the rich sources of hypothesis formation and testing which exist in the other person; and to the testing of his hypotheses in real actions in a real world.

But this is a digression, and I should like to return to certain limitations which apply to these three ways of knowing.

I trust that I have made it plain that no method of knowing is infallible, that there is no royal road to scientific certitude. As Dr. Polanyi has remarked to me, "Every way of acquiring knowledge is risky." Whatever approximations to the truth we are able to achieve in the behavioral sciences will not come automatically through following one approach to knowledge. There is no such thing as a "scientific methodology" which will see us safely through.

I believe that recent history shows us that we make a serious mistake when we attempt to use one of these channels of knowing in isolation, without reference to the others. Thus the behaviorist frequently regards himself as using only the objective mode of knowing, and sees the other modes as objects of scorn, or at least completely unnecessary to a developing science. Some current existentialist thinkers on the other hand, seem equally passionate in rejecting the objective way of knowing, relying entirely on the subjective and phenomenological ways of knowing.

Another type of mistake is made when we confuse or equate these very different modes of knowing. It is of the utmost importance to be entirely clear as to the mode we are using at any particular moment or in any particular enterprise. When we become confused as to which avenue to knowledge is being utilized or attempt to equate the knowledge from these three modes, serious trouble arises. Much psychoanalytic writing exhibits this latter error to a painful degree.

The new third force in psychology seems hopeful in that it shows signs of being willing to use, with confidence and clarity, all three of these channels to knowing, in such ways as to advance and enrich and deepen our science. Individuals in this group do not seem to be afraid of using their subjectivity, their "indwelling" in their professional experience, as an explicit basis for their hypotheses. They build heavily on interpersonal knowing as a far richer mode of arriving at insights about nature and human nature than any purely external approach could possibly be. This is perhaps one of their most significant contributions. They recognize, too, the full importance of the objective mode in its proper place as one of the later phases of scientific endeavor. Thus I believe that their entrance into the psychological field will have important effects, and these I should like to try to spell out.

THE CONSEQUENCES

A MORE INCLUSIVE SCIENCE

One of the major consequences of this phenomenological-existential trend is that psychology will become a more inclusive and a more profound science. There are without doubt some individuals in this current of thought who maintain the hope that this new point of view will supplant the behaviorist trend, but to me this is both highly undesirable and highly unlikely. Rather it will mean, I believe, that psychology will preserve the advances and contributions that have come from the behavioristic development but will go beyond this. Psychology will now be capable of focusing on a broader reality, which will include not only behavior but the person and perspective of the observer and the person and perspective of the observed. It will recognize, as physical scientists have been forced to recognize, that "as human beings, we must inevitably see the universe from a centre lying within ourselves and speak about it in terms of a human language shaped by the exigencies of human intercourse. Any attempt rigorously to eliminate our human perspective from our picture of the world must lead to absurdity" (21, p. 3). It is from this absurdity that the new trend will rescue the science of man.

It is quite unfortunate that we have permitted the world of psychological science to be narrowed to behaviors observed, sounds emitted, marks scratched on paper, and the like. In an attempt to be ultra-scientific, psychology has endeavored to walk in the footsteps of a Newtonian physics. Oppenheimer has expressed himself strongly on this, saying that "the worst of all possible misunderstandings would be that psychology be influenced to model itself after a physics which is not there any more, which has been quite outdated" (18, p. 134). I think there is quite general agreement that this is the path into which our logical-positivist behaviorism has led us.

As I read the history and philosophy of science, there seems to me no alternative to the view that science in every field has advanced by discovering new perspectives, by theorizing in new ways, by utilizing new methods, quite without regard to the question of whether they fit into the then current tradition in science. While it is obvious that the newness of a method or a theory or a perspective is no guarantee of its heuristic value, it is nevertheless true that science should resolutely set its face against anything which would limit its own scope, or which would arbitrarily narrow the methods or perspectives of its own pursuit of knowledge.

Valuable as have been the contributions of behaviorism, I believe that time will indicate the unfortunate effects of the bounds it has tended to impose. To limit oneself to consideration of externally observable behaviors, to rule out consideration of the whole universe of inner meanings, of purposes, of the inner flow of experiencing, seems to me to be closing our eyes to great areas which confront us when we look at the human world. Furthermore, to hold to the beliefs, which seem to me to characterize many behaviorists, that science is impersonal, that knowledge is an entity, that science somehow carries itself forward without the subjective person of the scientist being involved, is, I think, completely illusory.

In contrast, the trend of which I am speaking will attempt to face up to *all* of the realities in the psychological realm. Instead of being restrictive and inhibiting, it will throw open the whole range of human experiencing to scientific study. It will explore the private worlds of inner personal meanings, in an effort to discover lawful and orderly relationships there. In this world of inner meanings it can investigate all the issues which are meaningless for the behaviorist—purposes, goals, values, choice, perceptions of self, perceptions of others, the personal constructs with which we build our world, the responsibilities we accept or reject, the whole phenomenal world of the individual with its connective tissue of meaning. Not one aspect of this world is open to the strict behaviorist. Yet that these elements have significance for man's behavior seems certainly true.

It is as clear to me as it is to the behaviorist that to enter these areas, which have always been thought of as the realm of the subjective, could lead to a morass of speculation and introspectionism. But the vital hope for the future is the fact that this does not necessarily follow, as I hope I can show. If this trend should lead only to a pseudo-science, as I am afraid the Freudian insights have done, then it would be tragic indeed. But there is increasing evidence that this need not, and probably will not, be so.

Let me sharpen the point I have been making. We need no longer live in an inhibited science of psychology. The trend toward a phenomenological, existential, self-theory emphasis in the field means that we can, with fresh vigor, open our minds and our thinking, our theories and our empirical research to all the significant problems of psychology. We can utilize all channels of knowing, not simply certain prescribed channels. We can permit the full creativity of thought of the psychologist to be exercised, not simply a narrowly inhibited and traditional type of thought. In this respect I believe that the psychologist will experience a new burst of creative freedom, such as has occurred in other sciences when old bonds and boundaries have been broken. No problem, no method, no perspective will be out of bounds. Men can work freely and creatively toward discovering the significant relationships between humanly important variables in the psychological realm.

NEW CLASSES OF VARIABLES EXPLORED

I have stressed the greater scope which this new trend will bring to psychology as a science. One of the consequences of this broadened scope is that there will be whole new areas of problems explored, of variables measured. I should like to give several examples of work that I believe herald the future direction. In each of these examples we find that the measures used have many of the qualities valued by the behaviorist. These are thoroughly objective measures, whose results are publicly replicable. Yet they are used without some of the philosophical assumptions of the behaviorist group. And they are used to measure variables which could only come from a profound concern with the phenomenological world of the individual, from a concern with the human being as a process of valuing and choosing, of being and becoming.

a) Meaning.—Consider first some problems connected with meaning. We may wish to investigate the possibility that when the structure of meanings within our phenomenal world changes, then our behavior changes. As an example, it seems probable that the meaning of the word "China" underwent a striking change of meaning in the minds of the Indian people when Chinese troops crossed the mountains into territory held by India and that a change in the whole patterning of behavior then ensued. It is an exciting thing to realize that, thanks to the ingenuity of Osgood and his co-workers (20), we have a precise means of measuring such a change in meaning, the so-called semantic differential. We could chart the course in "semantic space" of the meaning of the concept "China." We could determine its changing relationship to other concepts such as "friend," "strong," "black," "honesty," "democracy," and the like. We can also study the relationship between its changing meaning and various external behaviors. Or, to comment on another and perhaps more basic use of the tool of the semantic differential, we can determine whether semantic space has essentially the same fundamental dimensions in different cultures, the people of which speak different languages (19). We can determine whether divergent cultures have, in spite of their differences, an underlying generality in the way in which they perceive meanings. Here we see an impressive example of studies of functional relationships, using methods which are strictly operational, but dealing with problems of inner phenomenological meanings as they exist in the private world of each individual, and discovering orderly relationships between those meanings. What more intangible problem could be dreamed up than to measure the figurative space which exists between two or more meanings in a person's experience and the way in which these spatial relationships change over time? Yet this important existential area has been convincingly dealt with in a thoroughly objective manner, giving results which are replicable by any qualified scientist.

b) The self and related variables.—I should like to turn to another example or, rather, a cluster of related examples. An object of vast importance in the phenomenal world of each individual is his self. Many years ago the significance of this in psychotherapy was driven home to me, in spite of an initial prejudice against anything so vague, so unobservable, so tainted with introspectionism. Clients persisted in expressing themselves in terms such as these: "I feel I'm not being my real *self*"; "I wouldn't want anyone to know the real *me*"; "It feels good to let go and just *be* my*self* here"; "I think if I chip off all the plaster façade I've got a pretty solid *self* underneath." Gradually I became aware that change in therapy was very vitally concerned with the self—yet how could this ever become a part of psychological science?

I can well remember the mounting excitement I felt when a graduate student told me of the new Q-technique which William Stephenson (28) was presenting and the possibility that it might be used for tapping or measuring the individual's conception of, or perception of, himself. Since that time there has been a burgeoning of self-measurements. One can develop an adequate objective representation of "myself as an adolescent," "myself as I see myself now," "the self I would like to be," "myself as my mother perceives me," etc. It has given us a tool often inadequately understood and, without doubt, sometimes improperly used but, nonetheless, a tool for the objective representation of one of the most important aspects of the inner phenomenal world. Instead of measuring all sorts of peripheral behaviors, we can go straight to what is often hypothesized as the dynamic core of the personality and a most significant influence upon behavior, the self. Indexes derived from such measures, such as the correlation between the perceived self and the valued self, have proven to be a satisfactory measure of maladjustment and among the most satisfactory measures of change in psychotherapy (23, especially chap. 4 by J. M. Butler and G. Haigh). Most important of all, the possibility of giving objective representation to this meaningful phenomenal object has opened up various aspects of self-theory for empirical test (5, for example). The extent to which the self has become an acceptable object of study to psychologists is indicated by Hebb in his presidential address to the APA, where he says: "The self is neither mythical nor mystical, but a complex mental process. . . . It is not really remote and inaccessible in the laboratory, any more than it is in the clinic" (11, p. 743).

Closely related to studies of the self is the study of self-esteem, the degree of similarity between "the self you are and the self you would like to be." Shlien (25), in an ingenious and thought-provoking paper, compares a number of ways of measuring this completely phenomenological variable. Among other things, he constructed a physical device, completely abstract in its nature. It consists of two Plexiglas squares which may be placed edge to edge or overlapping to varying degrees or exactly superimposed one upon the other. The individual is instructed to regard one of these as the self that he is, the other as the self he would like to be, and to place them in their proper relationship to one another. Shlien produces evidence to indicate that this completely abstract, non-verbal, behavioral measure provided by placement of the squares is closer to the unique personal perception of the self-ideal relationship than is the same subject's sortings of a structured Q-sort. It shows that when we begin to focus on the problem of measuring phenomenological constructs, we can find all sorts of ingenious methods. One would, a priori, regard it as quite impossible to construct an instrument which would measure a certain abstract subjective value-feeling in different persons, taking into account that in each person such a value-feeling is based on a consideration of elements often unique to that person, and where even common elements are differently weighted by each person. Yet this is precisely what Shlien has achieved in a very simple fashion.

c) Further variables from the psychotherapeutic interaction.—I should like to stress still further the point that an investigation based upon a phenomenological approach permits us to test significant variables much more directly. Gendlin cites the example of a research in psychotherapy in which a rating of the degree to which the client focused on his relationship with the therapist—in other words, the degree to which he verbalized about it—was not found to be associated with outcome measures. But when the scale was reformulated in terms of the specific phenomenological experience it was intended to capture, the result was different. This time, cases were rated as to the degree to which the relationship was a source of new experience for the client, indicated by such client statements as, "I've never been able to let go and feel dependent as I do now." Such ratings were definitely associated with the outcome measures (8).

I should like to draw in some further examples, again from the field of psychotherapy. Attempts to study therapist behavior in any meaningful way have not met with much success in the past. Recently, much more positive results have been emerging. Based upon naturalistic clinical observation, it has been hypothesized that the degree of sensitively accurate empathic understanding experienced and communicated by the therapist in the relationship may have something to do with personality change in the client. Working directly with this highly existential-phenomenological concept, three different investigators (2, 10, 29) have developed different measures for the therapist's empathic quality in the relationship and have applied such measures to different groups of therapists, working with very divergent kinds of clients. In all three instances, a significant association has been found between the measure of the therapist's empathy and measures of personality change.

The most recent and carefully controlled study involved therapists working with a group of hospitalized schizophrenic individuals (29). Here the average empathy score in the case, based on ratings of recorded interview segments made by naïve raters, correlated very significantly with an independent measure of the degree and direction of personality change over therapy. Here is evidence of a significant and lawful relationship between two inner variables, both essentially phenomenological in nature.

This same research investigated a still more subjective feeling in the therapist (30). Ratings were made of the degree of his unconditional positive regard for his client—the extent to which he exhibited a nonevaluative, non-possessive warmth and liking. The measures of this elusive phenomenological quality also correlate very significantly with the independent measure of personality change over therapy.

Let me bring in two other illustrations. Clinically it has been felt that the way the client relates to himself and to his problems tends to predict the probability that he will or will not be able to change in therapy. One such hypothesis is that a willingness to discover new feelings and new aspects of himself, is a predictor of personality change. Another hypothesis has to do with the immediacy of the client's experiencing, whether he is remote from and unaware of his feeling life or is able to experience his feelings with immediacy as they occur. Instruments have been developed to assess the indicators of these highly subjective inner variables. Although the instruments are decidedly imperfect, some exciting findings are emerging. For example, in the group of schizophrenics mentioned above, a measure of the depth of self-exploration in the *second interview* correlates significantly (at the 1 per cent level) with the independent measure of personality change at the end of therapy one, two, or three *years* later. Even the assessment of the closeness of the client to his own experiencing shows a similar, though somewhat less significant, correlation (at the 5 per cent level) with the final measure of change. The client's manner of relating to his own problems at the time of the second interview is similarly related (again at the 5 per cent level) to the degree of change he shows throughout the whole period of therapy (31).

What is suggested by findings such as these is that, when we proceed directly to discover and measure objective indexes of subjective inner phenomenological events judged to be significant, we may more readily find lawfulness and order and predictive power than when we limit our conceptualization to external behaviors.

d) A personal learning regarding a phenomenological variable.—I should like to give a personal story of my own initial learnings in this respect, a story which dates back many years. A competent student, doing his graduate work under my supervision, chose to study the factors which would predict the behavior of adolescent delinquents. He made careful objective ratings of the psychological environment in the family, the educational experiences, the neighborhood and cultural influences, the social experiences, the health history, the hereditary background, of each delinquent. These external factors were rated as to their favorableness for normal development, on a continuum from elements destructive of the child's welfare, and inimical to healthy development, to elements highly conducive to healthy development. Almost as an afterthought, a rating was also made of the degree of self-understanding, since it was felt that although this was not one of the primary conditioning factors, it might play some part in predicting future behavior. This was essentially a rating of the degree to which the individual was open and realistic regarding himself and his situation, whether he was emotionally acceptant of the facts in himself and in his environment.

These ratings, on seventy-five delinquents, were compared with ratings of their behavior and adjustment two to three years after the initial study. It was expected that the ratings on family climate and social experience with peers would be the best predictors of later behavior. To our amazement, the degree of self-understanding was much the best predictor, correlating .84 with later behavior, while quality of social experience correlated .55, and family environment .36. We were simply not prepared to believe these findings and laid the study on the shelf until it could be replicated. Later it was replicated on a new group of seventy-six cases, and all the essential findings were confirmed, though not quite so strikingly. Furthermore, the findings stood up even in detailed analysis. When we examined only the delinquents who came from the most unfavorable homes and remained in those homes, it was still true that their future behavior was best predicted, not by the unfavorable conditioning they were receiving in their home environment, but by the degree of realistic understanding of themselves and their environment which they possessed (24). Thus the phenomenological variable proved to be much more closely related to future behavior than the assessment of the observable external environment, and the stimuli it provided.

The lessons which I only very slowly assimilated from this experience were these: (1) It is possible to measure phenomological variables with a reliability which compares with the reliability of measuring complex behavioral variables. (2) If our aim is to discover variables which have potency, are predictive, and show significant functional relationships with important externally observable events, then well-selected phenomenological variables may be even more likely than behavioral variables to exhibit such potency. The inner world of the individual appears to have more significant influence upon his behavior than does the external environmental stimulus.

Perhaps the examples I have given will suffice to indicate that the effect of this "third force" in psychology will be to open for investigation variables, and classes of variables, which will go far beyond the scope of our presently narrowed science. If my prediction is correct such constructs as "semantic space," "immediacy of experiencing," "unconditional positive regard," "self-esteem," are only early fore-runners of the many variables which will be hypothesized to be significant in human existence, and which will be studied empirically.

A NEW MODE IN PSYCHOLOGICAL THEORIES

In the realm of theory construction I believe this third current in psychology will have an invigorating effect—in fact, elements of such vigor are already emerging (3, for example). There will be more of a tendency to build theories which have connection with the fundamental problems of human existence. There are likely to be more developments of truly psychological theories to supplement some of the essentially physiological theories of the past. It is likely that there will be more freedom and freshness in theory construction once thinking has burst out of the bounds prescribed by a strict behaviorism.

I think that there are evidences that in the theoretical formulations which grow from this field, there will be more concern with process, or as Bridgman says, with "doings or happenings," rather than with "static elements" and abstractions. I believe that this is one of the important functions of theory. Some years ago I attempted to state this view, saying that:

Objective research slices through the frozen moment to provide us with an exact picture of the interrelationships which exist at that moment. But our understanding of the ongoing movement—whether it be the process of fermentation, or the circulation of the blood, or the process of atomic fission—is generally provided by a theoretical formulation. . . (22, p. 127).

An illustration of the kind of theoretical concept likely to emerge is provided by Gendlin (9) in his careful delineation of the preconceptual process of experiencing and the manner in which it functions in the creation of personal meaning. Here is a concept rooted in naturalistic observation, purely phenomenological in origin, of a process nature, which helps to bridge the gap between the subjective and objective in the way in which it lends itself to objective research.

At the risk of oversimplification, let me endeavor to give some of the main features of Gendlin's concept and the reasons he regards it as significant for the development of new theories and a more adequate science.

Experiencing refers to the ongoing feeling of *having* experience, "that partly unformed stream of feeling that we have at every moment." It is preconceptual, containing implicit meanings. It is something that is basically prior to symbolization or conceptualization. It may be known to the individual by direct reference—that is, one can attend inwardly to this flow of experiencing. Such direct reference is differentiation based upon a subjective pointing to, or attending to, the experiencing. The experiencing which is going on may be symbolized, and this symbolization may be based upon direct reference; or more complex symbolizations may develop out of it, such as those we term "conceptualization." Meaning is formed in the interaction between experiencing and symbols. Thus, as the individual refers to his experiencing the implicit meaning becomes symbolized into, "I am angry," or "I am in tune with what he is saying," or "I am uncomfortable with what is going on." Thus our personal meanings are formed in this interaction. Furthermore, any datum of experiencing—any aspect of it—can be symbolized further and further on the basis of continuing inward attention to it. Increasingly refined and differentiated meanings can be drawn by symbolization from any experiencing. Thus, in the last example, the individual who feels uncomfortable with what is going on may continue to refer to his experiencing and form further meanings from it. "I'm uncomfortable because I don't like to see another person hurt." "No, it is more than that. I resent his power, too." "Well, I guess another aspect of it is that I am afraid that he may hurt me." Thus a continuing stream of more and more refined meanings may come from a single moment of experiencing.

I have described this concept at some length, to indicate the extent to which this is an existentially oriented, phenomologically based concept. Yet as Gendlin points out, reliance upon this concept of experiencing can assist us to select and create scientific variables which are significant to the existential predicament of man and which can then be operationaliy defined and empirically tested. His thinking constitutes one step in transcending the subject-object dichotomy which plagues our thinking today.

I will do no more than mention other examples of theorizing which have their base in an existential-phenomenological orientation. The burgeoning of self-theory is an example (1, 16, 17). The redefinition of motivation, of stimulus and response, of learning, of the whole field of human psychology from a perceptual point of view, is well illustrated by the work of Combs and Snygg (7). The title of a recent volume by several contributors, *Perceiving, Behaving, Becoming* (6), is suggestive of a whole range of theorizing going on.

SCIENCE AND THE "UNREAL"

I should like to turn for a moment to the uneasiness which such thinking creates in the minds of many psychologists and perhaps in the minds of other scientists as well. The uneasiness stems from what they regard as the "unreal" nature of the referents in much of this thinking. What is to become of psychology if it turns its attention to such ephemeral, vague wisps of fog as experiencing, the self, becoming? What has happened to the solidity of a science which was built on a tangible stimulus, an observable response, or a visible reward? To such uneasy ones, I would like to point out the course of the physical sciences.

I am fully aware of the pitfalls involved in reasoning by analogy, yet I think we may learn something and perhaps be reassured by considering some of the developments in physics and mathematics, insofar as they are understood by this outsider. It seems quite clear that most of the recent striking advances in these sciences have come about, not through following the channel of logical positivism and operationalism—though their continuing contributions cannot be denied—but through the fantastic imaginings of experienced, insightful, thoughtful men. Such men have raised strange questions regarding the meaning of infinity, for example, and have developed strange hypotheses regarding it—infinity, which no one has seen or measured or even comprehended. These odd theoretical developments have resolved some long-standing mathematical problems. Or they have developed strange new constructions of space—formulations of types of space never seen and never really imagined but existing only in mathematical symbols. They have developed hypotheses about these new types of non-Euclidean space. The most famous of them all harbored revolutionary thoughts that perhaps neither weight nor the force of gravity exist and that time and space are one—thus robbing our universe of almost all of the solidity which it has for us. So far have these developments gone that a competent mathematician writes:

We should regard any theory about physical space then, as a purely subjective construction and not impute to it objective reality. Man constructs a geometry, Euclidean or non-Euclidean, and decides to view space in those terms. The advantages in doing so, even though he cannot be sure space possesses any of the characteristics of the structure he has built up in his own mind, are that he can then think about space and use his theory in scientific work. This view of space and nature generally does not deny that there is such a thing as an objective physical world. It merely recognizes that man's judgments and conclusions about space are purely of his own making (14, p. 429).

Yet we need to recognize that it is these subjective creations which have made possible the theory of relativity, the release of atomic energy, explorations in space, and many other advances in knowledge and technology.

If I may draw a cautious conclusion from this for the field of psychology it would be this: There is no special virtue attached to the policy of limiting our theories to observable behaviors. Neither, I would add, is there any *inherent* virtue in basing our theorizing on phenomenological variables. The fundamental question will be settled by the future. What theories will prove to be genuinely heuristic, leading to the discovery of significant functional relationships having to do with human life? There is at least as much reason to believe that theories based upon existential-phenomenological constructs will be successful, as to believe that theories based upon observable behaviors will be successful. A theory that postulates relationships between inner subjective phenomena not directly measurable may, like theories regarding non-Euclidean space, prove to be more valuable in advancing our knowledge than theories regarding observable behavior.

THE PHILOSOPHICAL VIEW OF MAN

There is one other consequence of this phenomenological-existential view in psychology. It carries with it a new philosophical underpinning for psychological science, which is, I believe, more fruitful and more human than the presently held philosophies.

Each current in psychology has its own implicit philosophy of man. Though not often stated explicitly, these philosophies exert their influence in many significant and subtle ways. For the behaviorist, man is a machine, a complicated but nonetheless understandable machine, which we can learn to manipulate with greater and greater skill until he thinks the thoughts, moves in the directions, and behaves in the ways selected for him. For the Freudian, man is an irrational being, irrevocably in the grip of his past and of the product of that past, his unconscious.

It is not necessary to deny that there is truth in each of these formulations in order to recognize that there is another perspective. From the existential perspective, from within the phenomenological internal frame of reference, man does not simply have the characteristics of a machine; he is not simply a being in the grip of unconscious motives: he is a person in the process of creating himself, a person who creates meaning in life, a person who embodies a dimension of subjective freedom. He is a figure who, though he may be alone in a vastly complex universe and though he may be part and parcel of that universe and its destiny, is also able in his inner life to transcend the material universe; he is able to live dimensions of his life which are not fully or adequately contained in a description of his conditionings or of his unconscious.

It is not my purpose to go deeply into the philosophical issues. I believe, however, that we are leaving behind the narrowly mechanistic philosophy which has tended to accompany behaviorism. I believe an increasing number of people would agree with the physicist, P. W. Bridgman, when he says, "It is evident that . . . the operational approach cannot be completely general and that it can by no means provide the basis for a complete philosophy" (4, p. 2).

It is my judgment, as I try to understand the vigorous thrust of this phenomenological-existential movement in a variety of other fields, as well as in psychology, that it represents a new philosophical emphasis. Here is the voice of subjective man speaking up loudly for himself. Man has long felt himself to be but a puppet in life—molded by economic forces, by unconscious forces, by environmental forces. He has been enslaved by persons, by institutions, by the theories of psychological science. But he is firmly setting forth a new declaration of independence. He is discarding the alibis of *un*freedom. He is *choosing* himself, endeavoring, in a most difficult and often tragic world, to *become* himself—not a puppet, not a slave, not a machine, but his own unique individual self. The view I have been describing in psychology has room for this philosophy of man.

CONCLUSION

Let me try to state very briefly, and in somewhat different terms, the consequences in psychology of this fresh new current in modern culture, which is so incompletely described by terms like existential, phenomenological, self-oriented.

It will make confident use of subjective, intuitive hypotheses formulated by the scientist who has immersed himself in his field of study and senses a pattern, an order, which he can perhaps only partially articulate.

It leads, I believe, to a naturalistic, empathic, sensitive observation of the world of inner meanings as they exist in the individual. The whole range and scope of the human situation as it exists in each individual is thus opened for consideration.

It leads to the formulation of heuristic concepts based upon such observation. In my judgment these concepts will tend to have more of a process-quality than do the psychological concepts of the past.

It requires careful definition of observable behaviors which are indexes of these subjective variables. It is recognized that variables of inner experience cannot be measured directly, but it is also realized that the fact that they *are* inner variables does not preclude their scientific study.

It is leading and will, I believe, increasingly lead to the imaginative development of clearly operational steps and operational tools for the measurement of the behaviors which represent these inner variables.

It seems quite evident that it will lead to a diminishing of the dichotomy between subject and object as it studies the relationships between the internal variables and such external variables as environmental stimuli, outward behavior, and the like. A study, for example, which relates the changes in the self-perceived behavior of an individual to the maturity of that individual's behavior as it is observed by his friends (23, chaps. 13, 15) brings more closely together the internal and the external world.

It will lead to theoretical formulations which will be as shocking to conventional psychologists as theories of non-Euclidean space were for conventional physicists. We shall be attempting to discover the functional process-relationships which hold for the inner world of personal meanings and to formulate these with sufficient precision that they may be put to empirical test.

It contains within it the seeds of a newer philosophy of science which will not be fearful of finding room for the person—both the observer and the observed—in his subjective as well as his objective mode. It will carry within it a view of man as a subjectively free, choosing, responsible, architect of self.

BIBLIOGRAPHY

1. ALLPORT, G. W. *Becoming: Basic Consideration for a Psychology of Personality*. New Haven: Yale University Press, 1955.
2. BARRETT-LENNARD, G. T. "Dimensions of Therapist Response as Causal Factors in Therapeutic Change," *Psychological Monographs*, LXXVI, No. 43, whole No. 562 (1962), 1–36.
3. BERGIN, A. E. "Worknotes toward a Science of Inner Experience." Paper presented at meeting of the New Jersey Psychological Association, December, 1961.
4. BRIDGMAN, P. W. *The Way Things Are*. Cambridge: Harvard University Press, 1959.
5. CHODORKOFF, B. "Self-perception, Perceptual Defense, and Adjustment," *Journal of Abnormal and Social Psychology*, XLIX (1954), 508–12.
6. COMBS, A. W. (ed.). *Perceiving, Behaving, Becoming*. Washington, D. C.: Association for Supervision and Curriculum Development, 1962.
7. COMBS, A. W., and SNYGG, D. *Individual Behavior: A Perceptual Approach to Behavior*. New York: Harper, 1959.
8. GENDLIN, E. T. *Experiencing and the Creation of Meaning*. New York: Macmillan; Glencoe: Free Press, 1962.
9. ———. "Operational Variables from the Practice of Psychotherapy." Unpublished paper given at APA Convention, 1962.

10. HALKIDES, G. "An Experimental Study of Four Conditions Necessary for Therapeutic Change." Unpublished Ph. D. dissertation, University of Chicago, 1958.

11. HEBB, D. O. "The American Revolution," *American Psychologist*, XV (1960), 735–45.

12. JESSOR, R. "Phenomenological Personality Theories and the Data Language of Psychology." In *The Phenomenological Problem*, ed. A. E. KUENZLI, pp. 280–93. New York: Harper, 1959.

13. ––––. "Issues in the Phenomenological Approach to Personality," *Journal of Individual Psychology*, XVII (1961), 27–38.

14. KLINE, M. *Mathematics in Western Culture*. New York: Oxford University Press, 1953.

15. KRECHEVSKY, I. " 'Hypothesis' in Rats," *Psychological Review*, XXXII (1939), 516–22.

16. MASLOW, A. H. *Toward a Psychology of Being*. New York: D. Van Nostrand, 1962.

17. MOUSTAKAS, C. E. (ed.) *The Self*. New York: Harper, 1956.

18. OPPENHEIMER, R. "Analogy in Science," *American Psychologist*, XI (1956), 127–135.

19. OSGOOD, C. E. "Cross-cultural Generality of Visual-Verbal Synesthetic Tendencies," *Behavioral Science*, V (1960), 146–69.

20. OSGOOD, C. E., SUCI, G. J., and TANNENBAUM, P. *The Measurement of Meaning*. Urbana: University of Illinois Press, 1957.

21. POLANYI, M. *Personal Knowledge*. Chicago: University of Chicago Press, 1958.

22. ROGERS, C. R. *On Becoming a Person*. Boston: Houghton Mifflin, 1961.

23. ROGERS, C. R., and DYMOND, R. (eds.). *Psychotherapy and Personality Change*. Chicago: University of Chicago Press, 1954.

24. ROGERS, C. R., KELL, W. L., and McNEIL, H. "The Role of Self-understanding in the Prediction of Behavior," *Journal of Consulting Psychology*, XII (1948), 174–86.

25. SHLIEN, J. M. "Toward What Level of Abstraction in Criteria?" In *Research in Psychotherapy*, Vol. II. Washington, D. C.: American Psychological Association, 1962.

26. SKINNER, B. F. *Cumulative Record*. New York: Appleton-Century Crofts, 1961.

27. SNYGG, D. "Mazes in Which Rats Take the Longer Path to Food," *Journal of Psychology*, I (1936), 153–66.

28. STEPHENSON, W. *The Study of Behavior: Q-Technique and Its Methodology*. Chicago: University of Chicago Press, 1953.

29. TRUAX, C. B. "The Relationship between the Level of Accurate Empathy Offered in Psychotherapy and Case Outcome." Unpublished Research Report, Psychotherapy Research Group, Wisconsin Psychiatric Institute, 1962.

30. ———. "The Relationship between the Amount of Unconditional Positive Regard Offered in Psychotherapy and Case Outcome." Unpublished Research Report, Psychotherapy Research Group, Wisconsin Psychiatric Institute, 1962.

31. ———. "The Relationship between the Extent to Which the Patient Engages in Depth of Intrapersonal Exploration and the Case Outcome of Constructive Personality Change." Unpublished Research Report, Psychotherapy Research Group, Wisconsin Psychiatric Institute, 1962.

32. WERTHEIMER, M. *Productive Thinking*. New York: Harper, 1945.

PARAPHRASE OF DISCUSSION

MEMBER OF THE AUDIENCE

The communication of meaning in any interpersonal relation is subject to the "distortions" arising in "the subjective world of the person being observed" and those arising in "the subjective world of the observer." How can such a communication be dealt with "scientifically"?

COMMENTS OF PROFESSOR ROGERS

"It sounds as though you are still operating under the optimistic notion that there is some kind of knowledge that does not include distortions." Distortion is possible in any undertaking. Whatever approach to knowing used, one must endeavor to "cut down on the distortion" as much as possible. In therapy, when one responds tentatively to a client's confused report and the client says, "That's *exactly* what I mean," it would seem that "there is probably not very much distortion in the understanding." At other times, attempts at understanding seem not to progress, in which case one looks "for means of reducing" the distortion.

MEMBER OF THE AUDIENCE

"Would you give me your idea of the structure of the 'self,' that is, what kind of model you use in your work?"

COMMENTS OF PROFESSOR ROGERS

"Self" can be defined in many ways, ranging from the philosophical to the empirical. The empirical definition Rogers uses is that the "self" is an individual's "perception of himself as the nodal point of relationships." It is this definition that is the basis for the measuring instruments being developed. A different definition of "self" would require a different "operational instrument."

Hilgard's definition of "self" in terms of both conscious and unconscious elements has "meaning" but is not useful "scientifically," since, by including the unconscious, one includes an "area in which, probably, you can get no agreement." The significance for empirical work is reduced. In contrast, if one limits one's self "to those aspects of the individual and his relationships to others and to the world that are available to consciousness, . . . there can be agreement as to whether or not you have a decent instrument for measuring it."

He would select variables not only on the basis of significance but, also, on the basis of there being "some chance of measuring operationally." "That is why I choose the kind of definition I do."

MEMBER OF THE AUDIENCE

The answer defines "self" but does not answer the question about "structure of self." Behaviorists make a structural statement, "that man is a machine" and they describe behavior as a function of that structure. "What is your structure? What function of self do you see that you can point at as a function of that structure?"

COMMENTS OF PROFESSOR ROGERS

He does not think of "self" in terms of "models" or "structures." If forced to it, he might find "a round globe with a node in the middle" acceptable.

Concerning "functional aspects of the self," there is some empirical evidence. Just one example—the relation between the person's conception of himself as a speller, good or bad, and the number of words he misspells.

COMMENTS OF PROFESSOR SKINNER

He had not felt it necessary to use quotation marks in the chapter Professor Rogers mentioned since it was entitled "A Case History," rendering any such marks superfluous.

More seriously, he wants to question "the order of events." No doubt Einstein said he had a sense of direction in his life. Skinner argues that the "direction," that is, the "obvious characteristics" of behavior, preceded and gave rise to the "sense." In the case history referred to earlier, although he used "very casual language" in reporting "getting tired of handling" a rat in a given way, he could have specified the actions or conditions which lead to the behavior he called "getting tired."

He has compiled a dictionary containing the "behavioral equivalents of lay terminology." He uses it to render "more precise" something said in lay language as well as to find, for talks to lay groups, some "simple word" for behavioral terminology. An example is "discouragement": "discouragement seems to be something you feel—extinction is the behavioral change. . . . The behavioral change occurs, and one may then describe it by use of the word 'discouragement.' . . . I am *not* convinced that the things Dr. Rogers sees and infers are the primary moving forces. They seem to me to be epiphenomenal in a philosophical sense or, at least, something which occurs after the important fact."

COMMENTS OF PROFESSOR ROGERS

". . . [T]he view of science that I was setting forth would make it possible to give empirical tests" to these questions. Perhaps one does behave in a certain way and then sense it as a direction. Perhaps one senses a direction and then moves in that way. One cannot be sure until one tests empirically. If one were "willing to admit phenomenological concepts as a part of psychological science," one could test empirically.

MEMBER OF THE AUDIENCE

[A question for both Drs. Rogers and Skinner on the positions of behaviorism and existentialism on the issue of determinism.]

COMMENTS OF PROFESSOR ROGERS

In scientific research he accepts the world as a determined world. He feels one cannot carry on research unless there is an underlying notion of a cause-effect sequence. "There would be nothing to study scientifically if that were not a part of your assumption. . . ."

He feels, with "equal strength," that this "is not the whole of the truth about life. . . . [T]he experiencing of choice, of freedom of choice . . . is not only a profound truth, but it is a very important element in therapy."

These seem to be irreconcilable, but for him, "they exist in different dimensions." An analogy is the wave-particle theory of light: the physicists have not only learned to live with, but have been helped in research by, their "appreciation" of the "paradox." In a somewhat similar way, the "perception of the world as a determined world" when one approaches it as a "scientist" and "the perception of another dimension of subjective freedom" in interpersonal relations form a paradox, "but it is a paradox that, personally, I would rather live with than kill off either half. . . ."

MEMBER OF THE AUDIENCE

When speaking of the "dimension of subjective freedom," is "subjective" used as a restrictive term on "freedom"?

COMMENTS OF PROFESSOR ROGERS

"I guess my most honest response to that would be: 'I do not know.' The experiencing of subjective freedom is a real thing—just as real as experiencing an inevitable effect from a preceding cause. . . . This is the paradoxical part—that neither of them seems limited. . . . Each seems quite complete within itself. . . ."

COMMENTS OF PROFESSOR SCRIVEN

The free will–determinism question is, in certain respects, closely analogous to questions about the nature of light. Quantum theory has, though not in a simple way, resolved the "apparent paradox" of the nature of light. Recent attempts by philosophers to reconcile free will and determinism seem, also, to indicate a difficult but satisfactory resolution to that apparent paradox. Both resolutions suggest the necessity for retaining the two halves of the respective paradoxes.

It is the necessity for retaining both halves of the free will–determinism paradox that leads to more general comments about Professor Rogers' paper. If we adopt the "existentialist position because . . . of the feeling of it for . . . free will, we are likely to find ourselves denying parts of the other approaches which are undeniable."

Not only do we need both halves of the paradox for a fuller understanding of behavior, but "trying to support one position because it looks more sympathetic" to a conception of man that we find attractive leads us to overlook subtleties and strengths of other positions and to "deny" the positions "on grounds where they cannot be denied." "Casually" viewed, the Freudian approach might seem to present man as "an irrational being irrevocably in the grip of his past," or the behaviorist view might seem to be one of man as "just a machine manipulated in various ways." "Careful analysis" of these positions will reveal that these casual impressions are "ill founded." For example, "there is no denial that the man involved is a very complicated machine, complicated enough to have room in his behavior for the aspects of behavior that Professor Rogers finds attractive. . . ." To reject this position on the grounds that it cannot account for the kind of behavior Professor Rogers refers to as "man creating himself" is "incorrect."

Further, supporting existentialism because of the emphasis it gives to a particular view of man can lead to misunderstanding. For example, Professor Rogers says that the approach to psychology he is advocating, "will make confident use of subjective, intuitive hypotheses." In context, the statement stands up, but should it become "quoted as a slogan," one would think of Rogers as standing for "subjectivism and lack of checking and the use of intuitive rather than verified claims . . . which, of course, he does not stand for. . . ."

Finally, concerning which theories will prove to be genuinely heuristic. Scriven thinks that for problems of prediction, control and explanation, both phenomenological and behavioristic formulations have a place, depending on the particular kind of question being asked. ". . . I am recommending, then, that one look on Professor Rogers' recommendations . . . as a difference of emphasis [rather] than as a categorical difference which reflects on the truth and falsity of the opposing positions. . . ."

Comments of Professor Malcolm

"I regret to be in a position of biting my philosophical colleague, but I do not believe it is true that developments in recent philosophy have shown that freedom and determinism can be reconciled. . . . I suppose the most famous classical position . . . that freedom and determinism are entirely compatible with one another was stated by David Hume. . . . John Stuart Mill restated it. Mort Schlick of the Vienna Circle restated it and reaffirmed it. A. J. Ayer has reaffirmed it. . . . I would say they certainly have not proved their case. . . . [A]nd I would say that even *more* recent developments in recent philosophy indicate that freedom and determinism really are incompatible and will remain so."

Member of the Audience

Is the third way of knowing, in fact, "a way of knowing" or is it "another thing to be known"? If it is a way of knowing, it must be surrounded with the same "objective safeguards" as those of the second way of knowing and hence is not distinct from the second except in the "thing to be known."

Comments of Professor Rogers

". . . [I]t is quite true that the same machinery of verification [as that used in the second way of knowing] comes in" when one wants to "translate" interpersonal knowing "into objective science." There is, however, a "different quality" to the "tool of empathy" when it is being used to check with a colleague "our understanding of something 'out there' " and that "same" tool of empathy "when we are trying to gain knowledge about another person [and] the empathy is directed toward him."

All three ways of knowing are necessary in a "mature science." The research on the response of schizophrenics to therapy is an illustration of this. First was the "purely subjective hypothesis" that the "way a person deals with his problems has some relation to how he is going to come out in therapy." Then comes "the gaining of more knowledge . . . through empathic listening to many people." And finally, one begins "to translate it into objective knowledge by creating a scale, by setting up all the conditions of operationalism to make sure that . . . these judgments are truly objective and . . . do relate to an independent measure."

Science does not begin with the statistical work nor when "you are running your subjects—as they say. . . . Science is a *much* more comprehensive venture than that. . . . I think we had better recognize the whole range of science and begin to trust, and not be afraid of, our own subjective thinking, feeling, experiencing when we have" been, as Polanyi says, "indwelling" in the material of our science.

COMMENTS OF PROFESSOR MacLEOD

"On what basis are you so convinced that you have understood your client better than Mr. Freud has understood his patient?"

COMMENTS OF PROFESSOR ROGERS

One must consider the number of biases one brings to a situation. He would feel that "someone working from a client-centered point of view" would bring fewer "preconceptions" to the therapy relationship than would a Freudian. He claims no greater personal perceptiveness than that of some of his friends who "operate from a strictly Freudian point of view" but thinks that a client-centered therapist, with a lighter "baggage of preconceptions" is more likely to come to an "understanding of the phenomenal world of [an] individual as it exists."

MEMBER OF THE AUDIENCE

It seemed to be suggested that, by careful use of all three ways of knowing, it might be possible to achieve scientific certitude. Also, it was suggested that "valuable constructs" could be developed by use of the "constructural methods" of the physical sciences. "Do you equate scientific certitude with valuable constructs, and, if not, what do you mean by scientific certitude?"

COMMENTS OF PROFESSOR ROGERS

There must be a misunderstanding. He argues that there is no such thing as scientific certitude, nor any methods for achieving it. This should be the lesson learned from the recent years in the physical sciences. While physicists are aware that their knowledge is useful and predictive, they are also aware that "most of their present day knowledge has 'incertitude' written all over the face of it." This is most pertinent for psychology because it is "much less developed."

MEMBER OF THE AUDIENCE

"Empathy" and "unconditional regard" are presented as vital to good therapy. "Of what variables are these a function?" Are they things "that a person *is* or can he be trained to be that way?"

COMMENTS OF PROFESSOR ROGERS

The development of a good therapist rests on a type of learning that has been studied little. There are differences between "experiential learning" and "straight cognitive learning." We know relatively little about experiential learning. It appears that the best way of training a therapist is to provide the beginner with a training "climate which is therapeutic . . . which has a large measure of exactly the same kinds of attitudes that you hope he will create for his clients later on. Yet that is *not* the kind of learning that has much status in the universities and it is *not* the kind of learning on which you get degrees."

MEMBER OF THE AUDIENCE

"What distinguishes 'experiencing' from 'symbolizing' in the interaction which forms meaning?"

COMMENTS OF PROFESSOR ROGERS

"I shall just give a brief answer to that, which I am not sure will be satisfactory. I think that the substratum of our experiencing does not consist of symbols, that symbolization is something that happens to it. . . . It is only when I attend to the experiencing in me that I realize" the meaning of it.

COMMENTS OF PROFESSOR SKINNER

The discussion has treated modern science as though "it had no real certainty, no notion of how it might be sure of anything." Skinner would argue that the "physical scientists are, indeed, at sea," not because they lack "scientific sophistication," but because they lack "psychological sophistication, particularly the implications of a science of behavior for epistemology." Much that has been written by physical scientists and mathematicians about thinking and intellectual processes is "ridiculously elementary" and "simple minded."

He thinks the position developed in *Verbal Behavior* could be applied profitably to the "analysis of scientific methodology." Not only Goedel's Theorem but "all paradoxes can be cleared up from a behavioral point of view." While "the physical sciences badly need a scientific epistemology," psychology does not "need the present muddle in the physical sciences."

COMMENTS OF PROFESSOR ROGERS

"In view of Dr. Skinner's remarks, I shall modify an earlier statement of mine about scientific certitude. I will say that it seems to me [that] science does not lead to certitude, except in the case of Dr. Skinner."

NORMAN MALCOLM

Behaviorism as a Philosophy of Psychology

As a philosopher I have a professional reluctance to make observations about an empirical science and especially so in the presence of some of its distinguished practitioners. I am emboldened by the belief that the dispute over the place of behaviorism in psychology is fundamentally a philosophical issue. In saying this I do not imply that it is an issue which cannot be resolved and with respect to which we must content ourselves with opinions or attitudes. On the contrary, I think that what is right and wrong with the viewpoint and assumptions of behaviorism can be clearly formulated.

A Failure To Disagree

Professor Rogers claims that behaviorism has had an unfortunate effect on psychology. It impoverishes psychology by excluding from its data the "private worlds" of people, the "flow of their inner experience," "the whole universe of inner meanings," the purposes, goals, values and choices of people, and their "perceptions of self." He calls all of this "the phenomenal world of the individual" (3, p. 119), and he says that "Not one aspect of this world is open to the strict behaviorist" (3, p. 119). He believes that psychology needs to be enriched by "a science of the inner life" that will attempt to find lawful relationships between these phenomena and "external behavior." A study which concerns itself with these "inner variables" must be added to empirical psychology if this science is to obtain any deep understanding of human life.

I am willing to bet (a small sum) that Professor Skinner finds this criticism puzzling, because he cannot see in it any specific theoretical issue that divides him and Rogers. Whether Skinner is puzzled or not, I am. I do not see that Skinner's behaviorism commits him to denying or ignoring the existence of the "inner variables" which Rogers thinks are so important. Let me explain.

NORMAN MALCOLM, Professor, Department of Philosophy, Cornell University.

Skinner is an exponent of a "functional analysis" of human behavior. He holds that every piece of human behavior is a "function" of some condition that is describable in physical terms, as is the behavior itself (4, pp. 35 and 36). The conditions of which behavior is a function are, for the most part, external to the organism, although sometimes they may be "within the organism's skin" (4, p. 257). The physical conditions of which behavior is a function are called "independent variables," and the pieces of behavior are the "dependent variables." A dependent variable is said to be under the "control" of an independent variable. The relations between independent and dependent variables are scientific laws. The aim of behavioristic psychology is to uncover these laws, thus making possible the prediction and control of human behavior. "A synthesis of these laws expressed in quantitative terms yields a comprehensive picture of the organism as a behaving system" (4, p. 35).

Skinner devotes considerable attention to what he calls "explanatory fictions." Some of his examples are being *thirsty*, or *hungry* (4, p. 31), being *absent-minded* or having *confused ideas* (4, p. 30), being *interested* or *discouraged* or having a *sense of achievement* (4, p. 72), having an *incentive* or *goal* or *purpose* (4, pp. 87–88), and the *intent* behind an action or the *meaning* of it (4, p. 36). All of these are examples of what some philosophers call "psychological" or "mental" concepts. I think that anything any philosopher would want to call a "psychological" concept Skinner would consider to be an explanatory fiction. In saying that they are explanatory fictions Skinner means that they are *not* explanatory. Take such an apparent explanation as "He is drinking because he is thirsty." Skinner says that

If to be thirsty means nothing more than to have a tendency to drink, this is mere redundancy. If it means that he drinks because of a state of thirst, an inner causal event is invoked. If this state is purely inferential—if no dimensions are assigned to it which would make direct observation possible—it cannot serve as an explanation (4, p. 33).

When you speak of a man's "purpose" in doing something or say that he has stopped doing something because he is "discouraged," you are not saying anything worth saying unless you are making a reference, perhaps concealed, to the independent variables which control his behavior (4, e.g., pp. 36, 72).

Skinner's remarks about explanatory fictions are sometimes slightly ambiguous. Sometimes he seems to be saying that there really is not any such thing as, for example, *a sense of achievement*. "We do not give a man a sense of achievement," he says, "we reinforce a particular action" (4, p. 72). When a man is said to be "looking for something," "There is no *current* goal, incentive, purpose, or meaning to be taken into account" (4, pp. 89–90). This would seem to be a denial that the man really has a purpose in doing what he does. But I do not believe that Skinner wants to be in the absurd position of really denying that people are sometimes encouraged or discouraged or that they have goals and purposes, anymore than he wants to deny that they get thirsty. Instead, he is trying to say how these terms are to be understood. Such terms as "meaning" and "intent," he says, "usually conceal references to independent variables" (4, p. 36). "Statements which use such words as 'incentive' or 'purpose' are usually reducible to statements about operant conditioning" (4, p. 87). Skinner will agree that people have purposes, but holds that meaningful statements about purposes are reducible to statements about functional relations between independent and dependent variables.

Let us come back to Rogers' criticism of Skinner. The purposes, goals, values and choices of people, their "private worlds," their "perceptions of self," their "inner experience"—all of those phenomena which, according to him, behaviorism cannot deal with, are examples of Skinner's explanatory fictions. Skinner would willingly accept them as significant phenomena insofar as they can be handled by functional analysis. If you can define them in terms of functional relations between external or internal physical variables and the observable behavior of people, then well and good. If not, then it is not clear what you are talking about.

What I find puzzling is that Rogers himself seems to admit this or at least to go half way toward admitting it. He allows that the study of the "inner variables," of which he speaks—"requires careful definition of observable behaviors which are indexes of these subjective variables. It is recognized that variables of inner experience cannot be measured directly, but it is also realized that the fact that they *are* inner variables does not preclude their scientific study" (3, p. 130). He foresees the development of "operational steps" for the "measurement of the behaviors which represent these inner variables" (3, p. 131). Skinner could retort that the observable behavior and physical conditions which are said by Rogers to "represent" the inner variables, either do or do not define them. If they do, then the "inner" has become "outer," and functional analysis can go full steam ahead. If not, then the expressions which allegedly "represent" inner variables have not been given any meaning.

My conclusion is that Rogers has not shown some theoretical flaw in behaviorism. Skinner could hold that Rogers' "science of the person" would fall, insofar as it has an intelligible subject matter, within the wider domain of functional analysis of behavior. It would be one branch or division of behavioristic science and not an alternative or addition to it.

THE PHILOSOPHICAL BASIS OF BEHAVIORISM

Behaviorism, in my view, is essentially a *philosophical* doctrine. Skinner is agreeing with this when he says that behaviorism is "a philosophy of science concerned with the subject matter and methods of psychology" (5, p. 79). Behaviorism, as a philosophy of psychology, is continuous with the philosophical doctrine of *physicalism*, which was expounded by Rudolf Carnap and other members of the so-called Vienna Circle. I will set forth some of Carnap's views on this topic in order to bring out the close resemblance between Carnap's physicalism and Skinner's behaviorism.

The basic thesis of physicalism, according to Carnap (1), is that "every sentence of psychology may be formulated in physical language" (1, p. 165). When put in "the material mode of speech," the thesis is that "all sentences of psychology describe physical occurrences, namely, the physical behavior of humans and other animals" (1, p. 165). Carnap says: "Our thesis thus states that a definition may be constructed for every psychological concept (i.e., expression) which directly or indirectly derives that concept from physical concepts" (1, p. 167). Psychological laws, too, are translatable into physical language (i.e., into language which describes physical conditions and occurrences), and therefore they are a subclass of physical laws (1, p. 167).

The pure philosophical principle behind this thesis is the so-called Verification Principle: "The meaning of a statement is its method of verification." As Carnap puts it: "A sentence says no more than what is testable about it" (1, p. 174). Thus a statement that I make about another person, e.g., that he is excited or angry, can mean nothing else than that he is behaving in such and such a way, that he will respond in such and such a way to certain stimuli, that his central nervous system is in such and such a state, and so on (1, e.g., p. 172). If we try to claim that over and above, or behind, these physical facts there is an inner state of excitement or anger, which is entirely different from the actual and/or potential behavior and the physiological state and which might or might not be present with these physical facts, then we are claiming something that we do not know how to verify. Our assertion that this person is angry turns out to be "a metaphysical pseudo-sentence" (1, p. 174). It might be objected that the person could *tell* us that he felt angry, and if he was a generally truthful person we should have evidence for the existence of an inner state of anger. Carnap's reply is that the person's statement does not inform us of anything unless we *understand* it, and we do not understand it unless we know what observable phenomena would verify it. As Carnap puts it: "If the sentence 'A was angry yesterday at noon' has no meaning for me—as would be the case if . . . I could not test it—it will not be rendered meaningful by the fact that a sound having the structure of this sentence came from A's own mouth" (1, p. 180). The fact that we rely on the testimony of people as a source of information about them does not relieve us of the necessity of giving a physical interpretation of the sentences they utter, an interpretation which will make those sentences testable. In Carnap's view the psychological concepts of ordinary language are a source of confusion because their reference to physical conditions and behavior is not sufficiently explicit. The clarification of these concepts will consist in "physicalising" them, i.e., in providing explicit behavioristic definitions of them. But, as Carnap says, "psychology is a physical science even prior to such a clarification of its concepts—a physical science whose assignment it is to describe systematically the (physical) behavior of living creatures, especially that of human beings, and to develop laws under which this behavior may be subsumed" (1, p. 189).

There is one important respect in which Skinner's behaviorism differs from the physicalism of the Vienna Circle. The question arises as to whether the physicalising of psychological concepts is to be in terms of the inner physiology of the human organism or in terms of its outward behavior. Carnap discusses the example of a sentence which says that a certain person is *excited*. He holds that this sentence has the same "content" as another sentence which asserts that the person's "central nervous system" is in a certain state and also that the person is making "agitated movements," or would make them on the application of certain stimuli (1, p. 172). His sample analysis of a psychological sentence refers, therefore, *both* to inner physiology and to outward behavior. This mixed reference is even more explicit in some remarks made by Carl Hempel, also a former exponent of physicalism. Discussing the psychological sentence "Paul has a toothache," Hempel asks "What is the specific content of this proposition, that is to say, what are the circumstances in which it would be verified?" He goes on to say that the following are some of the test sentences which describe these circumstances:

a) "Paul weeps and makes gestures of such and such kinds."

b) "At the question, 'What is the matter?' Paul utters the words 'I have a toothache.'"

c) "Closer examination reveals a decayed tooth with exposed pulp."

d) "Paul's blood pressure, digestive processes, the speed of his re-actions, show such and such changes."

e) "Such and such processes occur in Paul's central nervous system."

Hempel declares that the proposition about Paul's pain is "simply an abbreviated expression of the fact that all its test sentences are verified" (2, p. 377). It is evident that the alleged "content" of the sentence about Paul is a very mixed bag, containing references to both the outward behavior of weeping, gestures and utterance, and also to such physiological phenomena as blood pressure, digestive processes, and events in the central nervous system.[1]

Skinner is dissatisfied, rightly I think, with physiological analyses of psychological concepts. For one thing, he says, not enough is known about neural states and events for them to be useful in the prediction and control of specific behavior (4, pp. 28–29). For another thing, he has a "methodological" objection. He believes that holding that the events observed or inferred in an analysis of behavior are basically physiological "does not solve the methodological problems with which behaviorism is most seriously concerned" (5, p. 95). Skinner means, I believe, that behaviorism as a philosophy of psychology is trying to solve a problem that he calls "methodological" and that I should call "philosophical." The problem is, as he puts it, "how one knows about the subjective world of another" (5, p. 83). Now the fact is that we know a great deal about the "subjective worlds" of others. (Here I am formulating a line of thought that I hope Skinner finds acceptable.) That is to say, we know on a great many occasions in ordinary life when someone is *angry, tired, excited,* or *perplexed.* This common knowledge we have of the mental states of others certainly is not a knowledge of physiological processes, about which we are largely ignorant. It is Skinner's view that if behaviorism is to clarify the "testable content" of psychological concepts, it should not concentrate on the inner physiology of the human organism but rather on what lies open to observation, namely, physical circumstances and outward behavior.

Skinner says:

The practice of looking inside the organism for an explanation of behavior has tended to obscure the variables which are immediately available for a scientific analysis. These variables lie outside the organism, in its immediate environment and in its environmental history (4, p. 31).

---

[1] It should be noted that both Carnap and Hempel subsequently abandoned the view that the "cognitive meaning" of an empirical statement is equivalent to all or some of its test sentences. See Hempel's "The Empiricist Criterion of Meaning" [in *Logical Positivism*, ed. A. J. Ayer (Glencoe: Free Press, 1959)].

Carnap asserted that:

A sentence about other minds refers to physical processes in the body of the person in question. On any other interpretation the sentence becomes untestable in principle, and thus meaningless (1, p. 191).

Skinner could say, and I should agree with him, that this is a *non sequitur*. If the statement that a certain person is *discouraged* about something refers to his behavior and also to external circumstances which "control" that behavior, then the statement is testable; and it is far more readily testable than if it referred to processes in his body. Thus Skinner's brand of behaviorism explains psychological concepts in terms of outward behavior and circumstances rather than inner physiology.

Despite Skinner's justified dislike of physicalism's predilection for physiology, the basic aim of his functional analysis is the same as that of physicalism, namely, to achieve a clarification of psychological concepts which will make it evident that psychology is truly a physical science. Like the philosophers of the Vienna Circle, he is attempting to reduce mental concepts to physical concepts, although he has a clearer idea of the form this reduction must take. It may be surprising to some to think of Skinner as engaged in a typically philosophical undertaking of reducing concepts of one kind to concepts of another kind, and therefore I will substantiate this claim by quoting from Skinner. Speaking of occupational therapy he says:

It is of no advantage to say that such therapy helps the patient by giving him a "sense of achievement" or improves his "morale," builds up his "interest," or removes or prevents "discouragement." Such terms as these merely add to the growing population of explanatory fictions. One who readily engages in a given activity is not showing an interest, he is showing the effect of reinforcement. We do not give a man a sense of achievement, we reinforce a particular action. To become discouraged is simply to fail to respond because reinforcement has not been forthcoming (4, p. 72).

Skinner remarks that it is a "fundamental principle of science" to rule out "final causes." He goes on to say:

But this principle is violated when it is asserted that behavior is under the control of an "incentive" or "goal" which the organism has not yet achieved or a "purpose" which it has not yet fulfilled. Statements which use such words as "incentive" or "purpose" are usually reducible to statements about operant conditioning, and only a slight change is required to bring them within the framework of a natural science. Instead of saying that a man behaves because of the consequences which *are* to follow his behavior, we simply say that he behaves because of the consequences which *have* followed similar behavior in the past (4, p. 87).

It is fairly evident that in these passages Skinner is trying to give logical analyses, i.e., reductions, of various expressions that, on his view, mislead us. He is trying to tell us what becoming discouraged *is*, what being interested *is*, and what it *is* to do something for a purpose. He pays particular attention to the notion of *looking for something*, which describes an activity in terms of its purpose. He makes this assertion: "In general, looking for something consists of emitting responses which in the past have produced 'something' as a consequence" (4, p. 89). Here he is trying to tell us of what looking for something *consists*. He offers several "translations" of the sentence "I am looking for my glasses." He says that this sentence is "equivalent" to the following: " 'I have lost my glasses,' 'I shall stop what I am doing when I find my glasses,' or 'When I have done this in the past, I have found my glasses.' " He remarks that these "translations" seem "roundabout," but this is because "expressions involving goals and purposes" are "abbreviations" (4, p. 90).

These remarks I have quoted from Skinner make quite evident his role as a philosopher engaged in translating and reducing the misleading mentalistic expressions of ordinary language. These expressions have a disguised meaning. They are "abbreviations." Skinner's task is to unpack these abbreviations by making explicit the behavioristic variables to which they refer in a "concealed" way and which give them whatever intelligibility and usefulness they have.

I think it is easy to see what makes behaviorism attractive as a philosophy of psychology. It may be conceived of as a reaction against another philosophy of psychology (which I shall call "introspectionism"), the basic assumption of which is that each of us learns from his own case what pain, anger, fear, purpose, and so on, *are*. Each of us first of all takes note of, and identifies, his own inner experiences and then surmises or infers that others have the same inner experiences. I believe that Wittgenstein has proved this line of thinking to be disastrous (6). It leads to the conclusion that we do not and cannot understand each other's psychological language, which is a form of solipsism. Worse than this (if that is possible), it leads to the result that one's identification of one's own inner experience might be wrong without one's ever being the wiser. Not only might it be the case that what I identify in myself as "anger" is not what others identify in themselves as "anger"; but also it might be that what I identify myself as "anger" is a *different* something each time, although I *think* it is the same. If it were something different each time then I should not be identifying anything. Whether this were so or not could not be determined, either by myself or anyone else. Introspectionism assumes that each of us makes *correct* identifications of

his mental states. But if it makes no sense to determine that my identification is right or wrong, then it does not *have* a right or wrong,
and therefore it is not an *identification* of anything. Introspectionism
is a self-refuting doctrine, because its assumption that each of us
obtains his mastery of psychological concepts from introspection actually leads to the collapse of the notion of inner identification.

One does not have to accept the verification principle "whole hog"
in order to acknowledge the strong point of behaviorism. The refutation of introspectionism, on purely philosophical grounds, proves that
our concepts of mental states and events cannot be divorced from
human behavior. As we noted previously, this problem cannot be
avoided by the maneuver of holding that *verbal* behavior is a sufficient
foundation for our common psychological concepts. Skinner is keen-
ly aware of this point. He says:

We cannot avoid the responsibility of showing how a private event can
ever come to be described by the individual or, in the same sense, be
known to him (4, p. 280).

Skinner puts the point with equal sharpness in his paper for the present
colloquium. He talks about a case in which some students applied
various psychological terms to the behavior of a pigeon. They said,
for example, that the pigeon *hoped* for food, *expected* reinforcement,
and so on. Skinner is willing to say that the students were reporting
what they themselves "would have expected, felt, and hoped for under similar circumstances" (5, p. 91). But he goes on to emphasize
that they must have learned these terms from a "verbal community"
which

*had access only to the kinds of public information available to the stu-
dents in the demonstration.* Whatever the students knew about themselves
which permitted them to infer comparable events in the pigeon must
have been learned from a verbal community which saw no more of their
behavior than they had seen of the pigeon's (5, p. 91).

I believe that Skinner has stated here an absolutely decisive objection
to introspectionism. The intelligibility of psychological words must
be based on something other than the occurrence of those words.
That we have a common understanding of them proves that their use
has to be logically connected with other public behavior.

THE FALLACY OF BEHAVIORISM

I have been trying to give an account of the hard core of logical
truth contained in behaviorism, which gives it toughness as a philosophy of psychology. But now I want to disagree with behaviorism.
The Achilles' heel of this doctrine lies in its treatment of psychological
sentences in the first-person-present tense. The same error occurs in

physicalism. Let me begin to explain this by considering Carnap's sample sentence "I am now excited." Carnap says that the "rational support" for this sentence lies in such sentences as "I feel my hands trembling," "I see my hands trembling," "I hear my voice quavering," and so on. He goes on to remark that the sentence "I am now excited" has the "same content" as the "physical" sentence "My body is now in that condition which, both under my own observation and that of others, exhibits such and such characteristics of excitement" (1, p. 191). Carnap is obviously assuming that when a person says, "I am excited," his saying it is based, in part at least, on his observations of the state of his own body. The truth is that it would be a rare case in which a person said that he was excited on the basis of noticing that his hands were trembling or his voice quavering. I do not say that it is impossible for such a case to occur. A man who had narrowly escaped some danger might notice afterwards, perhaps with surprise, that his hands were trembling, and he might conclude that he must be very excited. In the normal case, however, a man does not *conclude* that he is excited. He says that he is, and he is; but his utterance is not the result of self-observation.

The point comes out very strikingly when we consider first-person reports of bodily sensations, e.g., "I have a headache." It would be completely mad if I were to say this on the basis of noticing that my face was flushed, my eyes dull, that I was holding my head, and had just taken some aspirin. If someone were to say, *on that basis*, that he has a headache, either he would be joking or else he would not understand how the words are used. The same is true of a first-person perception sentence, such as "I see a black dog." On the basis of observing that another person's eyes are following a black dog, *I* can say "He sees a black dog." But it would make no sense for *him* to say, on the basis of noticing that his own eyes were following a black dog, that he sees a black dog.

The natural temptation to which behaviorist philosophers have succumbed is to assume that first-person psychological sentences have the same "content," or the same verification, as the corresponding third-person sentences. It looks as if that must be how it is: nevertheless, that is not how it is. I can verify that another man is excited, by the trembling of his hands. But I do not verify in this way that *I* am excited. In the normal case I do not verify it at all. By observing you I can verify that you have a headache. I do not verify that *I* have a headache. I can verify that the animal in the field is a brown cow. I cannot verify, in addition, that I *see* a brown cow. In the case of another person I can verify both that there is a brown cow in the field and that he sees it.

The notion of verification does not apply to a wide range of first-person psychological reports and utterances. Another way to put the point is to say that those reports and utterances are *not based on observations*. The error of introspectionism is to suppose that they are based on observations of inner mental events. The error of behaviorism is to suppose that they are based on observations of outward events or of physical events inside the speaker's skin. These two philosophies of psychology share a false assumption, namely, that a first-person psychological statement is a report of something the speaker has, or thinks he has, observed.

The mistake of assimilating first-person to third-person psychological statements is quite obvious in Skinner's thinking. He refers to an imaginary case in which we ask a man why he is going down the street and we receive the reply "I am going to mail a letter." Skinner says:

We have not learned anything new about his behavior but only about some of its possible causes. The subject himself, of course, may be in an advantageous position in describing these variables because he has had an extended contact with his own behavior for many years. But his statement is not therefore in a different class from similar statements made by others who have observed his behavior upon fewer occasions. . . . [H]e is simply making a plausible prediction in terms of his experiences with himself (4, p. 88).

The truth is that normally when a man tells you his purpose in doing something his statement is in a different class from a statement made by somebody else on the basis of observation of him. If you see someone rummaging about in the papers on his desk, and remember that when he had done this on previous occasions the rummaging had come to an end when he grabbed hold of his spectacles, you might reasonably conclude on these grounds that he is now looking for his spectacles. But it would be weird if *he* were to reason as follows: "Here I am rummaging about on my desk. When I have done this in the past my activity has terminated when I have caught hold of my spectacles. Therefore, I am probably looking for my spectacles"! If you heard a man make such a remark and believed that he was not joking, you would thereafter regard him with suspicion, because of the craziness of the remark.

Skinner is puzzled by such utterances as "I was about to go home," "I am inclined to go home," "I shall go home in half an hour." He says that they "describe states of affairs which appear to be accessible only to the speaker. How can the verbal community establish responses of this sort?" He thinks a possible explanation is that when the language is learned while the individual is "behaving publicly," "private stimuli" come to be associated with the "public manifestations." The rest of this possible explanation is that:

Later when these private stimuli occur alone, the individual may respond to them. "I was on the point of going home" may be regarded as the equivalent of "I observed events in myself which characteristically precede or accompany my going home." What these events are, such an explanation does not say (4, p. 262).

For Skinner "private stimuli" would mean, of course, physical events within the individual's skin. The fact that Skinner regards this hypothesis as a possible explanation of the utterances, even though he does not know what the private stimuli would be, shows how unquestioningly he assumes that such a remark as "I am on the point of going home" must be based on the observation of something.

Undoubtedly people sometimes decide to go home because of physical disturbances within their skins. But it is wrong to suppose that the announcement "I am about to go home" is a prediction based on observation. Normally it would be outlandish to ask a man what the observational data are on the basis of which he is predicting that he is about to go home. The announcement "I am about to go home" is normally an announcement of intention. Announcements of intention are not based on the observation of either internal or external variables, despite Skinner's assumption that they must be.

Skinner would reply that surely the announcement or the intention is under the *control* of some variable. Perhaps so, depending on how ambiguously we use the word "control." Normally a man would have some reason for going home, e.g., that it is supper time. We might express this in some cases by saying that the fact it was supper time "determined his decision" to go home, or was the "controlling factor," or some such thing. We usually expect there will be something which controls a man's intention, in this sense. But if we mean "control" in Skinner's technical sense, according to which y is under the control of x if and only if x and y are connected by some *functional relationship*, i.e., by a *law*—if this is what we mean, then I will say (quite dogmatically, because I have not time to go into it) that we have no ground at all for believing that either intentions or announcements of intention are under the "control" of anything.

CONCLUSION

Behaviorism is right in insisting that there must be some sort of conceptual tie between the language of mental phenomena and outward circumstances and behavior. If there were not, we could not understand other people, nor could we understand ourselves. If a small child says "I am hungry" while rejecting food, we consider that he has not quite learned what to say. Or if he says this while rejecting food and going for drink, we think he has confused the words "thirsty" and "hungry." More subtle failures to master the correct use of language may be noted with other psychological terms. But when on several occasions there is the right correlation of behavior and circumstances with the child's utterance of a psychological term, we conclude that he has mastered its correct use. By having behavioral criteria for the truth of some third-person psychological statements, we are able to determine whether someone has a correct understanding of a good many psychological terms.

But then a remarkable development occurs. The person who has satisfied our criteria of understanding those terms begins to use them in first-person statements in the absence of the former behavioral criteria. He says that he is *angry* at someone or *anxious* about something when we should not have supposed so from his demeanor. Probably he will be able to give some reason for his anger or anxiety. The interesting thing, however, is that in a great many cases we accept his testimony. We conclude that he is angry in a case where, if we had been judging solely on the basis of our former behavioral criteria, we should not have supposed it. We use this testimony as a new criterion of what he is feeling and thinking, over and above and even in conflict with the former behavioral criteria.

The first-person psychological sentences must be correlated with behavior up to a point. But they quickly go beyond that point. People tell us things about themselves which take us by surprise, things which we should not have guessed from our knowledge of their circumstances and behavior. A behaviorist philosopher will say that if we had known more about their history, environment, and behavior, we should have been able to infer this same information. I do not believe there are any grounds for thinking so. The testimony that people give us about their intentions, plans, hopes, worries, thoughts, and feelings is by far the most important source of information we have about them. This self-testimony has, one could say, an *autonomous* status. To a great extent we cannot check it against anything else, and yet to a great extent we credit it. I believe we have no reason to think it is even a theoretical possibility that this self-testimony could be supplanted by inferences from external and/or internal physical variables.

If a study of mankind does not regard man's possession of language as an essential difference between man and the lower animals, then I should not know what was meant by "essential." Within the whole body of language the category of first-person psychological sentences has crucial importance. Man's puzzling status as a subject and a person is bound up with these first-person utterances, having the two striking characteristics I have tried to point out: First, that for the most part, they are not made on the basis of any observation; second, that they are "autonomous" in the sense that, for the most part, they cannot be "tested" by checking them against physical events and circumstances, other than the subject's own testimony. If we want to know what a man wants, what he is thinking about, whether he is annoyed or pleased, or what he has decided, the man himself is our best source of information. We ask *him* and he tells us. He has a privileged status with respect to information about himself, and not "because he has had an extended contact with his own behavior for many years."

In the beginning of my paper I said that Rogers had not, in his contribution to this colloquium, expounded a telling criticism of behaviorism. He does, however, make some remarks which hint at the criticism which I believe to be cogent. For example, he says, by implication, that behaviorism "transforms everything it studies into an object" (3, p. 113). I have argued that behaviorism fails to perceive self-testimony in a true light. It mistakenly assumes that when a man tells you what he wants, intends, or hopes, what he says is based on observation, and, therefore, he is speaking about himself as if he were an *object of observation*. Behaviorism also assumes that these first-person utterances, since they are observational in nature, could theoretically be replaced by the observations of another person, although this might require "technological advances." Behaviorism, in other words, fails to perceive that self-testimony is largely autonomous, not replaceable even in principle by observations of functional relations between physical variables.[2] Perhaps the best way to sum up behaviorism's shortcoming as a philosophy of psychology is to say that it regards man as *solely* an *object*.

BIBLIOGRAPHY

1. CARNAP, R. "Psychology in Physical Language," *Erkenntnis*, III (1932–33). Reprinted in *Logical Positivism*, ed. A. J. AYER. Glencoe: Free Press, 1959.
2. HEMPEL, C. G. "The Logical Analysis of Psychology." In *Readings in Philosophical Analysis*, eds. H. FEIGL and W. SELLARS. New York: Appleton-Century-Crofts, 1949.
3. ROGERS, C. R. "Toward a Science of the Person." In *Behaviorism and Phenomenology: Contrasting Bases for Modern Psychology*, ed. T. W. WANN. Chicago: University of Chicago Press, 1964.

[2] In his brilliant review [*Language*, XXXV (1959), 26–58] of Skinner's *Verbal Behavior*, Noam Chomsky shows conclusively, I think, that Skinner fails to make a case for his belief that "functional analysis" is able to deal with verbal behavior.

4. Skinner, B. F. *Science and Human Behavior*. New York: Macmillan, 1953.
5. ———. "Behaviorism at Fifty." In *Behaviorism and Phenomenology: Contrasting Bases for Modern Psychology*, ed. T. W. Wann. Chicago: University of Chicago Press, 1964.
6. Wittgenstein, L. *Philosophical Investigations*. New York: Macmillan, 1953.

PARAPHRASE OF DISCUSSION

Comments of Professor Skinner

The feeling of desertion and loneliness which Professor Skinner reported following Professor Koch's paper is partially allayed. He is, in general, "pleased and heartened" by Professor Malcolm's clarifications of the behaviorist view. Perhaps agreement can be reached, even with respect to first-person statements.

To counter Professor Rogers' suggestion that the behaviorist has a "corner on certainty" as well as to introduce a discussion of first-person statements, he confesses it is true that, when he was interpreting in what senses a man might report that he was going to mail a letter, he erred in omitting "the other kind of information which would be available to the man." He did not mean to suggest that such a statement "is merely a translation of statements about past instances," although, more often than we realize, "we *do* attempt to explain what we are doing by looking for external or historical variables rather than these immediate, felt impulses, or whatever it is that is the alternative." The story told of Norbert Wiener points this up. Having finished a talk with a colleague on the campus, Wiener asked, "Which way was I going when I met you?" "You were going that way." "Good, then I've had my lunch."

This kind of evaluation of our actions in objective terms must be pointed out. For example, it is possible to account for his presence at the symposium "in terms of public events [which] . . . could be adequately translated . . . in terms of statements of external contingencies." However, it must also be pointed out "that there are uniquely private events which often take over." These events are under "control of terms which have to be learned from a verbal community which is in contact *only* with the public event." The importance of the possible "test sentences" of statements about toothaches is that they point to "what the verbal community could have known in teaching a person to describe himself as having a toothache."

When speaking of such things as toothaches, it is clear that "extraordinarily powerful and irresistible stimuli . . . almost entirely control" the response. It is not so clear that "private stimuli" are as important in such things as "intentions." Statements of intention, such as those of "going home," may appear to be describing inner states, and one might try to search for the "private stimuli" suggested by such a formulation. However, these statements of intention are more readily understood in terms of "mands" and "softened mands" than in terms of descriptions of states of an organism. We should not take statements such as "I am thirsty" to be descriptions of any state of the organism just because the statement has the syntactical form of a description. No state has been analyzed to be described. This is a "softened" form of a "mand," i.e., a statement designed to elicit responses from others. There is "an enormous family of responses" of this kind, most of which are cast in the syntactical form of first-person descriptive statements. Semantical and syntactical analyses of such responses can be misleading if one mistakes an eliciting response for a descriptive response. Most, if not all, expressions of intention are forms of "mands"—warnings, alerting a listener, preparing a way, and so on.

An additional source of understanding some statements that appear to be statements of intention might be found in an examination of "the conditions under which the verbal community forces the individual to discuss himself." One condition is that in which we attempt to establish conditions under which we can react most effectively to another's actions. To that end, children are trained, from the beginning, to give statements which will warn us, alert or prepare us. In this training, children are taught to pay attention to the variables which operate on their behavior and to report in traditionally abbreviated forms of first-person statements of intention.

A final point, on a different subject—about the differences between animals and men: "I quite agree that the great step taken by the human race was bringing the vocal musculature under operant control so that language could be elaborated." While some "lower organisms have been shown to bring vocalization under the control of reinforcement," the behavior is "trivial." However, the point made about Darwin is still correct—he *wanted* to show there was no great difference between animals and men. To do so at the time he was writing, he had to "face the question of consciousness and rational power." Were he writing today, he would have to face the question of verbal behavior. Skinner "would argue" that analyses of verbal behavior indicate that it "is a very special kind of behavior but [that] there is nothing by way of processes involved that would distinguish it from non-verbal behavior and hence [verbal behavior] would not distinguish man from the [other] animals."

COMMENTS OF PROFESSOR MALCOLM

Occasions do arise in which one depends on external cues such as Professor Skinner refers to—being momentarily distracted, a person might be reminded of what he had been doing by some such clue. "But these exceptions prove the rule." The very fact that the story about Wiener is amusing indicates that it is "an oddity . . . , that it cannot be used as the paradigm of first-person psychological utterances."

Professor Malcolm does not understand what is meant by "private events taking over." "What *is* the private stimulus that takes over . . . in place of the external, observable behavior . . . so that I say I have a toothache?" To say the stimulus is the toothache would not solve the methodological problem because, to Skinner, "the private stimulus is always a *physical* event inside the skin of the organism." If the report of a toothache is based on observation, the observation must, in Skinner's view, be of a physical event. "What would the physical event be?" Even more puzzling: what would the physical event that is observed be in the case of statements of intention?

Skinner does not "solve any problem" by the "move from external physical variables to private stimuli." His move in the direction of analyzing first-person statements as softened mands rather than as descriptive statements based on observation is a "more hopeful" and "more sophisticated position . . . but it does not really seem . . . to be adequate. . . ." There can be many cases in which a first-person statement cannot be construed as a request, command, warning, or preparatory statement. It will have the syntactical form of a report; it will not be a request, and it will not be based on observation. That is the "paradoxical nature" of a "first-person psychological utterance" which leads to the description of such utterances as "autonomous" in character.

COMMENTS OF PROFESSOR ROGERS

He felt that he and Professor Malcolm were, in many ways, in agreement, yet not operating "on the same wave length." It had not been his purpose to point out "any theoretical flaw in behaviorism." "There is a lot about behaviorism that I accept. I was simply trying to go beyond it."

He feels that his emphasis on the "fact that we can obtain evidence from the internal frame of reference of the other person" through "interpersonal knowing" is "along the same line as [Malcolm's] point that first-person sentences have a status of their own. . . ." He is puzzled over the fact that, while Malcolm sees the "first-person" questions as indicating a basic difference with Skinner, he does not seem to see Rogers' stress on evidence gained from internal frames of reference as indicating a "similar basic difference."

He doubts that Skinner would be willing "to accept the existence of the kind of inner variables" that are derived from interpersonal knowing. He has found Skinner to be "consistent" in thinking of himself in the "same objective third-person terms" used to describe others. Skinner has in the past accepted as correct, characterizations of his behavior as being the result of "a chance schedule of reinforcement"; in the present symposium, he described how he got himself to work on a paper in terms of arranged contingencies, and he indicated yesterday that the phrases in the case history "should have been in quotes . . . [because] they are not the real subjective things . . . [but are] unfortunate and operantly conditioned way[s]" of saying things.

On these grounds, Rogers feels he has a "very genuine difference" with Skinner "in the extent to which we give reality to the subjective field of the person." The point of view he holds leads to "investigation of a whole range of variables which would not be considered [in] Dr. Skinner's conception of science. . . . [T]here certainly is a very real pragmatic difference in the kind of science that issues from Dr. Skinner's views and mine."

COMMENTS OF PROFESSOR MALCOLM

Of course there is a basic difference in the points of view of Rogers and Skinner, but Rogers, in his paper, did not make "a really cogent attack on behaviorism." Skinner could appropriately reply to Rogers that, as long as one must have external indexes of the internal variables and must establish correlations between the indexes and other behaviors, one is doing a functional analysis of behavior.

The question as to whether or not Skinner would accept the inner variables "pertains to the typical ambiguity of behaviorism." Watson, for example, seemed, on the one hand, to be denying that consciousness exists, but, on the other, he tried to say what thinking *is*—tiny movements of the speech apparatus. The ambiguity resides in only seeming to deny the existence of thinking, while, in reality, one is giving an analytic reduction for the term. A similar ambiguity runs through Skinner's writing to some extent. "I still hope and believe that, if it came to the pinch, Skinner would admit that people do get depressed, tired and hungry, annoyed, and so on. . . . The only position for Skinner . . . as a behavioristic philosopher, is to say that his quotation marks mean that this is a term for which he is going to give a reduction. That is, the quotation marks around 'discouragement' or 'sense of achievement' . . . do not mean that there is not any such thing as sense of achievement or discouragement; [they] mean that [these are] misleading term[s] that confuse people, which will have to be analyzed in terms of relations between external and internal variables and behavior."

That Malcolm and Rogers do not operate on the same wave length is not cause for discouragement. Rather, grounds for encouragement can be found in the coincidence of wave lengths at the point where it is apparent that they were talking about the "same phenomenon" in discussing interpersonal knowing and the autonomous status of self-testimony.

COMMENTS OF PROFESSOR SKINNER

It seems agreed that a statement of intention can be, in some cases, "a fairly objective description of the evidence we have of our probable future actions," or can be, at the other extreme, "something like a social gesture." In between these two "is this debatable ground." He is convinced that "there are some private stimuli involved, but the kind of connection they have with the verbal response" is not clear. He has analyzed many such examples in a chapter called "The Impure Tact." He is uncertain as to "the mode of control [by the private stimuli] over the verbal response" and is "not disturbed" at the possibility that the mode of control "might turn out to be something which would cause the whole argument to fall."

"As to the quotation marks, I think that Mr. Malcolm has more or less stated my point on that." The question, though, is not whether such statements or terms are meaningful, but rather, what is the order of events. "I believe, in general, these [descriptive terms such as tired, discouraged, etc.] are ex post facto, a posteriori descriptions of changes in my behavior rather than the causes of what I did afterward."

MEMBER OF THE AUDIENCE

Professor Malcolm agrees with Skinner that information can be gained from third-person observational statements, and he agrees with Rogers that information can be gained from first-person statements. He insists, however, that nothing can be gained from the attempt to reduce most first-person statements to an observational base—they are "autonomous." It is suggested that the insistence on the autonomous nature of self-testimony is puzzling in view of the almost universal tendency to seek such reductions. For example, if a person were to report that he had a headache and yet he, himself, could observe no physical or physiological stimuli in himself and no other observer could observe changes, the person would be very puzzled. It is suggested, therefore, that the interest in achieving reduction of first-person statements to functional, observational terms arises in the attempt on the part of a person to gain "more security about [his own] first-person statements."

COMMENTS OF PROFESSOR MALCOLM

When a person reports a headache, he reports it and does not seek justification for that report by looking in the mirror, or taking his temperature, or asking someone if he looks as though he has a headache. He might ask for help in determining the *cause* of a headache, but he does not ask for help, from his own observations or those of others, in determining that he *has* a headache.

The puzzlement, which is justified, is a philosophical one, arising from the assumption that the statement "I have a headache," being an indicative sentence about a state, must be based on observation. "That is why, as a philosopher, you have an inclination to believe that, somehow, this sentence must have an observational base." This is a subject for philosophical inquiry, and the assumption should not lead one to suppose that, in ordinary life, "we do somehow connect the statement 'I have a headache' in some loose way with a state of my body or my external behavior such that, if I did not see the right correlation, . . . (I) would wonder whether I was really justified in saying 'I have a headache.' "

MEMBER OF THE AUDIENCE

Yet, unless the realization of having a headache were, at the same time, tied in very closely with these other experiences which can be verified, one would be very puzzled.

COMMENTS OF PROFESSOR MALCOLM

There must be some misunderstanding here. "Does this [headache] make any difference in your activities . . . do you say 'Well, I had better not go to the concert'?" [From the audience: "It does affect my activities."] This is a different case. It is true that it would be a "piece of nonsense" to report having a headache and not have *some* correlated change in behavior, but that does not imply that the statement, "I have a headache," "is made on the basis of a reduction of some kind [from] my activity. . . . I do not verify that I have a headache by noticing that I have declined an invitation to go to the concert."

MEMBER OF THE AUDIENCE

First, a question about first-person statements not being reportorial or observationally based: What about a report of a headache in which details as to position, intensity, and movement of the ache are contained? Second, what does it mean to say that first-person statements are autonomous? To say such statements are not based on observation does not say what they are. " 'Autonomous' does not help."

COMMENTS OF PROFESSOR MALCOLM

The question about what is meant by "autonomous" introduces a topic too large to discuss here.

In answer to the question about a detailed report of a headache, three points are made. First, in most cases we *report* our sensations, and only under special circumstances, e.g., a request from a physician, do we "observe" them. Second, while it is true "there is a kind of thing called 'observation' which applies to some bodily sensations in some cases, . . . it is not the kind of observation that behaviorism wants, . . . it is not an observation of external or internal physical variables or correlation between them." "It is an entirely different use of the word 'observation.' . . ." Third, while it *might* be permissible to say we "observe" bodily sensations, "one has not the faintest idea what it would mean to 'observe' one's intention, or one's desire" or other "psychological phenomena."

COMMENTS OF PROFESSOR KOCH

Professor Malcolm's paper lessens "whatever cynicism" Koch might have felt about the prospects for analytic philosophy. A great deal of what Malcolm had to say is consonant with what Koch would feel to be the necessary consequences of the "analysis of definition" he presented in his own paper.

One consequence of his analysis that might not result as a consequence of Malcolm's analysis is the conclusion that behaviorism, by virtue of its eagerness "to universalize the language community . . . [by] achieving objective definitions," has "given us a simplistic picture of the nature of communication." To elaborate, behaviorism seeks for definitions on which one can achieve "wide consensus—universal agreement." It does this by attempting to link concepts to "simple objective indicators . . . which depend on relatively crass discriminations." Koch's analysis argues that "any adequate reconstruction of what goes on in communication" will reveal that the "concepts which we have, as operationists and logical positivists, tended to represent as definable in terms of very simple and crass discrimina-

tions are not, in fact, so definable." An examination of what a member
of the language community *does* when he applies or understands concepts given these simple, objective criteria will reveal that what is involved in this application or understanding is frequently "an extraordinarily subtle discrimination of an often rather delicately contoured
property or relation, or, sometimes, [of a] highly embedded or
masked relation in a . . . very complex manifold of events. . . . In general, our paradigms for specifying what we are doing when we are
communicating in science, *even* when we are talking about concepts
having external references" are "enormously simplified."

Further, this analysis suggests that any questions about the sensitivity and competence of the observer apply as pertinently to members of the language community using concepts having external reference as they do to members when "trying to describe a subtle and
highly embedded property or relation of his experience. . . . The fact
that one is, in the first instance, dealing with concepts having external reference does not necessarily make the communicative process
less indeterminate, labile, defective, probabilistic . . . than would be
the case with respect to communications in terms of . . . first-person
report. . . ."

The question of the relation between report and experience is "one
of the most complex questions that mankind could well raise." It has
been "bypassed" by psychology in recent times. Some little can be
said about the relationship now, but not much. It is not, however, a
question that is "closed, in principle, to progress."

In another vein, Koch feels that the "defense of behaviorism" developing in the symposium "reflects an absolute contempt . . . for
subject matter. . . . It seems to me there is an absolutely Philistine and
almost malicious attitude toward the universe involved in the constant
reference to 'experience' as the 'field of private stimulation.'" It
exemplifies the "constant, ubiquitous importation of . . . vaguely disguised experiential meaning into a quasi-objective vocabulary. . . .
This thinnest of all metaphors—'stimuli,' 'stimulus,' something presumably associated, in its early history, with end organ activity—now
becomes all of experience. . . . I would be happy to say what we have
been hearing could be characterized as the death rattle of behaviorism,
but this would be a rather more dignified statement than I should like
to sponsor, because death is, at least, a dignified process."

MICHAEL SCRIVEN

Views of Human Nature

O UR TASK is to assess the behavioristic and the phenomenological approaches to psychology. My special task is to comment on the papers of Professors Koch and MacLeod. As they have already told you, sickness struck them down while their work was concluding. This had the minor consequence that, unlike Professor Malcolm, I have had little or no more time to reflect on the papers I am to discuss than you have. I am afraid this has probably led me to overlook, or do scant justice to, some points I should really discuss in detail, and I am afraid it has certainly prevented a tidy synthesis of what I do have to say. Please forgive me for this relative disorderliness.

INTRODUCTION

I do not believe one can assess the merits of these two approaches to psychology today without having some view about the nature and future of psychology in general. At a certain very early stage in the history of thought, anthropomorphic explanation, animism, was the best bet. It was the rational form of explanation at that time. At later stages, where the rigid laws governing natural phenomena were becoming more apparent, it seemed superfluous to say that it was a god who drove the sun across the sky. And today this kind of explanation in the field of natural phenomena is mere superstition. Behaviorism, at least in its methodological form, represents the same kind of tough-minded economizing approach that has very frequently paid off in the history of psychology. Professor Skinner's analogies with, for example, the fate of the doctrine of essential spirits in chemistry, indicate that he clearly sees himself in that tradition. The question is whether that tradition at *this* time and with *this* subject is the appropriate one, or whether we should not, by now, be turning back to see whether we have thrown out the baby with the bathwater, the in-

MICHAEL SCRIVEN, Professor, Department of History and Logic of Science, Indiana University.

dispensable data along with the superfluous interpretations and ramblings of early introspectionism.

Such a question is not likely to be decided correctly by ourselves or by budding theorists today without considerable knowledge of the arguments on both sides that have been so thoroughly aired in the past, a claim which is well supported by the historical scholarship exhibited by the distinguished contributors to this symposium. They exhibit an interest in history which makes the disregard—indeed contempt—for the history of psychology in the normal departmental curriculum an unfortunate and crippling prejudice. In no other subject are the historical arguments still current, and they are likely to remain current forever unless the upcoming student is made to realize that his brilliant insights about the dispensability of mental states, for example, fall short of originality by about fifty years. The issue between behaviorism and phenomenology will not be resolved if allegiance to one side is treated as a form of departmental religion, as if it were the liberalism-conservatism issue. The shotgun divorce of philosophy and psychology is surely no longer an adequate justification for forcing the beginning psychologist to repeat for himself, and perhaps never transcend, philosophical errors long since exposed as such. I recall hearing the chairman of one of the most distinguished departments of psychology in the English-speaking world say in a lecture that he thought the most important unsolved problem in psychology of perception was the problem of how we come to see things the right way up when the image on the retina is inverted. Now those of you who do have some familiarity with the history of the subject will understand that this is an important problem, but only historically; the solution to it has been propounded several times but never any better than when it was first propounded some forty years ago. It is unfortunate that one should have to spend that kind of time and involve oneself in that kind of confusion through an attitude to the history of the subject which I think is based upon emotional reaction rather than upon an assessment of its value.

In the light of the history of the issue between behaviorism and phenomenology, and the current successes and failures of psychology, what can we say about the relevance of these two approaches today? I am going to argue that, in what is now their only tenable form, they are at least compatible, if not in one man, at least within the subject. There is not just room but a proper place for each. In the past there have often been supporters of both sides doing good work, but they have characteristically offered war cries that were in direct opposition to each other. Today the war cries strike me as calling for work on different problems or different aspects of the same problem. Seven years ago I wrote what has the dubious distinction of being, I think, the longest and most detailed treatment of Skinner's position in the literature, in which I came to conclusions which largely overlap those of Professor Malcolm. But I think that Professor Skinner's position, as he put it in his paper in the current symposium, is a considerably more flexible one, and he seems to view his occasional statements that would be directly incompatible with the position of the phenomenologists as being indications of emphasis, rather than as the most fundamental planks in his platform.

First of all, then, I am going to outline the picture of psychology that now seems to me the most plausible, completely uncontaminated as I am by any practical participation in the subject. Within that framework I shall indicate what I take to be the proper location of the behaviorist and phenomenological camps. Then I shall turn to the particular discussions of these positions with which I am here concerned and indicate where I think they need minor surgery or medicine, the result of which, I believe, would reveal them as playing the role that I have indicated in my more general remarks.

THE NATURE OF PSYCHOLOGY

The apparent shortcomings of psychology have nothing to do with its alleged youth. This is partly because it has no youth, the rational study of behavior being the oldest field of human knowledge. People have played gambling games and fought one another for too long to act entirely stupidly in all fields of the study of human behavior—given that rational behavior has some survival value. And it is partly because its crucial shortcomings, if this is what they are, are ineradicable and hence will not pass with its youth. We are prone to think of psychology as young because it has not been long since it developed its own instrumentation, a new terminology or systems of terminology, and its own departments and professional apparatus. We may decide to regard this as the occasion to award the subject the recently struck medal labeled "Science," a term which we sometimes think of as being old but which, of course, was coined only in the nineteenth century at a meeting of the British Association.

If we do decide this is the occasion to call psychology a science for the first time, we then consign the labors of Aristotle, Hobbes, and others to the pre-scientific limbo. But the youth of the science is not, then, in any way an explanation of what are often thought of as its adolescent shortcomings, its lack of satisfactory comprehensive theories, its lack of precise and highly general laws—the features which distinguish it from the paradigmatic astronomy and mechanics. Our explanation has slipped away, for the interesting question simply becomes: Why was it so long *before* psychology the subject became psychology the science? After all, the reasons for developing the science were always there—the need for predicting human behavior and explaining it and classifying it being, indeed, much more pressing than the reasons for developing the science of mechanics or that of astronomy. No lucky breakthrough, no crucial discovery in other fields, no particularly brilliant investigator was responsible for the birth of the scientifically labeled subject. No, the reason why psychology is in its present state is that, by its very nature, it will never be in a very different state and, indeed, has probably never in the past, even in its pre-scientific past, been in a very different state. We are misled by the trappings of statistical language, the gadgetry, and the unreadable volumes of research findings; or, in other cases, we may be misled by the clicking of cumulative recorders.

There is no doubt that in a very straightforward way we have a great many more facts of a psychological kind than we ever had before. And we do understand some things in psychology better than we ever have before, though most of the classic examples which people are prone to put up—for example, in the attempt to produce an analogy between Newton and Freud—rest upon a failure to comprehend what is involved in the claim that understanding of human behavior has been achieved in these cases.

The position that I am outlining may appear, at first sight, to be a distressingly obscurantist one; but it is not, for I do not wish to deny, indeed I confidently affirm, that knowledge of some kind and, indeed, discoveries of very great importance, are, and will continue to be, forthcoming in psychology. I wish only to claim that a certain kind of fundamental discovery—the kind that unified astronomy and mechanics (the law of gravitation) or the kind that retransformed the whole of physics (relativity being one example and quantum theory another)—is wholly impossible in psychology. In the unspoken religion of science this is often thought to be a sacrilegious claim, just as the indeterministic claims of quantum theory were frequently and still are occasionally viewed as sacrilegious. It is especially irritating to a scientist, after all, thinking of his busy labs from which he has been led into the lairs of the philosophers, to be told by a philosopher that there are limitations on what he can do in his labs. But in both cases, the case of psychology and the case of physics, the religious approach is inappropriate. We can retain our fervor in the search for causal explanations and scientific progress and, indeed, improve our chances of success if we do not have an inappropriate idea of the areas where this is likely to be found. Indeed, we merely waste our efforts and corrupt our perception of new phenomena and theories and new suggestions for research if we retain an inappropriate picture of the capacity and expectations of our subject, be it psychology or modern physics. The scientific approach does not depend in any way on the idea that a Newtonian or Einsteinian revolution is possible in a subject. The relevance of behaviorism and phenomenology to psychology depends on this point. Why do I think that such radical developments are impossible in psychology?

Psychology as a science is essentially defined or limited in three ways, the first of them unique. The first fact is that the territory of psychology is, in a curious way, sharply restricted by common sense.

If we began work upon the psychology of the Martians, supposing that there is such a race, or the inhabitants of the first planet of Tau Ceti, which is rather more likely to have life on it, then it would be a matter of great excitement to discover, for example, that many of them exhibit symptoms of extreme inebriation upon consumption of one six-ounce bottle of Pepsi-Cola. But if we were to produce the corresponding fact about alcohol as a contribution to modern psychology, it would not be regarded very highly by the populace or by our supervisor. If we were to discover that most Martians become quite exhausted after running a mile in six minutes and are unable to repeat this performance immediately, we should again have discovered something of great importance about them and about their capacities for exercise and locomotion. This is not something which modern psychology can produce as one of its contributions to our knowledge of the human organism. And, in this peculiar way, which extends into the whole realm of motivation, of perception, of verbal behavior, of operant conditioning—indeed, almost every realm of psychology— we find, if we view the study of human behavior as an enterprise to produce systematic organized information, that a colossal quantity of this information (a point which Skinner has often emphasized) has already long since been snapped up and incorporated in our ordinary language. It has either been incorporated in the very meaning of the concepts themselves or become a stock part of the body of truisms which we all know about human behavior. Psychology as a science must begin beyond that level, and that level was founded upon fifty thousand years of close observation of human beings. There was a certain amount of nonsense involved in those observations, and a great many of the explanatory schemata of the early days can now readily be seen to be without foundation. But if we look at the level of empirical laws, then we can see that we have already winnowed out much of the easy material for the scientific study of human behavior. We are faced therefore with a task which Galileo never faced, which Newton never faced. The fact that they never faced this task made it possible for their subjects to undergo the kind of fundamental change and unification which those individuals contributed to them.

Had we been allowed to begin at the beginning with human behavior, as we might with Martian behavior, we might find it of tremendous excitement that both liquid and solid nourishment are required by human beings, and so on. These kinds of discoveries are not open to the science of psychology.

Common sense indeed does two unkind things to us: it not only steals the easy pickings from the field of study of human behavior, but it passes on to the science of psychology a set of extremely embarrassing questions, because the everyday interaction of human beings leads them to need much more than their common-sense knowledge quite frequently. The meteorologist often curses his misfortune in being stuck with the task of predicting precipitation, a very delicate function of many conditions which he can predict in themselves with great but frequently insufficient accuracy, measured by the criterion of the public's need. Similarly, the experimental psychologist (unlike the astronomer) is quite good at predicting many effects under laboratory conditions but finds these are not a good basis for predicting what people want to know about the success of college students, marriages, executive trainees, different ways of teaching physics or reading, etc.

The second limitation on psychology, for which it cannot be blamed but which radically affects our assessment of its capacities, is that its territory is restricted and, indeed, constantly being annexed by other sciences—biochemistry, biology, genetics, biophysics, physiology, neurophysiology, and so on. At a certain point an explanation of behavior must be ruled out as being an explanation of behavior not in terms of psychology but rather in terms of brain structure, genetic characteristics, the digestive processes, and so on. There are many examples of this kind. As we press against the frontiers of more efficient prediction and more thorough explanation, we discover ourselves often forced in through the skull or down the nervous system in other parts of the body—a fact which has led many people in the field (as it has on innumerable historical occasions before) to argue that the true future of psychology lies elsewhere, e.g., in neurophysiology. This is, of course, a future which exists after the grave, since that stage is no longer psychology.

These recommendations, therefore, have a certain double-edgedness to them. They are on a par with the suggestions, which have been popular for a hundred years or more, that chemistry should be abandoned in favor of fundamental physics and a large computer, into which you feed the data about the fundamental particles and the conditions in which you intend to mix them and from which you expect to receive information as to the results, thereby avoiding any contaminating contact with test tubes and the like. This is an interesting but peculiar view. It is peculiarly attractive for some people—particularly people with strong yearnings toward unified science—but there is something essentially impractical about it. I would like to go into this point at some length, but I shall not. I shall rely on your common sense (although I think I might be able to undercut it if I made an effort) to see that we are constrained by the definition of the subjects here to deny the term "psychology" or "psychological explanation" to explanations which simply use variables from other subjects as they are commonly recognized; although they may in fact explain molar behavior that can be regarded as psychological behavior.

The practical circumstances of the problems which common sense and technical requirements pass along to us as the problems of psychology prevent this idealistic solution—using the complete structure of the brain at the particle level and the large computer—because it is typically the case that we can only use such a device if we can feed it data which are microscopic, too, and such data are inaccessible. It may well be true that we could predict the behavior of human beings, uncertainty effects apart, given a sufficiently large amount of data about them and the construction of their brain, and a large computer. However, it is only too clear that the requisite data would include a postmortem and a total history; and the computer itself has not yet been constructed. Consequently, this does not provide us with anything like a practical approach, if, indeed, it even provides us with a comprehensible alternative to the approach of the psychologists who are looking for laws and theories which are concerned with molar variables at both the independent and dependent end.

Psychology thus begins facing the handicaps that much of the information about, and explanations of, human behavior have been stolen by common sense and that many of the novel ones are about to be stolen or may be stolen by other sciences. It is therefore in a peculiarly deprived position. If it deprives itself also of its own history and the discussion of philosophical issues I fear that it will suffer unnecessarily. Its condition is already sufficiently difficult to make of it a special subject which must be viewed as not, in any important way, analogous with the classical mechanical and physical sciences. (It is actually very like contemporary sub-divided physics, or geography, or—to turn from the sublime—contract bridge.)

I now turn to the third difficulty. It is perfectly easy to demonstrate that a great many psychological problems are not going to admit of a precise, simple, Newtonian solution in terms of accessible psychological variables. We are interested in the prediction of college or marital success, in the effect of different styles of teaching or therapy on the recipients, in the etiology of neuroses, in the explanation of the moon illusion, in the analysis of misunderstandings in communication, in the development of the moral sense in children, in the structure of power alliances in groups, and so on. These are all problems that come straight to us out of our everyday experiences and that we, as psychologists, cannot ignore. Yet it is demonstrable with respect to many of these problems that the controlling variables lie at least partly outside the range of the psychologist's investigations.

The effects of this vary with different aspects of the science. I take the three major tasks of the science to be prediction, explanation, and what I call "the problems of static organization," which are classification and summary. I take the problem of control to be largely a problem of what we frequently refer to as technology, though it is sometimes part of applied sciences insofar as it is different from the problems of prediction. Now with respect to prediction, it is important to notice a crucial difference between conditional and unconditional prediction. Many of the problems that psychology comes up against in its interaction with the world are problems where an unconditional prediction is required. We want to know, as the astronomers wanted to know, when the eclipse will occur, not if I can manipulate the position of the moon. We want to know whether this marriage will fail—not whether a marriage will fail if people are previously conditioned in the following way, this being a way that we cannot identify as being the way in which the people we are concerned with were conditioned. We want to know not just how (although of course this is often an important first step) an organism will be affected if we halve the rate of reinforcement; we want to know how this organism will be affected if it is switched from a high-protein to a low-protein diet. The relation of that to the rate of reinforcement is a complicated one, and often the gap between a known theoretical connection and an actual connection is the gap which proves to be the insuperable one in psychology.

Now many problems of unconditional prediction in psychology are simply unsolvable. To start with one type of extreme example, it would be interesting to be able to predict in precise detail the form of the next paintings that will be produced by a particular artist. It would be interesting to be able to forecast, speaking more generally, what the next revolution in art will look like. It would be interesting to know what a great scientist is going to think of next in the way of fundamental theories. But it does seem perfectly clear, not only that it is difficult for us to guess the data that we need for this, but that as a practical matter it would be unrealistic to suppose that we shall ever be in a position where we can do this exactly. Psychologists divide on that point. You sometimes find enthusiasts who are willing to argue that the difficulty of prediction of really important, novel discoveries, e.g., the next step in quantum theory, from psychological study of the antecedents, is only a case of practical difficulties. I would want to argue that it is a case where the number of variables on which we would need data and the time to which we would have to go back in the training schedule of the organism we are studying are such that we just are not going to be able to get it. By the time the scientist proves to be bright it is already too late to find out what we would need to tell what his next discovery is going to be, even if we had the required laws.

Often the dependent variables, as far as prediction goes, depend upon such things as genetic constitution, tumors, and the random stimuli that people encounter in their ordinary everyday uncontrolled behavior to a degree that makes precise prediction impracticable or, to put the matter more bluntly, impossible. There are too many cases where the problems that we wish to solve are demonstrably dependent for their solution upon information about, or control of, variables we cannot get at or cannot control because of the practical circumstances.

One is inclined to respond to comments of this kind by saying that this is surely no different from the situation in physics. We know what happens to falling bodies in a vacuum, but, when it comes to the way bodies behave when we drop them in air, we are not able to say very precisely what they will do. And, when it comes to the question of how a particular leaf falls from a particular tree on a particular autumn day, we are almost helpless. This is true, but nobody feels that it is very important to be able to predict the behavior of a leaf. If this were the kind of crucial problem in physics then it would be the case that physics would always be a subject of a very unsatisfactory kind. When it comes to the behavior of bodies falling in air—for example, missiles on re-entry—it turns out that we can, through one very simple procedure, obtain extremely satisfactory answers. Our theories do very little for us here. What we do is send up a large number of samples and study the effects. We then discover that we can get an empirical relationship accurate enough for our purposes. Unfortunately, in the case of psychology we find that although there is a great communality of, for example, the gross features of learning curves under particular kinds of schedules of reinforcement, the behavior of the particular individual human being or particular group of individual human beings with respect to a particular environmental reinforcement at a particular time in their adult life is highly unpredictable (with respect to the domain of accuracy beyond the common-sense level). It is unpredictable because of the lack of data we have about their long history of learning. And yet it is just this kind of problem which is crucial in psychology. If it were the case that the problem of predicting astronomical positions involved predicting the behavior of the planets to within a micron or an inch, astronomy would be in its infancy; indeed, astronomy would probably never get out of its infancy, because it is probably the case that the tidal influence on the motion of the planet effected by a storm at one part of its surface would be more than enough to throw its position off by such an amount. We would therefore be caught up in the necessity of predicting the weather on the planet itself and probably weather on other planets, too, before we could get to the point of predicting the orbit. Our chances of doing that in a precise way are again dependent upon our capacity for predicting the number of storms in intergalactic space or interstellar space, the storms of high-energy particles that we run into. These clearly effect the behavior under study in quite important ways, and these are generated in turn by the sun spots or by the decay and death of distant stars. We find ourselves then at a point where we would be unable, because of the openness of the system, to make any precise predictions to the degree that we are interested in. The good fortune of classical physics and the misfortune of psychology lie to a large extent in the kind of prediction problems which they inherit.

I add one further point about prediction. There are certain kinds of provable limitations on the prediction of human behavior which are worth mentioning. It is possible to prove, for example, that the behavior of an individual who has in his possession all the information about him that you have, is unpredictable if he wants it to be, because he will be able to duplicate any prediction that you could make; and, because of his motivational condition, he will in fact do something else. You may have all the information that can be known about a man at a particular time, but if he has it too, it will not predict what he is going to do. This fact leads to some interesting attempts to subvert determinism in various ways though, I think, unsuccessfully.

The story with respect to explanation is different. It is a classic myth of the traditional philosophy of science of the first part of this century that explanation and prediction are logically similar. They are, indeed, extremely different and the question whether explanation is possible is a quite different question than the question of when and whether prediction is possible in psychology. In particular, it is the case that the effect of unpredictable variables from outside the system, which will certainly spoil our predictions, can easily be handled within the explanatory system. There is no difficulty in explaining why something that was caused by an unpredictable storm happens. It is perfectly easy to explain that the rain was the cause of the damage. But it is very hard to predict *when* damage will occur because floods are very hard to predict. So explanation is, in this respect, characteristically simpler than prediction. On the other hand, it is sometimes more difficult because giving understanding often requires more than giving true statements (about the future). Predictions can be deduced from mere correlation laws, but explanation cannot. And there is the problem of "empty" explanations. I can, for example, produce for you an explanation of the weather which is simply a tautological one and in no way conveys understanding: it is raining because water was precipitated from the atmosphere. Some of the explanations that Professor Skinner objects to in common-sense psychology are of this kind. On the other hand, in the business of explanation we can add to the axioms and we frequently do. Physics has on several occasions gone down to the last ditch fighting against accepting some allegedly incomprehensible phenomenon—for example, action at a distance—and then has compromised by adding it to its list of permissible fundamental forms of behavior, that is, forms of behavior which do not require explanation. This is unfortunate in a certain sense, but it is characteristic of the procedure of enlarging one's understanding. And in quantum theory today the problem is whether or not you can be said to understand the effects in terms of the merely statistical theory. On balance, however, explanation in psychology is easier than prediction, but it is not without its own special limitations.

Finally then, with respect to the problems of static organizations of science, classification and summary, there are no crucial difficulties, since we have rather good technical vocabularies and can elaborate these, for which I see no special difficulty.

So I could summarize by saying that the problem that faces psychology is rather like the problem that faces, say, volcanology. One of the crucial problems that people are interested in is predicting when, or explaining why, a volcano erupts on a particular occasion. It is clearly dependent, at least sometimes, upon variables which are, at least in part, inaccessible. Galileo was lucky, and the problem that faces psychology should not be thought of as having any relation to the early stages of mechanics.

Comparisons can be helpful. Mathematical economics is a nice example of a subject which has been carried away by the idea that if you can make something mathematical, you are making it precise, and it brings out very nicely the way in which the crucial point is not whether you can produce a precise law governing an ideal case but how precisely you can relate the ideal case to actual cases. The history of symbolic logic, again, provides extremely illuminating comparisons for the history of modern systematic psychology. It was originally thought of by Leibniz and others as a marvelous way in which we would be able to solve all problems by using the universal language, the *ars characteristica universalis,* in which we would be able to formulate every problem in a form that the *calculus ratiocinator* could handle, and we would then just go through the operations prescribed by the rules and would have the solution to the problem, whether it was ethics, logic, or whatever. Today this must be thought of as a hopelessly unrealistic picture: symbolic logic has become a minor branch of mathematics of some intrinsic interest but of little value for solving typical logical problems. The reason is simple: the encoding is as debatable as the original problem, and the precision of the calculus is of no more value than the precision of a good watch when one is unsure of the accuracy with which it was originally set. It is not true that psychologists, in general, view as hopelessly unrealistic a position that is essentially identical, in its epistemological foundations, to that view of the capacities of symbolic logic.

If one asks what it is that I am attempting to rule out as a possibility, then I would say I am making a distinction between the possibilities of *indefinite* improvement in a subject's capacity for prediction and explanation and the possibility of *unbounded* improvement with respect to each problem area in a subject. I am not placing any limitations on the future progress of psychology, if by that you mean the likelihood of constantly improving efficiency in prediction or constantly enlarging thoroughness in explanation, but I am saying that it in no way follows from this that you may conclude that any given limits of efficiency, say 85 per cent, in prediction, etc., in any particular interesting problem case will one day be attained. To err about this is a simple but serious logical mistake.

What follows from this set of comments about the nature of psychology, as I see it, for the general procedures of the subject? It seems clear that limited laws, laws governing certain ranges of behavior in certain sets of organisms under certain conditions, are already available, and we may expect to greatly increase the extent of these. It is also clear that limited explanatory theories, referring to particular kinds of perception or misperception and to particular kinds of motivation situations, etc., are already available and can be refined and enlarged in number. In general, I am emphasizing what we might call a local government point of view for psychology. Local government is not incompatible with national government; indeed, it is helped by it, and it helps it. But, for many purposes and in large countries, local government is more efficient and should be thought of, in general, as being a highly viable form of organization. In many sciences, this emphasis is more appropriate; modern geography is a good example. Specifically, in psychology this leads me to one or two suggestions which bear on the symposium's topic.

First, it seems to me, we should, methodologically speaking, start taking seriously the paradigms of informative partial descriptions and analysis. Psychology was responsible for the creation of a large part of modern statistics and has been responsible for a great deal of its development. Yet it has never fully adopted the crucial point of view about statistics—that statistics provides us with exact ways of describing complex situations and data by selecting out certain parts or aspects of it. It is by no means the case that statistical language is the only appropriate language for psychology. Wherever we can avoid it we should avoid it. We have precise laws (with limited ranges) of a non-statistical kind in the field Professor Skinner has so impressively mined. It is also the case that we should concentrate more carefully on causal statements and causal laws. This has little to do with the problem of tracking down exact general laws, except that if you happen to find general laws you can sometimes produce causal claims from them. The reverse is not the case. You can identify the causes of disease without knowing all the conditions required for a law. You can identify the causes of certain kinds of mental disorder without being able to say what every relevant variable is. This is part of the epistemology of incomplete information, and it is the kind of model with which psychology should concern itself. It should abandon the idea of the vast systems of highly precise differential-equation-governed laws, which are of some importance for physics and of virtually no importance in the social sciences. The search for these—apart from their informational poverty—is an energy-consuming impediment to the attempts to find useful causal relations.

Secondly, and not unconnectedly, it would do psychologists no harm, though they are likely to find the suggestion objectionable, to mine the resources of ordinary language considerably more thoroughly than they have. The present tendency to introduce nine technical terms for motivation concepts, rather than to take the trouble to find out what we ordinarily mean by the fourteen terms we already have, leads to a proliferation of jargon which constitutes one of the most important barriers to understanding the work, and also one of the most unfortunate features for those of us who are interested in presenting results in a form which makes understanding of its subject matter possible. The naïve idea persists that the imprecision of ordinary language is primarily due to the carelessness of its users. On the contrary, it is chiefly due to the statistical spread of the subject matter, and frequently no greater *usable* precision is obtainable.

In specific, rather than methodological, terms it seems to me clearly the case that one should abandon the direct search for super theories of learning, super theories of development, and super theories of mental illness or perception. These have proved themselves to offer a redescription rather than an explanation, which is the danger into which psychologists, like us all, are particularly prone to fall. The tendency is to extend a useful explanatory theory into other realms, where its value is nonexistent except in making the smell of the account attractive to other users of this scent. At the other end of the scale of investigation, it seems to me, the practical problems of psychology—the many problems that we face all around us about how to improve the methods of learning, methods of perception, methods of retention, and methods of therapy—are an excellent point at which to begin. It is possible to list a long series of important issues of this kind to which psychologists have given negligible attention over the years. If we pile up against this the contributions to the *Psychological Review* on minor points of learning theory that have made absolutely no significant contribution to anything at all, we ought to feel depressed. I have in mind, for example, such little things as the problem of the autoinduction of anesthesia. Now it would be nice if we had procedures for autohypnosis that would enable us in cases of serious accident to induce anesthesia in certain parts of the body. There is a good deal of literature, from Salter on, to suggest that this may be possible, but it is not exactly a major research problem of contemporary psychology. I suspect the theoretically interesting consequences would be no less exciting than those of the usual rat experiment. The automatic induction of sleep in a subject by some routine procedure which one can easily learn would be a rather major benefit to mankind. It is not, by any means, outside the purview of current theories of learning, and it would, it seems to me, be something that would again be (very) likely to lead to interesting sub-theories, even if it did not contribute to the advancement of a major complete theory. The work of O. K. Moore and others on kindergarten hyperacceleration is a superb example (one of the few available outside Skinner's ambit) of exactly the kind I am supporting.

Now the important consequence for us in this picture of psychology is the possibility of different approaches in different areas. The physicist interested in cryogenics (low-temperature physics) should, by and large, act as a determinist, and he does. But his colleague, interested in particle interaction, should not and does not. Indeed, neither of them knows very much about, or thinks his own explanations very relevant to, the other's field. People think of physics in a monolithic way if they are outside it. Within physics determinism has its role just as indeterminism does. In psychology we can reasonably argue that the area of sensation will best be handled within the framework of a careful phenomenology, that of scheduled motor learning by a careful behaviorism, and so on. Now, of course, school learning, for example, involves trial and error *and* meanings; and psychotherapy involves the self, affect, and *S-R* learning, something from each of the three streams. Here the best view is undoubtedly the eclectic one. But this is not in any way to deny that the stubborn enthusiasts for one side, who incorrectly see the other as the dead hand of the past or the wild-eyed fanaticism of an impractical idealist, may happen to produce the best results. Of course, steaming somebody up to think that the only way to do psychology is via phenomenology and that all behaviorists are wicked may well turn out to be a good way of getting him to do something worthwhile, but it is certainly an unfortunate comment on psychology if psychologists need to do this. Do we *have* to feed ourselves fibs as fuels for our forward movement?

It is now time for us to turn to an examination of possible difficulties with the versions of the contrasting positions put forward here. In the case of Koch's paper (I elevate the contributors to the sainthood by referring to them without professorial or doctoral prefixes) we shall proceed backward: we shall examine Koch's criticisms of behaviorism in order to see whether we can allow some version of it a little more rope than Koch allows the archetype of behaviorism that he discusses.

The Present Symposium

The greatest significance, for me, of this symposium can be simply stated. There are no psychologists, alive or dead, who have made a greater contribution to the crying practical concerns of psychology, particularly the improvement of learning and teaching, drug evaluation, and psychotherapy, than those now present. Their methodological formulations are thus of the greatest importance to the student and practitioner of the subject, since they feel compelled to them, not merely vaguely attracted by them. They see these positions as the mainsprings of the direction and details of their research; and, in the form they present them, there certainly appear to be explicit inconsistencies between them—for example, in the acceptance or rejection of the causal efficacy of mental states. I must, therefore, suggest certain criticisms in order to reconcile these positions as bases for compatible, though not identical, approaches.

Before I do this, it may be salutory to identify the large number of general philosophical issues which the participants have, unavoidably, I think, introduced. There is no hope that I could talk about these, and I mention them only to remind you of their involvement, to indicate topics you may wish to raise in discussion, and to emphasize again the appropriateness (and tardiness) of the birth of Division 24 of the APA. Cumulative recorders may click away without theories to help them, but if we want to understand their records we shall need to devise some explanations devoid of some of these philosophical difficulties. This, I think, explains Professor Skinner's love-hate relationship with methodological theories: on the one hand, he is anxious to stress the fact that the true science of behavior proceeds without them; on the other hand, he almost never turns down an invitation to a symposium at which he can stress the importance of his own methodological theories. I think this springs from his own honesty about seeing the extent to which he is, by his work, committed to a methodological position, which he then attempts to make as sound as he can.

I am going to list the other philosophical topics that have been deeply involved, on stage and behind the scenes, in the course of this symposium, each of which requires a great deal of discusison. Such discussion, I think, would benefit the psychological theorist or the person interested in the application of psychological theories or even the person who is simply interested in theory as a means toward doing good research. (*a*) Theories of definition. (*b*) The nature of and the criteria for evaluating theories themselves or (*c*) laws or (*d*) explanations (I think here for example of Professor Skinner's remark about the impossibility of explaining perceptual illusions by "slippage" laws. That strikes one offhand as being more or less directly incompatible with his own procedures of explanation but it would require considerable examination to see just whether it is or not.) (*e*) The relation of science to philosophy. Professor Koch, for example, suggested that the philosophy of science now rests on psychology or needs psychological underpinning. (*f*) The relevance of computer simulation to psychological theories. This is one of the most interesting of the recent issues in the philosophy of science; what is the significance of the fact that we succeed in developing a computer that is functionally isomorphic with human behavior in some domain for psychological theories about that kind of behavior? Does it contribute anything to our understanding that we have the wiring diagram of a computer that behaves—in output terms—just like a human being, for example, in solving mathematical problems. This is a problem on which a number of us are working, Colby at Stanford, myself at Rand, others of us at Argonne, etc. (*g*) The other minds problem. How do we know what is in another person's mind? (This is a problem of such antiquity I feel quite embarrassed to mention it, yet it is rather acute in the behaviorist-phenomenalist dispute.) (*h*) The problem of the inverted spectrum. Professor Bridgman's worry about maybe you see what I see when I see red when you see green, though you have been brought up to call it green, is a very difficult point to handle. (*i*) The mind-body relationship, especially with respect to a problem which never got sufficiently discussed—the problem of whether mental states matter *causally*. Professor Skinner often got to the point of practically admitting that we could have direct awareness of the existence of an inner state of the kind that we would normally refer to as, say, thirst. The claim at which he is balking is that it has any causal efficacy. He argues that it does not—and presumably it would be argued by some of the other symposiasts that it is this sensation which leads us to take steps to try and get our thirst slaked. Now that is the problem of whether mental states are epiphenomena. And it is a colossally difficult problem; one that needs a straight frontal attack. (*j*) The private language problem, the great problem of the *Philosophical Investigations* (2) (Wittgenstein's book to which Professor Malcolm referred) which Skinner referred to many times in talking about the community as a source of the language with which we use to describe our sensations. This ties in immediately with the problem which affects Professor MacLeod's paper all the time, the problem of the origin of the phenomenal language, the difficulties about setting up or identifying or using or testing of phenomenal language. (*k*) The difference between justification of methodological positions and ontological positions. There is a great deal of confusion between these at times, not particularly in this symposium, but even in this symposium a distinction between these two kinds of positions was not discussed enough, I thought. (*l*) The problem about what we may crudely refer to as "the nature of man," which was raised by a number of people and about which Professor Koch makes a number of remarks at the end of his talk (specifically his comments about modern psychology's image of man as being really a demeaning one and about there having been a mass dehumanization process or a deteriorization of culture, which is largely due to this image). I feel rather uneasy about this although it seems to me to be an interesting claim. And, finally, there is (*m*) the problem of reconciling free will and determinism, which strikes me as one of the important crucial issues between certain versions of phenomenology and behaviorism.

I am going to conclude with a specific discussion of some points, sometimes of a minor kind, in the two papers that I have been discussing by indirection, in order to try and get across to you some feeling for the ways in which I think that one can carry through the program of reconciliation of the *defensible* forms of phenomenology and behavorism. It is presumptuous of me to make comments about what I approve of in these papers, but it is unpleasant of me to make comments only on what I disapprove; and so I am going to be presumptuous rather than unpleasant. Turning first to Professor Koch, it seemed to me that a number of major themes of his paper were worthy of very hearty endorsement by a logician, and I want to say what they were. His condemnation of the logical analyses of definition theory (and explanation, though he hardly mentioned this) as used by psychological theorists of many past decades is absolutely right in two ways. As he pointed out, it not only is the case that these analyses are wrong, and have always been obviously wrong, for the other sciences on which they were allegedly founded, but it is also the case that they are not accepted by most logicians now. Secondly, his condemnation of actual practice in terms of these standards is well justified. I remember the glee with which I discovered that nobody actually produces operational definitions, even when they say they do. Hull's work is replete with examples of allegedly operational definitions. Within three lines of many of these he will insert an ontological addendum but still insist that the defined term has no meaning except as an intervening variable.

This kind of debunking exercise was performed excellently in the book *Modern Learning Theories* (1) by Professor Koch in discussing the Hullian theory, and nothing more ought ever to be necessary. It is dull to hear people preach operationism when nobody has practiced it—ever. (And if you think that maybe Bridgman was right in thinking that Einstein did, go and read that literature because that is not even on the way to being a caricature of the truth.) This kind of approach was, it seems to me, very damaging to psychology in several ways and Koch's criticism of it seems to me entirely justified.

As he suggests, the extension of *S-R* theory to the brain stands on its own merits as a piece of absurdity exactly parallel to the homunculus idea. If you are going to stick up for an explanatory system, do not work it to death, and if you think *S-R* theory can explain something, face the fact that it can only explain something because it does not get called on to do the same job in the brain. The same is true with explanations in terms of human behavior—animistic explanation.

My final point concerns the condemnation of certain aspects of existentialism. There is no question that it is doctrinally obscure, that part of its appeal is the fact that it is obscure, and that the appeal to it frequently arises from a lack of understanding of the alternatives. There is no worse basis for making an appeal. You then get out of the frying pan into the fire. None of that is to say it lacks all merit. Now then, Professor Koch, we come to the negative side of the ledger.

I have to put in a good word for analytical philosophy. Professor Koch has made two suggestions about it, that it was dead and that it was ludicrous, and I want to argue that two other things he says make this a little embarrassing for him. One is that he wanted to add that recent philosophy has shown a marked revival in all sorts of interesting fields like ethics, which I must point out has been largely, if not entirely, because of analysts. Moreover, almost every point that he made about definition—most of which I thought were extremely good —are very closely related to the points that Waismann and many other recent analysts make in the discussion of the open texture of language.

Secondly, I raise just a question. It did not seem entirely clear to me how his analysis of definition shows that the philosophy of science rests upon psychology. It seemed clear to me that some aspects of definition refer to behavior, but the exact nature of that relationship seemed to me not at all to demonstrate his conclusion.

Thirdly, I think that he underestimates certain versions of behaviorism quite seriously. Certain versions of Skinner's behaviorism, in particular the methological version on which I think Skinner is particularly keen, are, as I have argued above, important candidates for being good methodology in certain areas. We notice that it is characteristic of Skinner's behaviorism that he does not saddle himself with this apparatus of the logic of science, which Koch so rightly criticizes. I would, therefore, put in a plea here for making a very careful distinction between the standard forms of behaviorism and Skinner's, which really meets only two of Koch's five criteria for behaviorism, and these, in a rather special way.

So I would conclude by saying that Professor Koch's criticisms of behaviorism effectively destroy a specter which was, indeed, haunting and which has continued to haunt the subject. I think of behaviorism, as I know he does, as something which will leave its mark on a generation of graduate students now arising and will thus be with us for thirty or fifty years. I spend my life going around campuses and finding in each new psychology department a new burst of colossal enthusiasm; the leading lights of the graduate student body turn out to be enthusiastic, tough-minded positivists circa 1920. And they are now in their twenty-second year of age and, unfortunately, are likely to live a very long time. Some of them will presumably retain this approach to the subject. This is one reason why I believe that philosophy has an enormous influence on psychology though it has often been very bad. But that is, of course, because it was the wrong philosophy!

I conclude by turning to Professor MacLeod's extremely interesting paper and making some remarks about this, which are partly in the way of being questions. I particularly like—if Professor MacLeod will forgive me for liking some things in it, since he began by saying that he was relying on us to establish discord rather than harmony—the scholarly historical treatment, which I found most illuminating, even though I had often read about its development before. I think the use of the examples, which he went to the trouble of itemizing, admirable, and I feel that any discussions of this subject or related subjects in the philosophy of psychology that do not begin by laying down some examples become simply expressions of political views and may degenerate into political arguments all too readily. I think the distinction between phenomenology, introspectionism, and sensationalism extremely valuable and hope that this will be preserved intact in the published form. I think that the treatment of his conclusions vis-à-vis behaviorism was considerably more cautious than Professor Rogers', and I think, in this respect, easier to defend. Finally, I think that the insights into the conceptual confusions involved in the phenomenal constancy problem were extremely well put and are important stresses on an approach to that problem, which seems to me still to be a neglected one.

On the other hand, I am puzzled by a number of things in the paper. He says, as other phenomenologists or experientialists or introspectionists have said, that the self is really part of the phenomenal world, to use his words. This I have never found entirely clear. It may be that it is. I know that it is I who am talking, but this does not in any way show that the self is part of the phenomenal world rather than being a construct of it or a presupposition of experience; it is the distinction between these three which make the analysis of the self particularly difficult.

He says, about the phenomenon of disgust, that he feels that psychology has notably not told us what it actually feels like to be disgusted. Now I am not sure that is one of the tasks that psychology undertakes. It is not clear to me that even phenomenology should commit itself to that extremely difficult, if not paradoxical, problem. To know what it is to be disgusted is to experience a phenomenon, and the fact that that experience is irreducible is something which we may feel to be an important part of any theory; but to have to get to the problem of communicating that experience—presumably in words —strikes me as being a very awkward task to undertake.

I am not sure, to take another example from his discussion of meaning, that to use the extended sense of meaning, as he does and as writers characteristically have in this connection, is altogether helpful. He talks of the meaning of a point of light as including "that it is far and not near," and so on. It would take too long to go into this properly. It is, to some extent, a vocabulary problem, but it is, to some extent, a conceptual problem. It is a bit like a problem Malcolm hinted at when he said Skinner's position commits him to saying that you can see things even when they are not there. That kind of claim not only raises difficulties of a verbal kind, but it begins to set one's feet on a path which is different and that might lead to serious confusions. I am inclined to think, in the case of the point of light, that we may *notice* that it is far away, or we may *think* that it is far away, or it may *appear* to be far away; but it does not strike me as being clear that it has that *meaning*. This is not just hairsplitting, and I wish I had time to elaborate on why it is not, but unfortunately I do not.

Fourthly, I think he does not really discuss what is the crucial problem of the establishment of a phenomenal language itself, the establishment of communality of reference. As Professor Austin was often inclined to argue, when you get down to the dirty work there, it seems to turn out that you find yourself necessarily involved in the physical-object language. The ramifications of that point might lead one to become a phenomenologist with a great deal more sympathy for behaviorism, especially if one was really to try to develop the pure phenomenal language. In conclusion, it seems to me that although Professor Koch demolishes a great deal of the bad parts of behaviorism, I think he does not rule out either the possibility of a methodological behaviorism or its utility in certain areas. And the paper by Professor MacLeod seems to me to demonstrate that in certain problem areas in psychology, an attempt to avoid phenomenology scrupulously, as the behaviorist hopes to do, is at best fruitless, that the attempt to bring it in with care is not disastrous, and that one may expect this to continue to be so and to think of phenomenalism as not, in any way, an interim state of a feeble alternative to a complete behaviorism.

BIBLIOGRAPHY

1. KOCH, S. "Clark L. Hull." In *Modern Learning Theories*, ed. W. K. ESTES, pp. 1–176. New York: Appleton-Century-Crofts, 1954.
2. WITTGENSTEIN, L. *Philosophical Investigations*. New York: Macmillan, 1953.

PARAPHRASE OF DISCUSSION

COMMENTS OF PROFESSOR MACLEOD

Professor Scriven's analysis of the "rather difficult and occasionally ambiguous position of psychology" is a "very sound statement and one which we psychologists should take very seriously."

MacLeod wants to respond to three points raised in Scriven's "too gentle" criticisms of his paper. First, it may well be that the conclusions about behaviorism were "more cautious" and "easier to defend" than those of Rogers. "The topic . . . of the symposium . . . was the contrasts, or the alternatives, if you like, between behaviorism and phenomenology. . . . I would certainly suggest that these are not really two alternatives at all. They are two interesting approaches." They are "saying the same thing," and "if you try hard enough, you can translate what you wish to say into the language" of the other approach. However, to use the language of even the "best examples of behaviorism . . . [is] going at it the hard way." A lecture given in "Skinner's language" would take "twice as much time" to deliver as would "substantially the same lecture [given] in . . . ordinary English." In their attempts to be "parsimonious" in their assumptions and to "explain in terms of the very small and easily definable set of variables," behaviorists have developed distinctly non-parsimonious and somewhat "non-convincing" ways of saying things. Further, should one "begin by looking at . . . the fringy and fuzzy parts of experience as well as those parts of experience which stick out at us in brute fashion as simple things and events," he might find it not possible to achieve parsimony in the variables and assumptions used. Nevertheless, these are but two approaches.

Second, phenomenology, as an approach to behavior, does not require one "to move in the direction of" one kind of explanation rather than another; it should not be regarded "as representing, in any sense, a psychological system." MacLeod is "something of an eclectic" about explanations, regarding "the concept of explanation [as] itself . . . a very interesting phenomenological problem," "adequacy" of explanation seeming, as it does, to be dependent on "the experience of the individual." He is "very happy when we can relate the observed experience to something which our colleagues in physiology and neurology are discussing," but considers any such relationship to "have broadened the meaning" of the psychological phenomenon rather than to "have, in any ultimate sense, explained it." So, also, with behavioristic explanations.

Finally, he is not "satisfied with the way in which the 'first-person singular' has been dealt with" in the symposium. It is "virtually impossible" to make an "extended statement" without use of the first-person singular, but "most of our 'I's and 'me's' . . . are linguistic conveniences." However, even when the first-person singular is *not* being used as a convenience, "it has a wide variety of possible referents." The "me" in the statement "The point of light is in front of me" in a dark-room experiment has a phenomenological referent of "a very modest sort" compared to the phenomenological referent of the "me" in a therapeutic situation. These referents, different though they may be, cannot be excluded from our psychological descriptions. The fact that "I" and "me" can "occur in quite different fashions in different situations" should not lead us to discard them in our descriptions but should lead us to search for the referent of each "I" or "me" experimentally.

COMMENTS OF PROFESSOR KOCH

He is in general agreement with Professor Scriven with regard to the "positive analysis of the methodological position and prospect of psychology." Psychology *is* limited or restricted by knowledge developed before it began as a science. It *is*, in a qualified way, limited by the existence of cognate sciences. Finally, there *are* "principled limits on the . . . specificity levels . . . of prediction in psychology which are of the first importance if one is making rational estimates as to the directions in which psychology can go. . . ."

One point Professor Scriven makes must be further clarified before it is possible to determine if agreement can be reached. Scriven indicates that psychology can expect limited systematic formulations, that it must be a conceptually heterogeneous science, and that behaviorism and phenomenology may coexist. It is this last point which requires clarification.

If by behaviorism Scriven "means modes of analysis which link . . . independent variables of the sort that would be characterized at the present time as 'stimuli' with variables of the sort that would be characterized at the present time as 'responses' or 'behavior,' certainly there are many problems with respect to which such analysis is not only relevant but utterly sufficient. . . ." If he means the "knowledge of many periphery-periphery laws . . . generated by behaviorism . . . ," it must be said that, while this is "useful knowledge," it is more limited in its generality than is commonly supposed and, also, "requires frequent translation" to become useful. If by behaviorism he means "some set of theses of the sort that have been historically associated with behaviorism as a psychological tradition," even "that brand of neo-neo-behaviorism developed by Skinner," then "we face difficulties."

Skinner "has certainly discovered knowledge" through the actual empirical work he has done, and this work is certainly "closely tied up with" a "quasi-systematic" behaviorism. But this knowledge is "limited in its generality." Koch's experience in the animal laboratory has caused him to consider much of this kind of knowledge, even when it is "of a quite determinate sort, . . . so situation-bound, so local to unanalyzed conditions . . . of the experiment," as to be but ambiguously, if at all, applicable under altered conditions.

Further "and more importantly, . . . there are aspects of Skinner's thought and his style of thought which still are linked in definite ways with the neo-behaviorist tradition." The use of "crass and undifferentiating analytic tools . . . [which do] not register subject matter distinctions [that] would be very important both in behavioral analysis and in analysis of events inside the skin . . . is linked to a characteristic kind of assumption on the part of behaviorists . . . to the effect that you can write psychology . . . in terms of a homogeneous and highly simplistic vocabulary. . . . Now I point out to Mr. Scriven that when . . . Mr. Skinner was asked by a member of the audience yesterday how he felt about the problem of coexistence . . . his answer was extremely intolerant. I think this intolerance springs from Skinner's feeling that, in fact, this conceptual language of his is universally applicable to the problems of psychology and that it is rather unfruitful to think of conceptualizing problems in other terms." But psychology has to be a "conceptually heterogeneous" science. If even "the most libertarian neo-neo-behaviorist" would "permit" such conceptual heterogeneity, rather than insist on attempts to universalize the language community, Koch would "no longer have any objection to neo-neo-behaviorists. The indications, however, are otherwise."

Something "simply to note in passing" is the "impact of this extrordinarily impoverished set of conceptual tools on the people who have been influenced by this point of view." While Skinner looks upon the constructs as analytic tools, it is often the case that *some* "who employ the theory and do the research" see the point of view "as more or less constitutive of the structure of the universe."

Professor Malcolm pointed out that one implication of this restrictive analytic system "was that man, in effect, becomes an object." Koch points out the danger of "a simplification of sensibility."

MEMBER OF THE AUDIENCE

If we become explicit in stating exactly in what way and in which areas behaviorism is relevant, and explicit in stating exactly in what way and in which areas phenomenology is relevant, do we really have such a conceptually heterogeneous science as is implied?

COMMENTS OF PROFESSOR SCRIVEN

". . . [T]hink of the analogy in physics. There are areas in physics where deterministic methodology is defensible and areas where it is not. The fact that we can see that and say what those two areas are does not give us any kind of common subject matter theory in those two areas. I think the same thing applies to psychology." To be able to specify the kinds of variables which are relevant in different problem areas is not sufficient for a general theory.

MEMBER OF THE AUDIENCE

"On behalf of the students of psychology, I should just like to ask this: What is psychology?"

COMMENTS OF PROFESSOR SCRIVEN

To say "the scientific study of human behavior" is to include too much physiology and to load the answer in the direction of the behaviorists. "The 'scientific study of thought, behavior, feeling, and one or two other things like that' would not be a bad answer, but I think that is not really what you are after."

"What is left after I have taken away all those nice things like the Newtonian system?" Scriven has, in the past, been "violently attacked for corrupting the morale of . . . graduate students" by suggesting they could not "get major, overriding theories," but he does not feel one should handle adults by "feeding them fibs." Far more important than his apparently having taken away from psychology powers it never had in the first place is the "positive side" of his analysis. Rather than attempting to develop "super theories" from which specific consequences can be deduced, psychology should attend to more limited areas of behavior, effecting worthwhile results and, perhaps, gradually developing "local theories." An "exciting example" of this is the use of "automatic teaching machines connected to electric typewriters" in teaching very young children to read and write. ". . . [M]uch of the fascinating part of psychology is the part which has been definitely underdeveloped just because of the emphasis on 'super theories.' . . ."

Geology, the most historical of all sciences, is "an exciting and difficult subject." If one thinks of the problems of geography, geology, and physical topography—the questions of the ways in which valleys are carved, deltas are going to form, sandbanks go, and coastlines alter—one sees that these are not solved by deducing specific consequences from "colossal answers." Psychology "is not any different in its nature." One can "transform" these kinds of problems "into terms of problems about people. . . . If psychology was no more than very like geology it would still have every claim to being an exciting and legitimate science."

MEMBER OF THE AUDIENCE

Was the point of the paper that psychology is in a "miserable condition" because of the nature of the field itself rather than because of its adolescence?

COMMENTS OF PROFESSOR SCRIVEN

"I do not want to say that it is in a miserable condition at all. I want to say that it is in a position which many people think of as being unsatisfactory, or deficient, or immature, or adolescent, because they use, as a criterion, the standards of subjects which are wholly unlike psychology in ways that we can point out. . . . The crucial point is that . . . their criterion for immaturity . . . is . . . wholly inappropriate. . . ."

MEMBER OF THE AUDIENCE

"What is there intrinsic about psychology which is holding it back?"

COMMENTS OF PROFESSOR SCRIVEN

"That is to repeat a section of the talk, and I do not want to do that." Psychology has had "stolen from it large sections . . . , and it is immediately liable to have stolen from it other large sections by other marauding sciences and, thus, incidentally, it ought to feel a little sympathy for philosophy. . . ."

MEMBER OF THE AUDIENCE

"How do you feel about what is left after you have done all that?"

COMMENTS OF PROFESSOR SCRIVEN

". . . [T]his is a fine science, an exciting one, and, as long as you do not view it through the wrong sort of glasses, a rose-colored one."

MEMBER OF THE AUDIENCE

What is left is still adolescent?

COMMENTS OF PROFESSOR SCRIVEN

" 'Adolescent' is appropriate only if you have the *wrong* picture of what maturity is for a science. . . ." In many respects, physics presents a good comparison. It is not unified. "Nobody can relate quantum field theory to general field theory. Nobody knows what to do with particle theory. Nobody knows how to handle the behavior of liquid helium; . . . the plasma field is just beginning. We have local theories for each subject. . . . There is not an over-arching synthesis." But physics "never has a lower bound." One can move from level to level "and it's still physics." Psychology "definitionally" has bounds. If, in explaining behavior of some kind—schizophrenia, for example —one "move[s] into the brain," the explanation is not "still psychology." "To recognize these limitations is not to recognize 'handicaps,' or 'immaturities,' or 'difficulties' with the subject which we will, one day, overcome; it is simply to recognize its role in the structure of knowledge."

MEMBER OF THE AUDIENCE

If one is "talking about behavior . . . to start with" and finds that certain variables lie in another field "outside its domain," does that mean that one has "passed the problem into the other field"? Does the example given mean that schizophrenia has "suddenly become a physiological problem instead of psychological?"

COMMENTS OF PROFESSOR SCRIVEN

A distinction is made between a psychological problem and a psychological solution. Schizophrenia, being "human behavior at the macro-level," is a psychological problem. However, if one were to find that schizophrenia is a result of "genetic predisposition plus environmental impact of certain kinds of radiation fields on the brain which produces short circuits," this would be an explanation "in terms of physical variables of an identifiable kind" and would not be a psychological explanation.

MEMBER OF THE AUDIENCE

This is still not a physiological explanation because certain aspects of the environment were included. Perhaps what "you may be arguing is that these two fields which you are distinguishing between are not distinct."

COMMENTS OF PROFESSOR SCRIVEN

The environmental factors are included as precipitators, but "it is a physiological explanation because all the functional disorder is in the brain." Explanations of fermentation of yeast are still biochemical explanations even though a man, as an outside agent, might start the process.

MEMBER OF THE AUDIENCE

"In this last portion you seem to be saying that the only kind of explanation you can accept is 'reductive' explanation. What about what people have called 'constructive' explanation?"

COMMENTS OF PROFESSOR SCRIVEN

He does not mean to limit himself to reductive explanations. ". . . [M]uch of psychology demonstrates . . . the possibility of finding constructive explanations and psychology . . . is dedicated to finding [them]." It is important to recognize, though, that "there is no *guarantee* of there being such" explanations. It might be that, in certain areas, reductive explanations are the only ones possible.

MEMBER OF THE AUDIENCE

[The question could not be heard clearly. The questioner seemed to be concerned over the apparent impossibility of doing "pure or basic" as opposed to "applied and action" research in social psychology if one accepts Scriven's claim for the specificity of neo-neo-behaviorist formulations rather than Skinner's claim for their generality.]

COMMENTS OF PROFESSOR SCRIVEN

"I am not sure I got the real kick in that question. . . . [P]ure research in social psychology is among the most unproductive fields of human endeavor today," ranking only "with mathematical economics as being a kind of exciting game for people that like exciting games in this particular field, i.e., nobody except those who do it. . . ."

Concerning "Skinner's claim to complete generality, . . . when we start talking [in] Skinnerian language about complex features of poetic composition and about certain aspects of general social behavior, we are really performing the translation trick, not the explanation trick." This might lead us to think we have explained but it is really "the disease of the jargonier." It is important to distinguish between being able to talk about something in a particular vocabulary and understanding it in that vocabulary. The test as to whether a vocabulary "imparts new and genuine understanding" is its "capacity to predict new relationships, to retrodict old ones, and to show a unity where previously there was a diversity," not its capacity to produce an " 'aha' feeling."